BIOGRAPHY OF
LORD DUNSANY

BIOGRAPHY OF
LORD DUNSANY

Mark Amory

COLLINS
St James's Place, London
1972

William Collins Sons & Co Ltd
London · Glasgow · Sydney · Auckland
Toronto · Johannesburg

Frontispiece photograph
Radio Times Hulton Picture Library

First published 1972
© Mark Amory 1972
ISBN 0 00 21486 0 000 211484 4 (BNB May-Aug 72)
Set in Monotype Baskerville
Made and Printed in Great Britain by
William Collins Sons & Co Ltd Glasgow

PART ONE

Birth till 1914

1878 – 1914

I

Foreword

MANY authors of fiction are accused of being unable to write with sustained interest of anything but themselves. This was so far from being the case with Lord Dunsany that he was his own least successful subject. The three volumes of autobiography – which he explains at the outset were written to please his publisher, not himself – try to describe the artist, but attempt little impression of the man, and even then are most enjoyable when with anecdotes or descriptions of scenery, he wanders away from himself altogether and approaches the territory of his other books. This sympathetic failure stems less from a self-effacing modesty than from a remarkable lack of interest in any human character, including his own. In his story he leaves many arbitrary gaps, saying little of his childhood and less of his family. Though the unhappy childhood of the sensitive author is not a new theme and interest in a man does not entail interest in his distant forbears something must be said of each to throw light on the man he became. Nor is the recital of his shooting successes, leavened with a list of his writings, a complete portrait of the later years. All of which preamble is designed to defend myself against the question: 'In the light of his autobiography, is your book really necessary?'

Believing those three volumes to be largely unread nowadays, I have plundered them, stealing anything of interest. The same approach to his other work is more dangerous. One book, *The Curse of the Wise Woman* seems to be autobiographical and there are passages from others which I have quoted to throw light on his life. It is rarely possible to prove that he is drawing directly from his own experience, but details can be checked and otherwise I leave it as my opinion that a passage is revealing, while admitting that I could be mistaken.

An imbalance, shared by many biographies and autobiographies, has been caused by the tendency of the famous to jostle their way to the front. Yeats in particular appears more prominently than his relationship with Dunsany warrants and appearances by Shaw, Wells and Kipling might have been curtailed if they had been less distinguished. I do not mean that I have implied that Dunsany knew them better than he did, only that he had other, closer, friends whose reputations do not demand for them so close a scrutiny. A reigning monarch can drop in for tea and be recorded, a neighbour may have dined every month for ten years and be left out. A further distortion is that when famous men or events do appear, I have made no attempt at an objective portrait of them. They are seen through the eyes of either Lord Dunsany or his wife with an occasional reminder from me that this may not be the whole truth. This is also and particularly true of Irish politics on which they naturally had strong views. There are not, I hope, any uncorrected errors of fact.

That I am heavily indebted to the Dunsany family for the use of letters and Lady Dunsany's diary will be readily apparent. My debt is far greater than that. I have asked Lady Dunsany literally hundreds of questions and stayed with the present Lord Dunsany while I questioned his servants and ransacked his attics. Lady Mary Clive, a favourite niece of my subject, has helped me with notes on people and places she remembered and, reading through the manuscript, saved me from many mistakes, as has Edward Plunkett. I am also indebted to Lady Sarah Cumming-Bruce, Lady Agnes Eynston, Lord Longford, Miss Gladys Cooper and Mr Patrick Mahony for information and opinions, to Dr Miles Gogarty for allowing me to quote at length from an unpublished essay on Dunsany by his father Oliver Gogarty, and to Miss Hazel Littlefield for allowing me to quote and draw on her *King of Dreams*.

Forbears.

There have been Plunketts living at Dunsany Castle, 20 miles north-west of Dublin, since 1190 when it was built, with perhaps a short gap around 1530 when Meath was ravaged by plague so that 'many a castle was left unguarded and many a noble corpse unburied'. There were inevitably other moments of uncertainty. The family have held for three centuries that they are of Danish origin and settled in Ireland in the 10th century before the Anglo-Norman invasion. Marriage linked them with the new rulers and Dunsany was a castle of the Pale, a link in the defensive chain established by the Normans. Plunkett is said to be a corruption of 'Blanche Jenet' and the coat of arms over one of the gates to Dunsany is supported by two white jennets.

Sir Christopher Plunkett was Deputy Governor of Ireland before 1430 and his two sons John and Christopher, who were the ancestors of the Fingall and Dunsany families, at first held their land in common. John lived in Killeen, another castle about half a mile from Dunsany. It is said that when they decided to divide, the boundary was fixed by the wives of the two brothers having a race. Each started from her own castle and a fence was put up at their meeting place, John's wife winning a few yards for the Killeen estate. The losing Lady Dunsany (Christopher had been ennobled in 1439 by Henry VI) at first worshipped in the same Church at Killeen as her sister-in-law but after a religious squabble she declared she would never set foot in the Killeen Church again but would build a church at Dunsany identical in every way except that it should be one foot greater in height, in width and in length. The story has long been believed, though the family thought it over-scrupulous to check the measurements. It was dismantled probably by Cromwell and later the windows bricked up as the hounds were kept in it and would otherwise jump out.

Thus the family early established and generally was on good terms with the English. A Dunsany was in the English Parliament under Henry VII and another, described by one of his descendants as 'a sort of small Essex', received from Elizabeth I an enamelled cup which is still at Dunsany. However, the same descendant had cause to say: We were always fighting in those days but always upon the wrong side. We fought for Perkin Warbeck and for Lambert Simnel.' On the wrong, or at least the unsuccessful, side once more, a cavalier Dunsany, Patrick, supported Charles I against Cromwell and paid heavily for doing so. While her husband was a prisoner in Dublin, Lady Dunsany defended the Castle and, as Lecky said, was 'torn weeping from the scene of her former happiness and was exiled to Connaught'. Much land and a fine home was forfeited and though Charles II restored Lord Dunsany to the full privileges of his rank, all his estates were not recovered. More land was lost when the first Dunsany to be called Randal, fought for James II and failed to recognise the victory of William III. This time the family were under attainder for several generations. In 1713 Edward, Lord Dunsany, who became a Protestant, allowed the family fortunes to ebb to their lowest point. The education of his heir, another Randal, was so neglected that he could not write his own name at sixteen, but at that age he went off to the Court of Spain where he had cousins and soon acquired the necessary accomplishments. When this Randal inherited, the castle was in such a state of disrepair that he decided to abandon it if the roof proved faulty; however it was sound and he stayed. He had the attainder reversed and his seat in the Irish House of Lords allowed. Then he set to work on what remained of the property, clearing up the castle and park and having an inconveniently close road shut by Act of Parliament. The inhabitants, not altogether surprisingly, continued to use the old road and he is said to have stood on the bridge throwing trespassers bodily into the water if they tried to cross. He was a large man.

In the rising of 1798 the family held a consultation as to whether to defend Killeen or Dunsany, as it was impossible to defend both. They decided upon Killeen, so Dunsany was abandoned and possessed by the rebels. As they made to sack the cellar, a move which would very likely have led to total destruction, the brewer who supplied the family said, 'Boys if you enter the old Lord's cellar it shall be over my dead body.' In return the family drank no other beer than that supplied by his representative, though it was not good and so a relief when the firm eventually failed, as did the rebellion.

The 13th Baron Dunsany lived much abroad but on the night of his death in Brussels his ghost appeared in an archway at Dunsany. His son Edward was also often away, fighting against Napoleon and the Americans in the Coldstream Guards and living for several years in Italy. He had the unpleasant experience of opening his paper at breakfast one morning to see the Reversion of the Family Estates offered for sale, 'the present incumbent being over eighty'. His heir, Randal, was the ne'er-do-well the incident suggests and the family fortunes sank once more. The 16th Baron, Dunsany's grandfather, was a prudent younger son who once more restored the situation, bought back land and acquired some coal mines which later became valuable. He left everything but the castle directly to his grandson, the subject of this book, not easing thereby the boy's relationship with his father, who naturally resented being skipped. The grandfather spoke in the Lords, and his father and his two uncles, Horace and Randal, were all in the House of Commons; it seemed that the family was planning to dominate British politics, but Randal, the eldest son, died young and Horace went abroad. His father was a remarkably fluent speaker and the House of Commons used to fill when he got to his feet. He once described some dish that he had cooked at Cambridge, which simmered until something began to rise to the surface, when you had to put in a spoon and stir it till the scum went down again. 'In the same way,' he continued, 'when I am speaking in the House and I see the Speaker beginning to rise, I put in something relevant and he sits down.' Witty and charming, if not practical, he married Miss Burton, a cousin of the most fascinating of nineteenth-century explorers, Richard Burton. Some of his unstable brilliance and occasional melancholy may have come to Dunsany through his mother.

WITH Dunsany Castle the enduring link between so many ups and downs over so long a period, it is perhaps a disappointment to find that Edward Plunkett was born in London, at 15 Park Square near Regent's Park. Yet if significance is sought in a circumstance which clearly has none, it was not so inappropriate. The Dunsanys had lived in Ireland for several hundred years but remained not Irish but Anglo-Irish. They had often lived abroad and often married foreigners. Their values and their friends came largely from the English upper classes though they certainly added something of their own. In a rebellion their instinctive loyalty would be to the government of Westminster, though we have seen that this was not always so. In nothing is a family tradition so powerful as in putting forward various alternative careers as an acceptable way of life. His family had not been interested in money, nor in the efficiency which leads to money, and Dunsany[1] followed them. They had been soldiers, politicians and country gentlemen and he was in turn all of those things. When he found that he wished to write and could do so it was a break with tradition. He believed his father would have written well, but talked instead, and his Uncle Horace was in the thick of the Irish literary set and was a strong influence on him; but he did not foresee his work, nor was it put in his head by the example of relations.

Born in 1878, Dunsany remained in London long enough to have memories of the rooms at 15 Park Square, and to buy an air-balloon with a penny, and be given a halfpenny change. Then he moved to Kent and a house called Dunstall Priory near Shoreham where his mother lived. He loved it immediately and for ever.

From the road you see a short white tower and then the small rectangular house set among trees going up the hill

1. For simplicity I shall call the subject of this book Dunsany throughout and distinguish others. Naturally he was called Edward Plunkett before he succeeded.

behind and with fields sloping away before. 'As much trouble
to run as a big one,' Dunsany's wife was to say, but it looks
neat, compact. Two vast stone urns now guard the entrance to
the unpretentious drive and on the house itself Dunsany placed
blue dragons and chinese warriors. It has changed little in 150
years, hardly at all in the last fifty, and the cause of its considerable charm remains in a clutter of curious objects that are
there because somebody liked them; everything has been used
and enjoyed, rarely arranged. As a small boy, Dunsany admired an orchestra of Dresden frogs – which are still playing in
the same place. Through the doorway of his father's study he
glimpsed 'a picture of a holy man of the east, with a toad
sitting on his head and a china figure of a diver caught by an
octopus and many more strange things with a kind of magic
about them . . . that room hinted that, if there was not actually
magic in the world, there were at any rate eerie things under
the moon, and, far away, strange gods.'[1] Now there are many
more, a large china elephant ready to carry a maharajah, a leaf
across which a snake wriggles, contorted Eastern peasants –
but he so caught his father's taste that it is not possible to guess
which of the two acquired which grotesque or charming piece.
His father showed him part of the cellars but not all, leaving a
little unknown and therefore thrilling. Mystery and imagination
were what Dunsany admired and Dunstall set the scene for
both.

As much as the house, he loved the country. When he writes
long afterwards of the lizards roaming in the chalky soil and the
butterflies on the oaks that grew on higher ground his affection
is obvious. The woods and valleys were empty of man. He saw
a hare for the first time and, 'if ever I have written of Pan, out
in the evening, as though I had really seen him, it is mostly a
memory of that hare'.[2] He enjoyed things that were unexplained
like the brilliant lights moving in the sky, presumably on the
evening of some November 5. Tediously asked what he wanted
to be when he grew up, he replied, 'A giant' (an ambition he
almost achieved). Soon he had a pony and a butterfly collection, more important to him than the stamps which preceded
it; and then moths; and later still fossils. When Dunstall was

1. *Patches of Sunlight* by Dunsany.
2. ibid.

let he cried and though a house was rented in the same valley, the return to Dunstall was a great moment. He cried each time he left during the next years and this was several times, for London or for a house at Clifton in his father's constituency. His father was distant though kindly; his mother's moods were uncertain and his childhood was lonely and unhappy. He failed to find the comforting cook and butler who seem to have stood in as foster-parents for others of his generation and he failed also to unite with his brother Reggie, who was only two years younger. Reggie is not mentioned in his autobiography and his own account of these years make him sound like an only child, almost like an orphan.

Dogs, which he loved, entered his life early but not happily.

I can remember seeing the mad dog when I was out for a walk some time round about my seventh birthday. He was lying by himself under a hedge, that was three or four yards from a path along which we were walking. I remember I pulled at the hand that was holding mine, so that we walked a little wide of the mad dog. Children are apt to be secretive but I cannot now remember the exact reason that prevented me saying a word about the mad dog that I alone had seen . . . we came safely home to a house where we lived with two mastiffs; and they were both mad. They died howling, shortly afterwards.[1]

Education loomed. An unwanted governess came and was as irksome as he had feared until 'one day I suspected that the dative was not to her what it was to Caesar; and soon I found that of Caesar, to or for Caesar, and by, with or from Caesar were all much the same to her. After that lessons were easier!'[2] A year later at the age of nine he went to a local boarding-school with about twelve other boys. He liked it and was the third generation of Plunketts to be nick-named Blanket. A well-written if under-punctuated letter postmarked 1889, when he was eleven, chirpily conveys his misfortunes:

My dear Mamma
I have been very unlucky lately first I got chilblains then a boy got in an awful bait with me and kicked my foot so that I could not walk on it, when that got better next day I had a sore throat and headache which lasted four days before it was found out, when it

1. *Dog Days* (Dunsany papers).
2. *Patches of Sunlight*.

was I was sent to bed. Now I have got toothache worse than last
time in a permanent double tooth. We played the Wilkinsons and
although we got four goals running it was six all; they are giants
and funks all the same. I hope your foot is all right now.

Your affectionate son,
EDDIE PLUNKETT.

He stayed until a few months before his 12th birthday when he
went to Cheam, a typical English preparatory school with a
hundred boys; all German masters were called Fink, all French
masters Bun and the butler Jumbo. The headmaster, who had
taught Dunsany's father, was liked as well as feared and had a
gift for imaginative abuse, once calling a boy a 'confusticated
piece of toasted cheese'. Dunsany cried when he went, which
was natural, but also when he left. Years later he wrote:[1]

... I think I owe most of my style to the reports of proceedings in
the divorce court, were it not for these my mother might have
allowed me to read newspapers before I went to school, as it was
she never did. I began reading Grimm and then Andersen. I
remember reading them in the evening with twilight coming on.
All the windows of the rooms I used in the house in Kent where I
was brought up faced the sunset. There are no facts about a sunset,
none are chronicled in Blue-books. There are no advertisements of
them.

When I went to Cheam school I was given a lot of the Bible to
read. This turned my thoughts Eastward. For years no style seemed
to me natural but that of the Bible and I feared that I never would
become a writer when I saw that other people did not use it.

When I learned Greek at Cheam and heard of other Gods a great
pity came on me for those marble people that had become forsaken
and the mood has never quite left me.

When I went to Eton the housemaid forgot to call me, or only
half-called me rather, on the morning of the Greek exam. I therefore took a lower place than I should have and less than three years
later, when I left to go to a crammer, where my education ceased,
my knowledge of the classics was most incomplete. But incomplete
in a strange way for they had implanted in me at Cheam and Eton
a love of the classical world of which I knew almost nothing.

And then one day imagination came to the rescue and I made
unto myself gods, and having made gods I had to make people to
worship them and cities for them to live in and kings to rule over

1. To Frank Harris in 1912.

them, and then there had to be names for the kings and the cities and great plausible names for the huge rivers that I saw sweeping down through kingdoms by night.

At Cheam he also learnt chess and liked it so well that later he saw it as a danger, for he could imagine succumbing to the temptation to do nothing else. He won the school tournament in his second year and all his life took great pleasure in chess victories. His reading was not extraordinary but as well as Grimm and Andersen he was now told that Xanadu was the finest poem in the *Golden Treasury* and read it and found that this was true. He also managed to grapple with all the tales of Edgar Allan Poe – quite a tough proposition. A taste for the fantastic and for imagined landscapes full of strange creatures and cities with exotic names was already strong, though his own work was rarely to contain the macabre cruelty of Poe and Grimm. All boys of his generation and class knew the Bible well and, aided by the divorce court reports, he knew and loved it better than most. When told to read the lament of David for Jonathan and then write a précis from memory, he instantly saw that no précis could be adequate and so learnt it by heart and wrote it out. This display of precocious good taste earned him no credit and he supposed that the master merely thought he had been cheating, and cheating in a most unimaginative way at that.

When Dunsany was ten his grandfather died and his father, though as an Irish peer he could have continued in the House of Commons, preferred to retire to Dunsany. He was not well and his health was not improved by heavy drinking, various drugs or self-inflicted experiments with Röntgen rays.[1] You could be X-rayed at Dunsany in 1900 but not in a hospital before 1905, and in 1918 Sevenoaks hospital borrowed the equipment from Dunstall. Also his marriage was not happy and, though there was no legal arrangement, his wife remained in Kent, so that they were effectively separated. The boys shuttled from parent to parent across the Irish Sea.

Dunsany's mother was beautiful but also lonely and neurotic and she could be unreasonable. When Dunsany and Reggie were quite small they had been out for a walk with their

1. An X-ray discovered by Wilhelm Röntgen in 1895.

governess and had seen Queen Victoria. They excitedly told
their mother who gave them a furious scolding for mingling
with the crowd and so risking infection. This sort of incident
could occur at any time. There had already been blazing,
shouting quarrels and were to be more. The brothers might
have turned to one another for comfort but Reggie was of so
different a temperament, shy and withdrawn where Dunsany
was affectionate and boisterous, that they never got on well.

At the same time they were both so obstinate that a small matter
could grow into an argument that lasted for days. Dunsany said
later that his mother always had a favourite son, though it was
not always the same one; but it was more often Reggie.

Their father in Ireland was more evenly affectionate but
aloof. In a novel[1] Dunsany says of an Irish house:

It was built by a forbear of ours who was a historical character, but
it is just about that time that the history of Ireland begins to be
fabulous, so that it is truer to tell you merely that the house was very
old. Of the period of its furniture and its fixtures I can tell you at
once: it was no period at all. As chairs and such things wore out they
were replaced in different generations, and the only thing that they
all had in common was that they were all bought by the same family.
There is a right and a wrong place for antiquity; it is right in walls,
wrong in carpets; wrong too in curtains and wall-paper and hearth-
rugs. We had antiquity everywhere.

The correctly antique walls were massive, grey and covered
with ivy that was kept neatly trimmed. Jackdaws nested in it
and Dunsany sometimes ate one of their eggs raw on his
porridge. A fine large building, Dunsany Castle lacks only a
view as it was built to guard a road and the road naturally, but
unfortunately, does not run over the hill tops.

Here he made a friend. John Hawksley, a cousin, whose
parents had died, came to Dunsany frequently and was adept
at remaining on good terms with both brothers. A gentle con-
siderate boy, he was depressed once by wounding a rabbit that
crawled back into its burrow. 'It'll be dead by now,' someone
comforted. 'But that's so horrid for the other rabbits,' he
replied. Dunsany's unhappiness and uncertainty during his
school-days perhaps help to explain why he remained so

1. *The Curse of the Wise Woman.*

sensitive to criticism and eager for praise, and his wish to escape to an utterly fantastic, beautiful and unreal world. In an obvious way he remained a schoolboy all his life enjoying the jokes and games he had missed. If his own account makes these years sound decent, almost ripping, it must be remembered that he set out to record only happy memories. His real feelings may be shown better by his thought at the end of some holidays when thirteen weeks of school loomed ahead and he was pondering on things left undone: 'I suppose I shall feel the same about my life when I come to die.'

II

Dunsany was pleased to have been at Eton, whither he was sent in 1891, and, admittedly a crude test of affection, in due course sent his son. He went to a famous house, that of Mr Cornish. His tutor he remembered as a venerable figure, who in a classroom would occasionally look up and say 'Don't'. If the boy addressed was foolish enough to reply 'Don't what sir?' Mr Cornish would continue, 'Very well write out the dictionary'. Silence for about ten minutes. 'How far have you got?' 'Down to ’αββα – father, sir.' 'Very well you may stop.' Dunsany says little else of Mr Cornish but was fond of Mr E. L. Vaughan to whose house he went when Cornish became Vice-Provost. Dunsany's banishment of unhappy incidents makes his account of Eton brief and even then what he recalls is rather dismal.

He was jeered at, when, not knowing that it was the emblem of Harrow, he wore a cornflower in his buttonhole; he did not have the correct clothes to go to the school concert and so sat alone in his room listening to the school song joyfully sung from afar; he translated some Latin verse into English hexameters and pentameters, but realising that it was rash to show any interest in poetry he copied it out as prose and, hurriedly corrected, it was accepted as such. A true prose work claiming to be a translation from Homer (slightly altered) and entitled 'Early School' begins 'And when the heavy-footed maids appeared we roused us from out our beds and hastened to school with rapid feet. Then took we council among ourselves and I spake unto the rest saying "Harken unto my words my comrades for we are in evil plight in that we have not brought our well-

smudged extra work, neither have we laboured over the same
with goodly toil wherefore my comrades we are in evil plight
seeing that poena-compelling Carter is a lawless man fearing
neither the laws of beaks nor boys".' In spite of the death of a
boy who is late and poena-compelling Carter's refusal to
accept their right-well-fashioned excuses there is a happy
ending for 'when it drew nigh unto 8 o'clock we departed
from out the well-built school-room with windows on either
side and got us unto our respective houses grieving for our
beloved comrade yet well pleased to have escaped from dreadful
fate and from poena-compelling Carter.'

His other poetic gesture was to learn lines of Horace by
heart because he liked the sound and did not mind being
ignorant of the sense; this emphasis was still with him ten years
later when he was first published.

His skill at cricket and chess failed to furnish him with any
notable triumph. He enjoyed going for cross-country runs and
once he got lost and found an old man on a chair watching a
sewage farm. 'I did not know that people set any store by
sewage, or that it needed watching; and seeing the old man
there in the late twilight, seated among the willows and not
knowing where we were, impressed a scene that is in my
memory yet.'[1] He wrote a little poetry but showed it to no one,
not even to Mr Cornish who was sufficiently perceptive to ask
if any existed. He learned to enjoy Tennyson as well as Horace.
But these are not the pleasures of a boy who would fit easily
into Eton in the '90s. His reports can be presumed to have been
bad, though he never saw them. His description of his own
industry supports this: 'I am not at all sure that idleness could
ever be achieved at Eton, although my father thought it could.
If he was wrong and if "poenas" defeated idleness before it had
time to put forth its luxurious growth, as I think they invariably did, then in saying that I idled at Eton I claim to have
done a thing that I never really did; the will being there but
not the opportunity.'[2]

In his most autobiographical book,[3] the hero is shooting in
Ireland.

1. *Patches of Sunlight.*
2. ibid.
3. *The Curse of the Wise Woman* 1935.

And sitting there with the bog all around me, and with that soft wind blowing, the thought suddenly came to me that in a few days I should be back at Eton following up the intricacies of some Greek verb.

'I go back to Eton on Thursday,' I said to Marlin [the game-keeper].

'That's a fine school,' said Marlin.

'It is,' I said.

'Don't all the gentry send their sons there?' he said.

'Some of them,' I replied.

'Sure, there's no school like it,' he said.

'There is not,' said I.

'But sure there's no use going back to it,' he said.

'I'm afraid I've got to,' I answered.

'But if you were too ill to go?' said Marlin.

'I'd have to be very ill,' said I.

'Begob,' said Marlin, 'there's diseases that men know nothing about, that Dr Rory over at Clonrue knows the same as an old woman would know the name of her cat.'

Dr Rory helps and Eton is postponed in the book, and though in fact Dunsany was not an orphan and did not therefore have the power to succumb to such a temptation, the attitude towards Eton – a good school as schools go, but to be avoided if possible – was his. In the same novel 'my feet had the fields along the left bank of the Thames wherever the beagles led them; a flat land with heavy soil I should say and deep wide ditches and white mists always rising up at evening; that is as my memory sees it . . . It was very soon after this that I went back to Eton, to the calm old buildings, the red may and the chestnuts, and then the willows.' His last half was so cold that the Thames froze over and they roasted an ox on it.

When he was sixteen his father, who had decided, or rather had always known, that he should go to Sandhurst, took him away from Eton and sent him to a crammer, mainly for mathematics which he always found prosaic and lacking in charm. Then and later he regretted leaving Eton, suspecting his father of wishing to economise on the fees.

Frank Harris attributes the sides of Dunsany of which he disapproves to these three years.

... but then he went to Eton and he is still suffering from that infection. Eton made him an athlete it's said, and taught him to play cricket, but it also taught him to sneer at Woman's Suffrage and to revere the House of Lords.

At Eton he lost a little of his Celtic kindly humane manners and learned 'good form'; instead of prizing Celtic equality and the Kingdom of man upon earth, he came to believe in British Imperialism and the world-devouring destinies of the British Empire ... all this imperialistic foolery I put down to his Eton training and, of course, in the last resort, to his want of brains.[1]

Harris never knew Dunsany well enough, let alone before or while he was at Eton, to estimate his amount of Celtic kindly, humane, manners at any given moment. But it is true that he had at least half of a conventional upper-class upbringing, and that he accepted the vast bulk of conventional upper-class views thus offered.

The first cramming establishment was not too bad. It was in Dublin, so he could go to Dunsany at weekends. During the holidays from Eton he had been taught to shoot by the keeper. At first he disappointed his father by not liking it as much as the cricket matches nor the boating and riding which were rival occupations. Then he took to shooting snails with an air-gun from what he considered a fair distance. His father ridiculed this, comparing it unfavourably with the pursuit of lion and rhinoceros. But the keeper had foretold that he would soon take to shooting and care for nothing else so much, and he was right. It was never to be finally decided whether Dunsany was a writer who shot or a sportsman who wrote.

There was not enough activity at Dunsany to occupy his already considerable energy, a state of affairs that was to continue. Indeed his whole life can be seen as an effort, sometimes successful, to smother a basic loneliness and uncertainty in distractions, to fill up his time. When he was unoccupied he became depressed, so naturally when he discovered a new interest he hurled himself into it with irresistible enthusiasm.

Dunsany did not yet know he was going to be a writer but his father knew he was to be a soldier. Nor did they particularly agree on other topics. His father was what Dunsany was to become – a brilliant talker rather than a brilliant conversa-

1. *Contemporary Portraits*; by Frank Harris.

tionalist. Most people were happy to listen to his flow of sharp wit and vivid metaphor, which was as well as they had little alternative. Dunsany admired this gift, but it did not make for easy intimacy.

The crammer sent good reports – suspiciously good. It was decided that their object was simply to give satisfaction to a fee-paying parent and in 1895 Dunsany was moved on to a clergyman in Norfolk. With only three other students life would have been drab indeed had he not found his tutor to be an excellent chessplayer who always beat him except on Saturdays when he was fatigued from composing his sermon. However there were two local clubs where he met with more success in spite of a simple ignorance of openings that an efficient opponent should have been able to exploit. He was asked to play for Norfolk while only sixteen but before he could do so he had been whisked away to the last and worst of his crammers.

This was Mr Wolfram's at Lee. He disliked it very much. One of the teachers was a poet, Stephen Phillips,[1] who gave him much to think about by telling him that he thought the finest line of English poetry was:

'Cover her face. Mine eyes dazzle. She died young.'[2]

He was still entranced with the cadence of Tennyson and found such simplicity a new approach. But, whether it influenced him or not, his own work was to lie somewhere between the two. He seems to have been rather impressed by the amount of work he did, but found time to write a poem which contains his longing for home as well as his dislike of Lee.

> When smoke into the ether went,
> Or dust along the highways whirled
>   With breezes from the downs of Kent,
> And mist about the houses curled,
>   Winds came at times and brought the scent
> Of roses from the outer world.
>
> But when the snow-clouds veiled the sky
> And dreary was the town of Lee
>   And carts unseen went rambling by
> And all was dull as death could be,

1. 1864–1915. Poet and dramatist.
2. From 'The Duchess of Malfi.'

> There came a whirring and a cry
> And geese went over to the sea,
>
> And brought us glimpses as they flew
> Of that which lived beyond the town
> Where rushes by the water grew
> And all the hills went sloping down
> To meet the moor, where ever blew
> The wind that turns the woodland brown.

The roses in the first verse were at Dunstall, the hills and water in the last are at Dunsany.

This was accepted by the *Pall Mall*, his first work to reach print. It earned him £1. However he was not so distracted that he did not pass his Sandhurst exams and he was relieved to go there. He found the life tolerable, though any later memory of it was clouded by the number of his contemporaries who were to be killed in the war. One who survived from his company was Lord Howard de Walden, a rather similar figure to Dunsany in that he was a peer with literary leanings who was often to be accused of being a dilettante. Lending unfortunate support to this slander they began a story together but did not finish it. On the other hand Dunsany had a great success with a pastiche of Kipling called *The Road to Camberley*.

A trip to Switzerland to recuperate from having his tonsils out was more inspiring. He had never been abroad and was amazed by the beauty of the Alps, which he enjoyed describing; a trick of the fading light gave him the line 'Rocks should not walk in the evenings,' which he used in a play years later.[1]

A letter to his mother which may have caused her to worry about her wild son shows neatly both the soldier and the writer. The opening is that of an unusually inarticulate young officer, but soon he is taking trouble to get right the description of a scene that has been carefully as well as breathlessly observed.

St. Moritz,
Engadine.
Dec. 21 '97

Dear Mother

I am writing to wish you a happy Christmas as I suppose you will get this letter some time around Christmas. I hope you're pretty

1. *The Gods of the Mountains.*

well. I am in pretty good health out here. Tobogganing is great
sport. We go on an average on the fast runs at about forty miles an
hour sometimes less sometimes a great deal more.

Although upsets are frequent one very seldom gets seriously hurt;
once I got pretty badly smashed but I have got over it now. We
go down lying flat head foremost and steering round the corners
with our toes.

We don't toboggan on snow here but on a smooth sheet of ice, so
it is pretty exciting. Once I tried some mountaineering on my own
hook without a guide. People don't go up as a rule in Winter as the
snow is very deep. On my way up the sun set; it was a wonderful
sight as it went down over the mountains and the lakes turned grey
and the snow a brilliant scarlet and then the crimson faded from
the sky and it was green and blue.

When at last I reached the top I suddenly realised that it was
night; it had quite suddenly grown dark and over the great grey
peaks the stars came sliding up. It seemed far steeper climbing down
than it did going up. There was nothing living in sight, not even the
pines as I had got above them. I had no idea of the way and had to
grope for my tracks in the dark. At night in the Alps the cold is most
intense. I had no gloves and once as I was climbing down I touched
a large slab of stone, and it came up frozen on my hand. I shook it
off but my hand was nearly paralysed by it and I had to knock it
about on the frozen snow to restore the circulation.

I was very tired and growing stiff and at the time I thought I
might never get back. Twice I lost my track but found it again and
I got home late that night. I was none the worse for it except that
the skin of my hands is still as if they had been slowly boiled.

I am off to toboggan again now.

Your loving son,
E. PLUNKETT.

III

Dunsany's father died when only forty-eight in 1899 and was
buried at Dunsany. Their relationship had not improved and
Dunsany had found it easier to appreciate his gifts from a
distance. His father left many debts which Dunsany paid, and
he also settled enough money on his brother Reggie to bring
in £500 a year, quite a decent sum for a young bachelor then.
Reggie resented being left nothing directly but did not appreciate that there was not much to leave. He had already em-

barked on his successful career in the Navy and the brothers
were not in close contact. Though he stayed at Dunsany to hunt,
often enough, Dunsany was never his home. Dunsany's uncle
Horace put himself in charge of the family affairs. Within
days of the funeral Dunsany had joined the first battalion
of the Coldstream Guards and not long afterwards, aged twenty,
set off for Gibraltar.

Dunsany himself ascribed much in his stories to this second
trip abroad. He rated those about the East above all others and,
firmly holding that Tangier is of the East, came to feel that
this first glimpse was the basic inspiration of his finest work,
though at the time of creation he imagined them works of pure
fantasy whose original source was his own mind. What he liked
best in his work was least realistic and therefore not to be pinned
down geographically. The designers of his plays and most of
his readers place his lands vaguely East of Suez with Egyptian
touches. 'Sunlight and desert and wandering men' he saw, and
added fancies drawn from conversation, china dragons or
Kipling. More specifically he remembered looking down on 'the
shining mass of Gibraltar at noon in midsummer,' while all its
population slept, and riding in Spain on an excellent pony
bought for £11. He wrote to his mother of the border where
'dogs run backwards and forwards, hiding behind tufts of
grass, smuggling tobacco which is tied round their necks. A dog
here fetches a good price according to how well he evades the
sentries, who shoot them when they can.' Two trips across the
straits to Africa were for less than a day each but 'how long do
you have to stand in an oriental street before you can get the
smell of it? How long does it take to see the flat roofs of a city
and a hundred people wallowing in the sunlight?'

Not long, for war broke out in South Africa and he left by
boat for Kimberley. Where a spell in Gibraltar might be
expected to leave a young officer a bit bored, a colonial war at
the farthest point of a strange continent could stir the blood of
any man, and that of an embryo writer who was attracted to
the vast solitude of Africa must surely churn with excitement.
Yet Dunsany took it very coolly. He responded more to the
land than the life and though he returned to Africa he went to
the south again only when he had no choice. He had no
scruples about fighting, which he regarded as an honourable

profession and, in times of crisis, a duty, and seems to have been a calm and efficient soldier in action. He did not get on with one of his superior officers, who once irritatingly remarked that he could have had an Irish peerage, only he had not bothered to take it up. Even his description of the first time he was under fire is detached, almost bored: 'It was absolutely flat all the way to the hills, and I have no wish to say anything critical of anyone's shooting, or to belittle some rifle that may be dear to its owner, but I cannot see why they did not get the whole lot of us. In the early part of that walk the bullets hissed, in the later part they cracked. When we got near the hills to which we were going, an enfilading fire broke out on our right, and the people in front continued their attentions. It was a low and rocky hill with a smooth slope on the far side and as we ran up it they got on to their horses. Our own people on our left had a higher hill to climb and when they got to the top and saw us on the top of our hill, they cheered. I cheered back and several men near me joined in. Then we walked down the other side into the Boers' laager.'

When he was in South Africa forty years later he took a taxi to the battlefields and discussed the war with the taxi-driver, who had been on the other side.

DRIVER: We watched you coming all the way.
DUNSANY: You were damned bad shots.
DRIVER: We were not.
DUNSANY: I wouldn't be alive if you weren't.

He was also at the battle of Modder River but notes in the same manner little more than that it was very hot in the day and very cold at night and of locusts, 'I remember very few green things near me before they came and afterwards there were none.' Later he worked as assistant Press Censor at Cape Town where he met and liked Kipling, who then went out of his life for twenty-five years. He made no attempt to meet him again but was delighted when he did. His 21st birthday passed unnoticed. When he left the army in 1901 he was glad to be free. If he still had no idea of what he wished to do, he was now certain of one thing that he did not.

IV

For a time Dunsany hunted in Ireland and found that it absorbed all his attention. His devotion is shown by a discovery: 'On Wednesday, when the Meath did not hunt, I used sometimes to go out with the Ward, a pack of staghounds that hunted much of the counties of Dublin, Meath and Kildare, but I soon found that one enjoyed hunting more by taking the Wednesday off.' He was offered and gladly accepted the Mastership of the Tara harriers which he hunted over the hundred square miles that lie round Tara through the 1902–3 winter. That spring he rode one of his own horses in a race in which 'there were as many falls as competitors. One horse did not fall at all and won; one fell twice, the rest of us had one toss each.' He came third.

There was also shooting. Returning with some rabbits on one occasion he fired an accurate shot at the bell as he walked towards the front door, so avoiding a tedious wait for the butler. The story was transferred indoors by an American admirer with the implication that he did it habitually, and the vision of Dunsany scattering bullets about the drawing-room, once conjured up, has proved durable. At Dunstall he still shot snails. Different pleasures had been suggested by a new friend, Jack Hope-Johnstone, whom he had met, inevitably given his way of life in Ireland, on the hunting field. In spite of this sporting introduction, what they really shared was an interest in literature. His relations said of Hope-Johnstone 'He's a terrible boy for the books' and for the first time Dunsany had a close friend who could understand and enjoy the imaginative side of his character, which might otherwise have been smothered for want of an airing.

Then there was the London Season. As a good-looking young peer he was asked 'everywhere' and, gregarious and friendly, he enjoyed himself, happily unconscious that his clothes were never quite right and that when he said whatever came into his head or acted on the spur of the moment, he sometimes gave offence. Friends called him 'eccentric' or 'mad'; others used harsher adjectives. At Ascot in June 1903 he was introduced to Lady Beatrice Villiers by a man who had already proposed to her.

Her first reaction, noted in her diary, was 'Delightful to meet, but not human enough to live with'.

Beatrice was one of the five children of the Earl and Countess of Jersey. Their eldest son was Lord Villiers, then came three girls, Markie, Mary and Beatrice, and then Arthur, the youngest. Her home was Middleton Park[1] in Oxfordshire, a large rambling Georgian mansion set among cedar trees, with mown lawns stretching away into the distance, a place where life could be very festive or rather dull but was always well-ordered and prosperous. The park was beautiful, the village was tidy and her parents were conscientious landowners who had a happy relationship with the people on their estate.

Lord Jersey also owned Osterley Park[2] in Middlesex which had been built and furnished by Robert Adam and was so elegant that the children did lessons in a schoolroom where furniture and walls were handpainted 'in the Etruscan style'. Osterley was near London and it could be reached by carriage or underground railway; Lady Jersey referred to it as a 'suburban' home, secure in the knowledge that no one would take her too seriously. It was ideal for weekend parties in the summer or for large garden-parties on Saturday afternoons. Henry James has described the impression it made on visitors in his story *The Lesson of the Master*. Lady Jersey was capable, energetic and well read and she collected interesting and distinguished guests – that they were also highly respectable may be deduced from the fact that she felt very daring when she invited the young radical politician, Joseph Chamberlain. Her butler showed his disapproval by commenting warmly on the next dinner-party, 'We had a very nice dinner last night.' She agreed that all had gone well. 'All very nice people,' he continued with heavy emphasis and left her to ponder the implication. Besides owning Middleton and Osterley, the Jerseys often took a house in London and they also had a house called Baglan on their South Wales property where the children were sometimes sent for a seaside holiday.

The outstanding event of Beatrice's childhood had been the

1. The house was demolished by the 9th Earl of Jersey in 1935 and a smaller one, designed by Lutyens, built on the site. This is now the property of the National Westminster Bank.
2. Now the property of the National Trust.

two years she spent in Australia. Lord Jersey was made Governor of New South Wales in 1890 when she was ten. He delayed his departure because his wife had typhoid but finally had to leave her to convalesce. When Lady Jersey was well enough to follow she took the four younger children, an English and a German governess, and the old nurse because the children cried so at leaving her behind. They left a bitterly cold England and made their way across an equally icy France, piled high with snow. At Mâcon there was an inn which had a courtyard with a balcony running round the inside. On this Beatrice saw the chambermaid with high-starched cap hurrying through the snow from room to room with a bedwarmer for each bed in turn. In Australia Beatrice was desperately home-sick. As the youngest girl, she did not have to play much part in her parents' official life, but Lady Jersey expected her children to make themselves useful when she needed them, and once asked her if she would like to open a children's bazaar. Beatrice did not dare say no. She was told what to say, and rehearsed it conscientiously but at the critical moment had to appeal for help before muttering that she declared it open and hoped it would be a great success. Then a little boy was brought forward and told to give three cheers for Lady Beatrice. Another embarrassing silence. When asked why he would not, he said that he had looked around the room and could not see three chairs anywhere. So if Beatrice had not done well, he had done worse; and she was given £1 to spend.

Lord Jersey came home in 1893. Educated by the governesses, Beatrice was highly intelligent, well read and soon used to the conversation of Cabinet Ministers. Shy, but not timid, she was also completely innocent of the ways of the world beyond the lodge gates. Even by contemporary standards her upbringing was severe. She was not allowed to play mixed hockey, which her friends did so much that to be a constant member of a team was almost like belonging to a club. They got up girls' games especially for her, but it was not the same. That she was allowed to hunt was a great concession. In 1898 Beatrice's eldest sister, Markie, married the Hon Walter Rhys, later 7th Baron Dynevor and heir to a castle in Carmarthenshire. The next year Mary married Thomas, 5th Earl of Longford. His house was Pakenham Hall, County Westmeath, but he was a soldier and they lived in many different places.

Beatrice thus became the only daughter at home, and though this brought her closer to her mother it also meant that she had to bear the brunt of her father's caprices; he had not moved with the times and Beatrice suffered from many irksome restrictions which other girls of her age escaped. When she had been going to balls for two or three years she was still not permitted to walk alone in London. It was important to her that Georgie Buller[1] should come to live actually in Lowndes Square as a journey which did not venture beyond it might be allowed unattended. At the same age she was eager to accept an invitation to stay with her sister Mary in Ireland, but was told she could not go as she was needed to play piquet with her father in the evenings. However her parents did take her on a trip to India where she found everyone much easier to get on with than she expected. When a girl of her own age, twenty, said 'My mother says I am too old and will never get married now. Nor will you,' she answered firmly, 'I think I may.' Asked at a party for women only if mixed evenings were more fun, already diplomatic she replied, 'Nothing could be more enjoyable than this.' Strolling round the garden in the evening, the son of a maharajah and Beatrice both lit cigarettes. 'An Indian youth,' he explained, 'would never smoke before his father.' 'Nor would this English girl,' she thought, having never smoked before. Though acute and self-possessed she was gentle and content to be out of the limelight. Her dashing elder brother, Lord Villiers and her sisters Markie and Mary were more forceful; so she obediently played piquet. She was always particularly fond of her younger brother Arthur and once they played cricket together for seven exhausting hours; but when her sisters had married, Beatrice's life became a little lonely.

Tall (six foot four inches, but he had met four men taller in the Coldstream), thin and very good-looking, Dunsany was an

1. Dame Georgiana Buller 1883-1953. Daughter of General Sir Redvers Buller, VC, Beatrice's greatest friend. She had an ugly clever face and was sympathetic, amusing and companionable. She was brought up in Devonshire and was Director of War Hospitals there in the 1914–18 war and afterwards started a home for crippled children in Exeter as well as one for disabled soldiers at Leatherhead. She never married.

extravagant figure anywhere and against all this correctness he was sensational; but not, unfortunately, a sensational success. He had no vices. Uninterested in racing and all forms of gambling, he was almost a teetotaller and smoked only an occasional respectable pipe, which in any case he gave up. He had no wish to appear unconventional, but somehow the impression he gave was wild, too enthusiastic, too uninhibited and too noisy. He persuaded Beatrice and a cousin to drop balloons from an upper window and shot them from a balcony with a toy gun – a cabman retrieved one he allowed to go floating down the street; with the same gun he shot fifty-three cats (they just looked round if they were hit) and a dancing bear (which did not notice). He had not learnt – he never did learn – to listen to his elders with patience and respect. He liked to talk and if he disagreed with Lord Jersey or anyone else he said so. He was bad at dancing, but did not mind; gestured towards conformity in dress, but did not achieve it. Once he travelled down to a garden-party at Osterley by train with Aubrey and Mervyn Herbert.[1] He claims that their mother, Lady Carnarvon, had asked him to look after their clothes and so suggested to Aubrey: 'Give your gloves to Mervyn, who hasn't got any and he will be all right. But you don't want them for with that hat nothing can make you right.' A moment later a woman wished to take a seat and was turned away by the guard who explained that it was reserved for those going to the garden-party. 'Well,' she said, 'they don't look like garden-party people.' Everyone laughed and Aubrey Herbert felt constrained to say, 'I am afraid that was my hat.' It all rings true enough except for Dunsany as the sartorial perfectionist. His formal clothes were adequate, his informal ones remarkable. 'He looks,' a friend remarked, 'as if he'd stood there naked and had his clothes hurled at him, leaving them wherever they happened to land.' He made no attempt to be tidy, and in the country wore rabbity clothes, commenting, 'Why spoil good ones?' Beatrice later addressed him as 'Pony' because of his shaggy look and one of his neighbours said to her wistfully, 'I thought perhaps he would get his hair cut after he was married . . .' (He called her 'Mink', partly because of a muff she often carried which he

1. The Hon Aubrey Herbert, son of 4th Earl of Carnarvon (1880–1923) MP for South Somerset 1911–1918 and his brother Mervyn (1882–1929).

once stuck to the ceiling with plasticine and partly, she thought, because of a confusion with 'minx'.) More important was the absence of religion. It had not been forced on him and he had not sought it, so, without any profound spiritual struggle, he was an atheist. Nor had he been confirmed. This shocked the Jerseys who were devout.

As Society was then small Dunsany and Beatrice met often enough. When he came to write he showed his first stories to her and she was very impressed and enthusiastic. He had not shown them to anyone, nor had anyone else ever shown his work to her; it was a great step in their intimacy. It is not true that he pushed her into a lake on purpose and proposed because she did not complain, but he did upset a canoe and the story has a certain truth to both their characters. In fact he proposed in the kitchen garden of Syon House during a garden-party on July 15th 1904, just over a year after they had met; the gardener, walking there in the cool of the evening, 'came by us once and then left us alone'.

Her family was not overjoyed; Lord Longford went so far as to comment to his wife, 'You shouldn't let your sister marry that undesirable Irish peer.' Two days before the wedding, Dunsany realised he had not bought a ring and had a dozen sent to Middleton, commenting of the jeweller, 'I hope he'll think I'm a Sultan'. In spite of all such difficulties Dunsany and Beatrice were married on September 15th 1904, when he was twenty-six and she was almost twenty-four. They had a country wedding. The parish church of Middleton Stoney is old and picturesque and stands inside the park gates. Lord Northland,[1] an army friend, was best man. They spent their honeymoon at a small house near Stoneleigh.

Beatrice had shown considerable courage. Her marriage was a great moment of emancipation, exciting but also frightening. In one step she left her friends, relations and cloistered security for a future in an Irish castle with fifteen servants to control, relations that quarrelled with one another and did not necessarily share her beliefs or standards, and a husband who was widely considered eccentric and had not yet found anything he wished to do. She knew nothing of sex, he scarcely more; it was

1. Thomas Uchter Caulfield (Viscount Northland), son of 5th Earl of Ranfurly 1882–1915.

never important to them. Soon after they were married he gave
her a clothes-basket full of his old letters and said, 'you sort
them,' from which she concluded that at any rate he had led a
blameless life.

Though Beatrice made friends easily with the country people
she was and she remained English and for the next twenty
years it was not easy to be a land-owning English protestant in
Ireland. There were problems and sacrifices apart from political
worries. She had to run a household, which had long con-
spicuously lacked a woman's touch. Dunsany had not been
reassuring, 'oh, there's an excellent housemaid', he said, 'she's
been very well trained by Reed [the gamekeeper]'. The game-
keeping approach to domestic problems had scored a success
when there were difficulties rewiring a bell through the thick
walls. The wire was attached to a ferret, and a squealing rabbit
held at the far end of the tunnel and all was done in no time. But
gentler methods were required; Dunsany Castle needed
modernising and improving and they set about buying carpets
and armchairs and sofas. It was much smaller than Middleton
– hardly large enough to put up a cricket eleven – and they
built on a billiard-room with two bedrooms and a bathroom
above it which they fitted out with specially designed arty-
crafty furniture. Dunsany bought anything that took his fancy
at an exhibition, generally the work of a contemporary crafts-
man or living artist. His taste was post-Morris and post-
Beardsley and his purchases soon came to look dated and are
only now coming back into fashion. In most Edwardian country
houses the men lurked in fastnesses of their own and only
appeared in the drawing-rooms at set times, but Dunsany
could not bear to miss any fun that was going and he was in the
drawing-room at all times of the day, pursuing the hobby of the
moment, however messy, among flowers and bibelots. Beatrice
managed the family with skill and never quarrelled with her
mother- or brother-in-law though she was necessarily present
when Dunsany did and could only be totally loyal to him. Her
family were always fond of one another and each was surprised
to see a family could be so different from their own.

Since the death of Dunsany's father, his Uncle Horace had
been his Trustee and almost guardian. Sir Horace Plunkett was
now fifty and a figure of some importance in Ireland. At twenty-

five he had been threatened with tuberculosis and the doctor offered him the choice of South Africa or the Rocky Mountains. He had chosen America and for over ten years he was a real, live, if part-time, cowboy. Leaving Ireland in the spring he stayed on and managed the ranch he and his partners owned beyond Denver, once won a buggy and harness playing cards, and worried about trouble with the Indians though not actually experiencing any. In October he returned to Ireland and with the death of his eldest brother Randal in 1883, the ageing of his father who died in 1889, and the lack of interest shown by John, Dunsany's father, and later by Dunsany himself, Uncle Horace year by year took over control of the estates. His interest in agriculture, first noticed when he named a hunter Silo, grew to a passion and in 1899 he became Vice-President of the Irish Department of Agriculture.

Though he did not read much he knew writers as well as politicians. In 1896 he had dined with Lady Gregory and met W. B. Yeats, 'a rebel, a mystic and an ass, but really a genius in a queer way, I believe.' Next year he found the poet, George Russell (A.E.) in a drapery shop and set him up rather un-suitably as an organiser and then editor of an agricultural magazine. When Dunsany was published in the *Pall Mall Magazine* he wrote[1] of 'some lines by a nephew of mine aetat eighteen. They are a happiness to me. If you knew the boy and his parents you would marvel at the product of his brain. He has a talent for chess and for upsetting things. He can draw a nightmare, but that he can write simple and rather musical English is a revelation that gladdens the avuncular heart.'

Kind and generous, Uncle Horace gave too much advice for too long and his relationship with Dunsany deteriorated and finally collapsed almost completely. In the meantime they played chess together, Uncle Horace gradually losing the upper hand but continuing to offer hints. He was not physically im-pressive and later, when they had quarrelled, Dunsany said that, not being so witty as his brother, Horace had borrowed remarks from Dunsany's father but repeating them had lost their point. In particular his father once referred to 'a little pagoda of lies stor(e)y upon stor(e)y' which Uncle Horace took up without understanding.

1. to Lady Betty Balfour 1897.

He appears in two of Dunsany's books both written after a quarrel over money. Uncle Horace had been accepted at his own valuation as a man of business and the world and had then acted – as trustees do – with less than adequate efficiency. The first account[1] describes without rancour their business relationship. 'An uncle, my father's younger brother, had now become my guardian. He was a man of charming manner and let me do what I liked; in return for which I naturally gave my consent to whatever he recommended in the affairs of the estate my father had left me. He often consulted me, always giving me two courses to choose from. Of some rents that were to be invested he would say: "If you would like the money invested at three and a half per cent in trust funds, I will do it for you; but if you would sooner have it invested at twelve per cent in a company that I can put it into which is equally good, you only have to tell me." And I told him.

'He never spoke of finance without smiling.'

His second appearance,[2] written four years further from the quarrel, is, surprisingly, more bitter. He is called Charles Peever and is once more the guardian of a financial innocent, this time the heroine Mona. He gets her a job in advertising (very bad in Dunsany's eyes), recommends her a losing horse (but 'Peever really thought the horse might win') and suffers a series of cutting little descriptions:

'It has come to my knowledge', said Charles Peever. 'It has come to my knowledge'. And he liked the phrase so much, so much better it sounded than the mere words 'I have heard' that he repeated it yet again. 'It has come to my knowledge . . .' She knew him well enough to be aware that his words were no mere indication of what he meant. He loved to be consulted over other people's affairs, and loved to direct them. It was difficult to say why this was: it was merely his idiosyncrasy. If one were to try to analyse it, which is rather tedious work, one might find that the muddle he used to make of his own affairs was on the point of forcing upon him a feeling of his own inferiority to the general run of educated men, and that he corrected this by advising and guiding others, very much as a blind helmsman, saved from the wreck of his ship, might take up the calling of pilot . . . He never said to anyone: 'I want to go to Ireland' or 'I am going to London' but always 'I have to go to

1. in *The Curse of the Wise Woman* 1935.
2. in *The Story of Mona Sheehy* 1939.

such-and-such a place'. The difference may not seem to have been worth making; and yet he never spoke in any other way of his journeys and it left the impression of a conscientious man, serving other people while the rest of us go here and there for our own idle amusement.

Of course he loses all Mona's money. But this was written after a row; for many years Horace Plunkett was a personage, a close relation and a friend. When he cut an Aubusson carpet in two for a conjuring trick it was accepted as showing his wit and sophistication.

Uncle Horace, whose feeling for Lady Fingall was widely known, would stay at her house, Killeen, one weekend and at Dunsany half a mile away, the next. Her character comes over clearly in her autobiography, not least in its title *70 Years Young*! Of Lord Fingal's proposal she wrote, 'I thought how nice he was and what fun it would be to live at Killeen. And I probably thought it would be fun to marry an earl too. And of course it was exciting to get engaged in one's very first season. So I said, "I think I would like to, awfully".' However she was very beautiful. They had run things before Dunsany's marriage and tried to continue to do so. After a few months Lady Fingall, dining at Dunsany, remarked to Uncle Horace, 'These tapestry chairs really do need recovering.' 'Yes,' interrupted Dunsany swiftly and firmly, 'but Beatrice and I have not yet decided what to cover them with.'

He hunted foxes and stags when hunting was available and all year attacked rabbits with a rifle, shooting a thousand in three months, a hundred of them on the run. There was never a pheasant shoot at Dunsany though he put down a few hundred each year. He preferred walking over the bogs with just the keeper.

Dunsany was greedy. He wrote 'Snipe – when properly cooked – and five minutes is quite long enough – is the food that gourmets are given when they have been good to the poor, and with their gluttony pardoned, have gone to heaven,' and with a couple for dinner, varied by a teal, woodcock or golden plover, claimed to shoot his dinner from October to March.

But he was aware of the paradox that those who really love the country are frequently those most dedicated to killing the creatures that live in it; and he, foremost amongst them, could not plead necessity. Though toying with the idea that the rabbits needed shooting, he admitted that there seemed to be just as many when he finished, hoped that he had minimised the gruesome need for trapping, but never really denied that he shot, or hunted, because he enjoyed it. Yet it nagged at him. After a lifetime of sport he wrote a strange poem[1] acknowledging an affinity with the birds who must surely hate him.

> When I am dead the birds
> That through the long reeds go
> Though they hear no man's words
> Those wondering birds will know.
> . . . And nought have I to say
> Against their myriad voice,
> Arising on that day
> To sing, Rejoice! Rejoice!

Cricket matches, sometimes one day, sometimes two, were an established feature at Dunsany, the home-team of friends and neighbours taking on the Free Foresters, Old Harrovians, Trinity College or a regiment. At the wicket Dunsany was a powerful and aggressive batsman, a slow bowler in spite of his height and a good slip-fielder; he played for the village, indeed his energy kept the game going, but he did not care to lose and would bowl all afternoon if that seemed the best tactic. Others had better not take more than their share upon them. When Paddy, a gardener, and safe fielder, moved to make certain of a catch off his own bowling in front of his captain he felt two large hands fasten over his and, though the batsman was out, 'It wasn't worth it.'

There might be twenty in the house and often wild games besides cricket were played. Harold Alexander,[2] not then so exalted, joined in a battle between canoes and punts which assailed each other with torpedoes loaded with dynamite, and when he was the only person not upset, decently dived in. A neighbour, Sir John Kennedy,[3] challenged Dunsany to a

1. *Mirage Waters* 1938.
2. Later Earl Alexander of Tunis 1891–1969. Field-Marshal, and C-in-C in the Middle East, North Africa and Italy, Supreme Allied Commander in the Mediterranean 1944.
3. 3rd Baronet 1856–1923, farmed in County Dublin.

spectacular duel with Vèry lights, which burn well but can be dodged, and fired a shot at the crowd, which was not too pleased, though all ducked successfully. There was no fishing, which was too inactive, nor croquet, though Beatrice liked it.

He was an early and enthusiastic driver and, though a friend of Charles Rolls, had an open Packard from 1904–1906; then, perhaps fortunately, for he drove furiously, he lost interest and hardly drove again. They had played bridge before they were married but he found the game went on tediously long and now Dunsany, who had been good, increasingly said they did not know the rules to avoid making up an interminable four. Crossword puzzles he used to curse and hold to be contemptible, but he often struggled with *The Times*. With chess the problem was to find opponents, Beatrice beating him only if he was very absent-minded. He enjoyed ping-pong but used tennis-scoring and in a play allows a character to say, 'You've made me lose my serve', a possible but unlikely remark. A forceful tennis player, quick at net and aggressive everywhere, he used to carry six or eight balls in his pockets and large hands when he was serving and sometimes varied rules to allow the ball to be played off overhanging branches.

In the evening he tolerated billiards but preferred something more lively like his invention 'Moucat'. Derived from cat and mouse it was played round, under and on a billiard table. Three men are blindfolded and have to catch in four minutes the one who can see. All players remove their shoes. The recommended technique for the pursuers is to link hands across the table and with one crawling under it to advance together. It is then necessary for the pursued to swing the lamps out of the way in order to have room to jump over their hands. Dunsany scored a brilliant success by grasping two pursuers by the hand while they were groping for one another so they took him for a friend. Not all hosts approve this game.

He revelled in acting and word-games after dinner, largely because he was very good at them, as happy writing parodies of Milton as taking the part of Drake in an historical tableau.

Once playing Dumb Crambo he had to represent shirt. He drew a screen into the drawing-room and retired behind it. A tail-coat appeared over the top, followed by a waist-coat, a tie, a collar and then a shirt. But he did not stop there; shoes,

socks and finally trousers appeared. With the excitement at its
height he walked out from behind the screen – fully dressed.
He had borrowed a second set of clothes. The yearning, the
sense of unease, that lay beneath the Edwardian games and
laughter, was never acknowledged, let alone understood.

Before his engagement it had been Uncle Horace who steered
Dunsany towards politics. Dunsany felt he should do something
and that was the sort of thing people – his family, his friends –
did. He had 1,400 acres at Dunsany, but no interest in farming.
So in 1903 he had joined the Tories, feeling correctly that that
was the party for him though he had little idea of his or their
policy. A. J. Balfour was their leader and Prime Minister. At
an informal meeting with the selection committee of West
Wilts. he was asked whether he was for men or measures. He
realised that there was a right or a wrong answer to this and
was pondering which to plump for, inclining a little towards
'men' when his patron, Mr Walter Long[1] butted in firmly with
'of course he is for measures'. That was the correct answer.
Later he found that Tariff Reform was an important issue and
he tried to find out what his Party's leaders felt about that.
They would not tell him, but he decided, again correctly, they
were for it, and so preached it up and down West Wilts. His
intellectual friend, Jack Hope-Johnstone enlivened the scene by
appearing there out of the countryside with a knapsack and
red braces, enjoying the effect he produced.

Dunsany was a tolerably conscientious candidate. Generally
he was an impulsive rather than a dogged reader. Impressed by
Thus Spake Zarathustra in Italy he read it all the way through
lunch. Now however he worked through a life of Pitt in several
volumes.

In spite of greatly preferring Ireland, a few months after the
wedding in 1905 they rented a house called Rood Ashton near
Trowbridge in Wiltshire. Dunsany's character was unusually
open for a politician and he held that 'you do not go before an
electorate to conceal your views but to make them clear'; a
doctrine to which most would give nominal assent, but few
would care to practise. He held frequent meetings and enjoyed

1. A friend of Uncle Horace and Dunsany: an MP for 40 years he had
been in the Cabinet as President of the Board of Agriculture, and was to be
First Lord of the Admiralty and created a Viscount.

speaking without notes or even preparation, welcoming hecklers, whom he found useful in that they introduced new themes and encouraging because they were easily out-manoeuvred. If he had continued along this path it is possible that he would have made a creditable MP, putting party loyalty above all else, allowing that others knew best on most issues, but occasionally lighting on some injustice that needed righting and, above all, livening up the House of Commons, as his father had, with irrelevant eloquence. It is difficult to imagine this role lasting long but it never came into being at all, for well before he fought an election he had discovered something he wanted to do much more.

Dunsany had shown his earliest tales to Beatrice before they were engaged, and been encouraged. Uncle Horace's life included the literary set so Dunsany had a slight acquaintance with Yeats, A.E., and others of those who made up the Irish Renaissance. This was now in full swing, and can be conveniently dated as having begun in 1893 when Yeats published a book called *The Celtic Twilight*. Dunsany had responded to A.E.'s gentle kindness immediately and offered to give some money to support a review he was to edit. George Moore reports that Yeats came along with a sneer, and said: 'I hear Lord Dunsany, that you are going to supply groundsel for A.E.'s canaries.' The sneer was enough to bring the project to naught. Aware of writers but not one of them, he was searching for something to do, to believe in, to build his life around and it may have been A.E. who revived the idea of strange pagan Gods in his mind. The final push towards writing had been a visit to Her Majesty's Theatre to see *The Darling of the Gods*.[1] *The Times* review opened: 'Little bundles tied with white sashes and topped with white mask-like faces under coils of jet-black hair sidle and slide, or bend low to the earth, or scamper like mice, uttering the little squeaks of mice . . . We at once know that we are in Japan, the Japan of the Western stage . . .' Though it was not quite the same fantastic oriental world as the one that already floated in Dunsany's head – less splendid, more quaint – it showed that such a world could be conjured up. Curiously it did not occur to him to write plays though he was to do so later. He began by writing portraits of the Gods of

1. By two Americans David Belasco and John Luther Long.

Pegana which he showed to no one but Beatrice. They have strange names such as Limpang-Tung and Skarl and Mana-Yood-Sushai. In rhetorical repetitious prose clearly influenced by the Bible he described their actions and their prophets, for example:

> Time is the hound of Sish.
> At Sish's bidding do the hours run before him
>   as he goeth upon his way.
> Never hath Sish stepped backward nor ever hath
>   he tarried; never hath he relented to the
>   things that once he knew nor turned to them
>   again.

or

And when it is dark, all in the hour of Triboogie, Hish creepeth from the forest, the Lord of Silence, whose children are the bats, that have broken the command of their father, but in a voice that is ever so low. Hish husheth the mouse and all the whispers in the night; he maketh all noises still. Only the cricket rebelleth. But Hish hath set against him such a spell that after he hath cried a thousand times his voice may be heard no more but becometh part of the silence.

Dunsany's Gods are a little more human and fallible than those of Egypt and a little less than those of the Greeks. Human beings appear only as prophets in relation to the Gods and their names are as exotic – Yonath, Yug 'Alhireth-Hotep etc. Most prophets are boasting liars:

'*Therefo e they said to Yug: "Be thou our Prophet, and know all and tell us concerning the werefore of It All."*

'*And Yug said: "I know all things." And men were pleased.*

'*And Yug said of the beginning that it was in Yug's own garden and of the end that it was in the sight of Yug.*'

When *The Gods of Pegana* was completed Dunsany made some drawings. In black ink, they show more imagination than technical mastery, as might be expected, and have a pleasing exuberance, but they are less striking than gloomier sketches of the same years. Of these a typical scene would show comfortless mountains under a chill brilliant moon while in the shadows is the suggestion of a creature something like a giant cockroach or spider but far more sinister than either. Bats appear frequently. A series called *Punishments in Another World* begins with Solitude, Criticism, Darkness, and Homesickness, the evils he dreaded as a boy.

Dunsany modestly felt that there were two men who might improve on his illustrations. One was Doré, whom he knew to be dead. The other signed himself S. H. Sime, and turned out to be living. He was tracked down and they began a perfect partnership. Frank Harris described Sidney Sime as 'a strongly built man of about five feet seven or eight, with a cliff-like overhanging tyrannous forehead. His eyes are superlative, greyish-blue looking out under heavy brows, eyes with a pathetic patience in them as of one who has lived with sorrow, and realises: "The weary weight of all this unintelligible world."

'From time to time humorous gleams light up the eyes and the whole face, mirth on melancholy – a modern combination.'

Sime's drawings were remarkably similar to Dunsany's and they had the same approach to the sinister, using the horrid implication of a hint rather than a statement of the demons that lurk out of sight; the whole enlivened by occasional dashes of humour. When they worked the wrong way round – Dunsany thinking of stories to go with Sime's pictures[1] – they were in such accord that no change of tone is perceptible.

Nobody else ever illustrated a story by Dunsany,[2] Sime worked in black and white and his style is inevitably reminiscent of Beardsley. He had a completely free hand always but there was never any difficulty and he became a great friend of the Dunsanys. Starting as a collier's boy he had worked underground for ten years meanwhile selling drawings done with coal to other miners before he managed to get to Paris. Perhaps because of his hard beginnings he had a distaste for work and used to say 'after forty no man ought to have to do anything but stretch out his hand for food.'

The Gods of Pegana was completed in 1904 and Dunsany arranged to pay for its publication. The publisher went broke. However a new one was found, Mr Elkin Mathews, and in 1905 he appeared publicly in print. He never had to pay to be published again.

1. *Book of Wonder.*
2. Except for book-jackets, which he did not control.

Naturally the Dunsanys were very excited and began a scrap book of reviews which were in time to fill over twelve volumes. The first crop was short and patronising, but almost none was bad, their general tone being summed up by *The Observer*, 'The book is full of grim and quaint fancies and the sheer originality of it encourages high hopes for Lord Dunsany.' It was a modest success. Neither side of the family took much notice of his appearance in print, except for his aunt, Mary Ponsonby, who thought he should use a pseudonym while Uncle Horace supported his right to appear in public without one.

Meanwhile he was still a Conservative candidate. The Conservatives had passed an Education Act which upset the nonconformists so that he was surprised to find that he was thought of as an agent of the Pope. He grew to like a 'sad and rather sweet'[1] tune, enough to forgive a poor rhyme and unfriendly words:

> Goodbye Dunsany. We don't want you.
> We want no candidate that will tax our food.

At one noisy meeting part of his audience began to sing it to drown his voice, but lost the rhythm. Dunsany snatched up a paper and beat time for them, until they laughed, one called out, 'We'll hear the bloody bandmaster,' and they did so.

Though enjoying the speeches he was not deeply enthralled by electioneering, which was time away from sport or literature. He once went over a wool factory with unprecedented thoroughness asking details of the work, but admitted later to his wife that he had really been gathering material for a story,[2] not seeking votes at all. The constituency had been Liberal before the Tory landslide of 1902 and when in June 1906 he lost by 1450 votes he was thought to have done rather well. Though he refers later to this contest almost as a sporting event in which he was glad to have put up a good show, at the time he still saw politics as a possible career and was disappointed by the result. He was re-adopted as the Conservative candidate though he was not to fight another election. While so few took his writing seriously, he was slow to do so himself, and saw it as an extra activity, not a career. However his gradual drift from

1. *Patches of Sunlight.*   2. *The Kith of the Elf-Folk.*

politics was not heart-breaking. If he had eventually to discard an occasional vision of himself rounding off a triumphant speech in the House of Commons amidst thunderous applause, it seems doubtful whether he ever considered what the subject of the speech might have been, or indeed noticed the need for it. In the same way he had never managed to get passionately involved with Tariff Reform or Education – the manner of politics held a certain charm for him, but in the matter he found little of interest.

At this moment Dunsany had everything – Beatrice, books to write, youth, health, looks, friends, a fortune, peace, two houses of which he was fond, a future – the list seems long enough. These were happy active years which he, and the whole country with perhaps less justification, would recall with nostalgia. A rough timetable evolved in the years after his marriage: winter and shooting at Dunsany, May and June at first in London, later in Kent, back to Dunsany for summer and cricket, September in Yorkshire always for partridges at Arden Hall with Lord and Lady Mexborough, then Scotland for grouse, before October and November in London. When a second tennis-court was built higher up a hill at Arden, he wrote 'Pleasant are thy courts below in the land of sin and woe, but I think your court up there is perfectly splendid.'

An important event in their lives altered the pattern a little. In August 1906 Beatrice had a son, their only child, and he was given the family name of Randal. Lady Jersey came to Dublin and was most annoyed when the papers said she had made the journey for the Horse Show in which she had a complete lack of interest. A bonfire was lit on the highest hill and twenty-one years later another was lit on the same spot. Beatrice wanted more children, Dunsany would probably have welcomed them but did not mind their absence. Randal had a nanny called Stidworthy whom he soon learned to control. Unfortunately she riposted by trying to bully Beatrice, than whom she was several years older, and she became a trial. Beatrice did not particularly like running a household, nor was she particularly good at it. Dunsany could be so difficult a master that she tried to be a gentle mistress, but this technique was not always successful. He thought a properly laid fire should catch if lit anywhere and once stood throwing lighted matches haphazardly into the grate until the supply was exhausted, when the maid was summoned and asked with great kindness to help. Dunsany's valet was butler for a few years, drank a bit, quarrelled with Dunsany a bit and died shortly after he left. After a dreadful stop-gap had departed, Mander arrived and ran everything until the second World War, arranging the *placement*, choosing wine, also having less frequent rows with Dunsany and, it emerged after he finally left, making rather more on the side than any butler should allow himself. He opened an antique shop in London.

Dunsany said he tried to write with poetry and humour. The poetry is everywhere apparent, the humour only creeps into the early work from time to time. What is most striking is what is left out. There is a complete lack of interest in any connection with the real world or in human character. Dunsany considered that to write about the familiar was a regrettable necessity for those who had not the imagination to conjure something beautiful from the air. He said of these early stories, 'I did not feel in the least as though I were inventing but rather as though I wrote the history of lands that I had known in forgotten wanderings.' Nevertheless he thought at this stage that the history of lands known in remembered wanderings was poor stuff to work into fiction and drew nothing consciously from first-hand experience; later he realised what had inspired many stories, often a strange or beautiful sight half-forgotten. As for character he had a remarkable lack of curiosity about people and their motives and did not think to try and understand them. Unusually self-centred, he saw the world almost entirely in terms of himself and his reactions but at the same time he was not in the least given to self-analysis. When people came into his plays and stories they remained less important than the language they spoke, the land they lived in and the situations that surrounded them.

He wrote at amazing speed and did not revise. When an idea came to him, he might turn it over in his mind for a day or two, probably being rather grumpy and abstracted while he did so, and then he would pour it down on paper. He had no interest in injecting a message or indeed any thought, though something of this kind might be discovered later. He wrote in 1916: 'I try sometimes to explain genius to people who mistrust or hate it by telling them it is doing anything as a fish swims or a swallow flies, perfectly, simply and with absolute ease. Genius is in fact an infinite capacity for not taking pains.'[1] And in 1934: 'My theory of the arts is that they are products of human emotions, that human feelings are their raw material, and that intellect should not be brought in except when absolutely necessary, to put the material together. The more the intellect is used, the less in my opinion is the man an artist, and the more he becomes a mathematician, a scientist or a trickster.'[2]

Dunsany had an intellect but did not care to use it on his work, his politics or indeed at all, except when playing chess. With this view, to revise or even pause for thought becomes interference with the proper creative process and he had the simple reverence for a creator, himself or another, which was common in his generation but appears romantic now. Living up to this speedy approach he wrote his most successful one-act play, *A Night at an Inn*, between an early tea and dinner. When a man from the BBC came to Dunsany, pleased with two short plays but wanting another on the same theme to complete a programme, Beatrice took him out for the afternoon while Dunsany wrote one. This is not typical, in that he usually required a few days before starting and would often have periods when he could not get going. There was not an inexhaustible supply of ideas to be rattled off, but when he did start, his progress was impressive. He wrote in pencil, coloured crayon or if in ink, with quills, often plucked from geese he had shot himself. Swan quills were even bigger and better, but not so easy to get. For ink-wells he found suitably shaped pieces of limestone at Eastbourne and elsewhere and kept them on the verandah at Dunstall. His writing was magnificent, fluent and whirling with great thick downstrokes; it looks as if it must be indecipherable and is in fact particularly easy to read. After his marriage Dunsany dictated to Beatrice except when she was absent or when she broke her arm and for a time could not write, and she evolved her own form of shorthand to keep up. He demanded absolute silence, which was not always easy to impose on the household. For an hour or two all was tense. No one must whistle. The saw-mill ceased. At Dunstall he had a

1. Letter to Stuart Walker.   2. Article: *Am I a highbrow?*

hut in the woods, in Ireland he retired to the top of a tower or to a cabin where a waterfall's monotonous roar drowned distraction. He would even lock the gate at Dunsany and once, when an importunate neighbour got through his defences, there was a terrible row. Hearing that the servant who had let him in was to be sacked, the neighbour came the next day to plead his cause. Dunsany was writing again.

When he became a literary man he did not change his way of life, though he thought it justifiable to recut a seal with the wings of Pegasus a little longer. He got to know some Irish writers he had not known before and those he had known he got to know better. They became more frequent visitors at Dunsany. But the basic pattern of his life was unchanged and because he was and remained very much a land-owning peer his work was brushed aside by many as the hobby of a rich man. In particular his wife's relations did not take it seriously. This hurt him deeply. His efforts to throw off this reputation as a dilettante were not aided by his swift and apparently carefree way of writing. It is pointless to wish that he had adopted a different method. He would not and could not have done so and perhaps a more meticulous approach would have beggared his work of its flow and richness, perhaps more care was taken than appeared. Nevertheless his work did not seem arduous and there are roughnesses and details that might have been smoothed away. People are quicker to grant serious intent to something that has demonstrably demanded hard work.

He wrote steadily. In 1906 Dunsany published *Time and the Gods*, a collection of tales – the word seems more suitable than stories – similar in style and content to *The Gods of Pegana* emphasising a theme only touched on there. Time, the servant of the Gods, turns out to be a scourge even they must fear, for, long after the great cities have been destroyed, they too will fall. It is a more substantial book than *The Gods of Pegana* and got more substantial reviews. Several agreed that there was a melancholy behind the prose, though those that disliked it called it pessimism. Otherwise it was not a case of catching the fancy of one and not of another; most found something to praise, usually the imagination, sometimes the style, and something to deplore, 'plangent repetition' or lack of profundity. Sime, who received nothing but praise the year before, varies from having 'ability – genius even – beyond question', to the more-in-sorrow-than-in-anger-abuse 'of Mr Sime's distinctly unpleasant illustrations we can only say that they contain all that is worst in the styles of William Blake and Aubrey Beardsley, without the redeeming features of either.' Each was credited about equally with being the sole justification of the book, though Sime was accused of betraying his partner's intentions, a treacherous act unnoticed by Dunsany. In all, the book got a mixed but more serious reception than *The Gods of Pegana* and marked a satisfactory advance.

Towards the end of the summer, to his surprise, he wrote for the first time a story with human characters and without Gods. He had been offered and bought a picture by Sime which showed, in indian ink as usual, a man 'much decomposed, hanging in chains, while three villainous people in ancient hats came by the light of such a moon apparently to cut the man down'.[1] In fact he asked Sime later and was told that they had come to sever the prisoner's hand in order to use it for magic. But Dunsany took a kinder view and wrote a version in which they are villainous but loyal and have come to bury the body of a comrade. In the spring he took his wife to Paris and a map which showed the outer boulevards named for French generals gave him the idea of a beautiful city guarded still by the heroes of the past and he wrote another story concerning human beings.[2] This he dictated to Beatrice as usual, about 5,000 words in two days with little hesitation or revision. During his usual routine of London and the season, Dunsany and cricket, Scotland and stalking, he continued to write and brought out a collection, *The Sword of Welleran* in 1908.

Among these dozen tales are the two with humans and two more,[3] which, being told in the first person, involve a human element. He was delighted by this broadening of his field and in fact the book makes an advance on every front with more humour and more plot but not falling away in the imaginative eloquence of his prose. Sometimes he is gruesome: 'And the savage lusting sword that had thirsted for a hundred years went up with the hand of Rold and swept through a tribesman's ribs. And with the warm blood all about it there came a joy into the

1. *The Highwaymen.*   2. *The Sword of Welleran.*
3. *The Ghosts* and *In the Twilight.*

curved soul of that mighty sword, like the joy of a swimmer coming up dripping out of warm seas after living for long in a dry land.'[1] Sometimes inventive – 'And the spell was a compulsive, terrible thing having a power over evil dreams and over spirits of ill; for it was a verse of forty lines in many languages, both living and dead, and had in it the word wherewith the people of the plains are wont to curse their camels and the shout wherewith the whalers of the North lure the whales shoreward to be killed, and a word that causes elephants to trumpet; and every one of the forty lines closed with a rhyme for wasp.'[2] Sometimes something in between, as when he introduces Sime's highwaymen:

In a tavern of foul repute three men were lapping gin. Their names were Joe and Will and the gypsy Puglioni, none other names had they, for of whom their fathers were they had no knowledge, but only dark suspicions.

Sin had caressed and stroked their faces often with its paws, but the face of Puglioni Sin had kissed all over the mouth and chin. Their food was robbery and their pastime murder. All of them had incurred the sorrow of God and the enmity of man. They sat at a table with a pack of cards before them all greasy with the marks of cheating thumbs.[3]

The subjects are somewhere between fairy-story and myth with talking hurricanes and a prince who slays a dragon, but there is also a movement towards the contemporary world in the damning of machines. Sime was on form, particularly when drawing 'a herd of black creatures larger than bloodhounds . . . they had large pendulous ears . . . and fawned about them disgustingly. Their eyes were horribly bright and ran to great depths . . .'

The reviews were good. Some claimed a position as old admirers and one stated the irritating and inescapable cry from which almost all prolific authors suffer. 'It is not we think quite so exquisite as the best of his former work . . .'[4] The number who found the meaning obscure or the moral doubtful was now more than met by those who took the stories, as Dunsany said they were to be taken, at face value. *The Times*

1. *The Sword of Welleran.*
2. *The Fortress Unvanquishable, Save for Sacnoth.*
3. *The Highwaymen.*   4. *Isis.*

Literary Supplement in a long piece found the title story *The Sword of Welleran*, 'the best Lord Dunsany has yet written, because it seems to mean more than the reader can explain, more perhaps that the writer consciously put into it. It expresses the desire that is growing among us for beautiful cities that we can love like human beings and it seems to tell us how our modern indifference for what men loved in the past may be stirred by voices from the past and how we may learn from our dreams to oppose that barbarous peril that threatens us.' This is a convincing compromise, for Dunsany did believe these things even if he had not meant to preach them in his story. His Celtic imagination and jewelled prose received the now routine admiration with a very few unfriendly adjectives such as 'selfconscious' or 'precious', and an astonishing number of separate reviewers found appropriate the phrase 'caviare to the general'. Dunsany might well have taken comfort from the idea that if his books did not sell in great quantities it was because they were too good, but he did not. The dedication was wistfully to 'those few known to me or unknown who enjoyed either of my former books'. He was easily discouraged. Beatrice could influence him if she was tactful but had once stopped him writing one story by suggesting that it needed a little more plot and was now cautious; on the other hand she persuaded him to introduce a girl into another,[1] to its benefit.

In 1908 she caught a cough which was attributed to the cold air inhaled as she drove to political meetings in an open car. One lung was affected and the best cure was said to be Egypt. So a boat was hired and with Lord and Lady Longford they made an expedition up the Nile to Aswan. If it is possible to choose a moment when Dunsany decided to be a writer then the decision was taken on this journey. The cough was cured and the journey a success but it has traps for anyone trying to connect Dunsany's work with his life. Though this was the farthest East he had ever been, the Eastern flavour of his stories was in fact becoming less rather than more pronounced. A story called *Idle Days on the Yann*, tells of the wonder of various cities encountered as a boat winds down a great river to the sea. One of these the narrator discovers when walking alone, '. . . as I came to the outer wall of the city I suddenly saw in it a huge

1. *The Curse of the Wise Woman.*

ivory gate. For a while I paused and admired it, then I came nearer and perceived the dreadful truth. The gate was carved out of one solid piece!'

The sailors seem to be Arabs, he had never made a journey by boat for pleasure before, nor seen the Nile. Yet the story was written a month before they set off, so that it can have been at most the idea of the trip that gave rise to it. In fact nothing was written abroad, but the temples of the old gods and the deep solitude of the desert were predictably to Dunsany's taste. Usually it is impossible to ascribe with certainty any work to an incident or place but a play written five years later owes its plot to a story about a lady named Nitocris, after whom their ship was named. They were told her story, which is not complicated. A Queen of Egypt, she asked her many enemies to dinner in a temple beneath the Nile and at the end of the meal, let in the water and drowned them all. Not altogether a happy choice of name for a boat, but there were no such mishaps. Also unscathed Dunsany climbed round the flimsy wicker furniture of an Egyptian hotel sitting-room without touching the ground. He was in good spirits.

He returned before his wife and scribbled letters or further paragraphs to letters almost daily, so there is a detailed account of these months. Most end with references to her cough or projected plans, which have been left out.

'Cleopatra',
Cook: Nile Service
Jan. 19th.

My darling Mink,
I've seen Kom Ombo again. We stopped there at about five, for forty-five minutes, after I had posted your letter unexpectedly at Darrow. I did not know we stopped on the way at all.

I was glad to see Kom Ombo, sacred to Sibik. Do you remember the Roman figure seated just inside the gate and the little things like Beastie just outside and the great columns and the pylon and the two black altars and the little underground place and the sort of walled street all around three sides and the usual gods and goddesses and Kings and the holy mummies of the crocodiles?

All these I saw again and left it just after sunset. Now a star has appeared over the glow and the hills are black.

An American and four of the women of his country formed the greater part of our party in the temple. They read constantly out of a guide-book and sometimes seemed to start a pillar or so too late so that Gods and King changed places or all moved up one and the Americans went on rapidly admiring as joyously as ever.

Now the dressing gong has gone . . . Now I go to bow myself facing towards London towards its Western end and to put upon myself black clothes and a painful shirt and a bow tie and to say 'Custom is custom and there is no fashion but the present fashion and I know not who was its prophet', first having made my ablutions and having cast away as unworthy the hairs of my chin.

After dinner

We have been twice ship-wrecked since dinner, but we are now getting off our 2nd sand bank and I have let myself in for a rubber of bridge.

The rubber is finished at last – Lady McKenzie was rather slow – but we are still on the sand bank and I think I shall go to bed . . .

Dunsany shared with his generation and class a patronising if friendly attitude to the uncultured Americans just as he shared a heedless anti-Semitism. Neither would cause him to be consciously unkind.

Mena House Hotel,
Pyramids, Cairo.

Thursday 11.30
. . . I didn't sleep at all badly and was very comfortable in the train, but arrived here pretty tired whereupon I set out to climb the 'great' pyramid. As I neared it I was set upon by a tribe of Arabs whose intention was to carry me to the top of the pyramid. I pointed out that I was going alone but this was ignored. Once unwisely I sat down and said I waited for them to go so they sat down beside me and I remembered that similar people under the same sort of circumstances sat down by Job for three days. I think they liked that better than walking fast which I also tried for a bit. After metaphorically spitting on their fathers' graves for a long time I bought the necessary ticket and got rid of all but one who said he was part of the ticket. Finally I escaped altogether from the last of them and started off up the middle of the pyramid driven partly by my fancy and partly from their exhortation to go up the corner. However they triumphed because after I had gone about 150 feet one of them overtook me going by the easy way. I was still climbing, but his help was exceedingly welcome and presently another man joined us. He said, and I thought truly, that no one had ever been that way before. Going by the ordinary way, either up or down, guides

are totally unnecessary for a man who can walk on the land without a stick, but the usual allowance of guides seems to be one for each hand and a third to push behind. The third joined on by the way when we got to the corner, but coming down I had about six.

Dunsany covered the inside of the pyramids with as much thoroughness and energy though 'the heat was great and the air not invigorating to anyone unaccustomed to an American hotel'. When he thought he had seen just about everything he heard 'of a place above the King's chamber in the Great Pyramid, forty-five feet of sheer rock with occasional notches in it. I have seen the Ascent this morning from the King's Chamber where I went again. It looks grim. It is the way to the Priests' Chamber and has not been done for five years. I am going to try it. The guide wants £5 and will not abate.'

He duly did some 'mountaineering in the hot darkness and saw the four small uninteresting chambers'.

January 23
Leaving Cairo

My darling Mink,
I have hated, and am still hating, leaving the country you are in and am only leaving it through indecision, not having made up my mind finally until 10.30 this morning. I don't in the least want to go to Dunsany without you . . . I should make a bad widower . . .

January 25th

My darling Mink,
Port Said is in sight, white and low with a dark curse hanging over it, and fishing boats are out. I have eaten a slice of seed cake and even that has not consoled me for leaving you.

January 26th
The first bugle has just gone for dinner so I shan't get far. There are no cricketers on board. The nets were up this afternoon and I assume that those who didn't play were not cricketers and certainly the rowdy lot that threw balls and stumps at one another were not and never will be now. There are one or two wild bounders on board but of course one notices the bounders first not because they are necessarily numerous but because they talk most and loudest.

January 29th
I think I expressed the above views, anyhow I got decent cricket

every day since. I have done a good review which has prevented me
writing to you at greater length.

January 30th 9 a.m.
entering Marseilles

I was very bored Monday, Tuesday and Wednesday; then on
Wednesday evening about tea-time I got to work on the Jap book,
reviewing as I went along. It has a lovely cover and beautiful
illustrations and pretty legends and folk-tales shockingly badly told.
There is a lattice work all over the cover and behind it the trailing
branch of a cherry tree and behind this a huge round harvest moon;
behind this is the inside of the book so I have called the review
Behind the Harvest Moon. And I ended so:

– And here I take leave of the fireflies and the plumtrees, and
shadowy moonlit temples and the snow and the spirits and peonies
and lotus lilies and swords and holy Fuji-Yama; all of which lie
behind the lattice and the cherry and the huge round harvest moon.
And I take leave of them with the words running in my head,
written by Robert Bridges to the nightingale: –

'Beautiful must be the mountains whence you come.'

I now have seven hours in Marseilles and must go and find out
what to do with them.

I said I was coming out again soon. Tell me by return what ship
Lord and Lady Jersey are coming by. Quite likely I shan't come at
all. How is the cough and what date now does the doctor say for
leaving Aswan?

Greetings to Mary
From your loving
PONY.

The greetings to Mary are an afterthought in a slightly different
coloured ink. But his next letter, started on the next day says
he 'bought a box of chocolates for Mary which I hope will
arrive in time. Marseilles is said to have some fame for its
chocolates'. France was cold and on February 1st

Here I am in London again and I find I like the sight of its
beastly mud and its abominable buses. Four weeks of travel in the
land of Cook isn't much but two months (I have utterly lost count)
in hotels, two months in the German Provinces of American Switzerland make one happy indeed at the sight again of a muddy step.
Also I have had breakfast and have been allowed to help myself out
of the dish and they wot of the difference between marmalade and

jam. Also I even enjoyed a dinner with Aunt Mary[1] and sipped warily at one glass of her champagne at 43 shillings *the dozen* as she herself confessed, but I think she gets it for less. Never dine with a widow. As a newly married lady wants to marry everyone, so one who has lost her husband seems to want to poison everyone else . . .'

In a couple of days he is at Dunsany, and, as he was rarely there without his wife, these letters are his own best account of his life there. Things have gone wrong in his absence.

That foolish woman Lady Fingall has put the staff and ladies of the hunt into dark blue collars. I don't know who she thinks she is imitating. The Percy hunt is the only I know of that have dark blue collars but the point is that it has nothing at all to do with the Meath.

Within ten days all is back to normal.

Dunsany Castle

My Darling Mink,
So sorry I posted no letter to you today but it is the only day I have missed since I left Aswan.

I was out all day on the big bog and that is why I didn't write till now.

It was not a windy day as it was last time I went, so the duck cleared off sooner, but I got one duck and twelve snipe and two teal. How is the cough? And what prospects have you of getting home by March 31st: if any? Aunt Mary has sent me selection of Francis Thompson's verse, it is difficult to judge poetry but he seems to me to be not very much inferior to Keats.'

My Darling Mink,
I wrote five poems yesterday. One I sent you, the sonnet and a short verse I enclose, and I also wrote about twenty-five lines of blank verse and one incomplete – and not very likely to be completed – piece of blank verse.

Spring

O, 'tis a glorious day; the green buds swell;
Now bloom anemones in alien lands,
And our woods are full of song.

1. Mary Ponsonby was sixty-one, a sister of Dunsany's father and to some extent a substitute for his mother when he was in Ireland. She had married Chambre Ponsonby in 1873 but he had died eleven years later.

I do not think today that Death looks well,
He wears a listless look, weak seem his hands
And he trails his feet along.

Dunsany Castle
Feb. 17

My Darling Mink,

I miss you very much since you ask . . . I heard the funniest story
that I ever remember. A man was on a restless horse that was
kicking about and managed somehow to get its hoof into the stirrup
iron, so the man said 'Well if you're going to get on, I'll get off'.

I think that is far funnier than the spinach story[1] and far truer. I
didn't tell you before, did I?

. . . I am delighted to hear about Lady Constance and my book
– good. I should like to have as many literary admirers as Keats had
while he lived. I think he had three.

Baby has written to you over the page [some blotches and
scribble]. I asked him who he was writing to and he said you and
when I asked him what he was writing he said 'Come back Mamma'
and then suddenly shouted it, so that you should hear.

Dunsany Castle

. . . Today was mild but I beat all the woods about the place,
trying the best bits in them for any cock that the frost of yesterday
might have put in. I got four of them and five rabbits. I went to see
the Holmes's child yesterday, she was there with her mother and a
small boy and a puppy. She looked very well. All but the puppy were
rather shy, so I talked most of the time to him until he wanted to
eat my clothes.

Alone, he shot and wrote a deal of the time and sometimes
went out or was visited by a friend. Relations with Randal, not
yet five, were variable.

Dunsany Castle
Feb. 25th

J.H.J. [Jack Hope-Johnstone] is very brilliant, we sat up till about
11.30 last night. I've now forgotten everything he said but some of
the things will recur to me, I expect.

Baby is possessed of one small devil I think. He said last night that

1. The spinach story concerns a man who picks up a lettuce and starts using
it to rub his forehead. A friend asks, 'What on earth are you doing with that
lettuce?' The man starts, looks aghast and replies 'Good God, I thought it
was spinach.'

he would not kiss me because I had taken away the lid of a box from him yesterday.

Dunsany Castle
February 26

My Darling Mink,
I turn from your nice long letter (enclosing my review) to answer your question 'what is a wolf-shot?' Wolf-shot is eights as I have discovered by unloading one of the cartridges with which that beautiful shikari provided me to go for a wolf with. The harvest moon and the cherry blossom is an error that I had thought of before I got the review (if review it is to be) typed, but I think I can call it the artist's error and not mine. I maintain that it is a harvest moon and that it is cherry blossom. Another point is that like as not they don't have harvest moons in Japan . . .

Sime said that the pictures he attended to were none of them finished, but he'll send some very soon. I will send you a rough sketch when he does. He doesn't want to keep the extra £10: He says too 'During the other night with Max Beerbohm I heard him say some extremely complimentary [sic] about your writings'.

Mr H.J. hasn't much to say against women's suffrage. He says there are 2 classes: 1, Intelligent Men; 2, Women and average men. The average man votes like a beast. Now the women say 'Why shouldn't we vote like beasts too?'

from your loving
PONY.

Dunsany Castle
March 6

. . . last night I sat down to write in the library and I started off to describe odds and ends as I thought I ought to be writing something; suddenly I got an inspiration and described, though very briefly, the Sphinx at Gizeh. Only 324 words I think but I will back my description against a combination of Lady Jersey and the London Library . . .'

Dunsany Castle
March 7

My Darling Mink,
We dined at Killeen last night and there came in addition to the home party nine from Tara.

I had to take in Mrs Moore-Brabazon. Her son you know is a most distinguished aeronaut. I told her how I make the stablemen tie ribbons round their cats so that I shan't shoot them and asked her if she would tie one round the neck of her son so that I should not shoot him by accident if he suddenly got up out of a patch of laurels. To which she replied, 'Oh, but an aeroplane is a great big thing'.

So perhaps a ribbon will not be necessary after all.

He enjoyed surprising people and was not averse to disconcerting them. When a woman asked him to write a Shakespearean quotation in a book, Dunsany wrote the Muscovite gibberish from *Love's Labour's Lost* and was unabashed when it was ill-received.

> Dunsany Castle
> March 10

'. . . I miss my nice Mink very much indeed. *Don't* play bridge. If your mother allows it for a moment a woman of her age ought to have more sense . . .

> Kildare Street Club
> Dublin

My Darling Mink

I'm sorry for poor Browne and his pestilence[1]-stricken multitudes although he has driven away Randal and me. Stidworthy and Olive [Randal's nanny and a nursery maid] like ghosts from an enchanter fleeing.

> Kildare Street Club
> March 15

Last night I went with other poets to the house of A.E. Seamus O'Sullivan was there, Count and Countess Markievitch, Mrs A.E., four or five whose names I have forgotten, the secretary who came with me, and a strange new poet whom A.E. has discovered and of whom I will tell you when I meet.[2] He seems totally without any education and his strange poetry is good and I like the man. One of his poems is quite astonishing. A.E. and I were both delighted with the proofs of his first book.

> Kildare Street Club.

'. . . I've told those tiresome Wiltshire people that I'll give them a week or ten days from April 2nd . . . Once Stidworthy took him (Randal) to an imitation seaside made out of asphalt and once I directed her properly to Merrion sands, when he brought back shells

1. The pestilence was scarletina.
2. Francis Ledwidge 1891–1917. Later he was generally accepted as Dunsany's discovery.

and gave me the biggest and Uncle Horace the 2nd biggest, but Uncle Horace's had a hole in it.

> United Artists Club
> Lincoln Place, Dublin.
> 21 March

My darling Mink,

Yesterday I took Baby to Merrion Sands after lunch and he digged and picked up shells and enjoyed himself very much.

Then we went back to Kilteragh and I wrote from four to nine and motored back to Dublin and had dinner and needed and obtained champagne. I did a tale of just about 2000 words which was a cross between Poe and Jacobs.[1] There is no fine writing in it, but there is imagination and the simple words that I use seem to give the situation all right. It is called *Poor Old Bill*. If the *Saturday* take it and use one tale every fortnight that will take me up to May 22nd. We need not fear plagiarism any longer. My style must be getting known and will probably influence some people but no one is going to rob me of an idea between my reading it to them and its appearance three weeks later in the *Saturday*. It was different before one had any literary position. Also ideas are no longer the all-important things they were to me. The thing is to start writing about anything and the ideas come, or if they don't I stop. A.E. is a marvellous genius.

I got a review yesterday. The man found fault with me a good deal because I did not quite come up to those classics *The Gods of Pegana* and *Time and the Gods*. He mentioned *Pegana* and *Time* with a kind of awe . . .

> Kildare Street Club.

My Darling Mink,

'. . . I'm so glad you've left Aswan, I am afraid you had a dreadful time and detested it. Look up Abu Boosh who is hanging about the first Pyramid, I forget his real name. He looks like a Chinaman . . . You ought to rejoice and delight in Gizeh. I did . . . I enclose a letter about nothing from The Great Irish Poet.[2]

> Kildare Street Club
> Dublin. M.24

My Darling Mink,

I forgot to tell you that when I suggested assisting Irish poets A.E. was for a paper that should give them an outlet. My offer of about £50 of course holds good if he wants a paper.

1. W. W. Jacobs author of *The Monkey's Paw*.   2. W. B. Yeats.

It will also bring them together to talk which stimulates the literary feeling. It is true that though Ireland is full of poets they don't trouble to write. I used to say so and now A.E. says it. But the paper will compel them to. Yesterday Miss Hamilton[1] at my request invited Yeats [or Yeates, as Dunsany at first wrote it] to share my hospitality at the Arts Club. (I was talking rather well there, Mink.)

Yeats mentioned an old idea of mine that he must have got hold of through Miss Hamilton. I had forgotten, so have you, but I recall it clearly now.

Yeats said I should write a little one-act play on it, it was such a good idea. I said I knew utterly nothing of the stage or how to write a play. He also said that if I didn't write it he thought he should have to get someone to steal it from me! Then I thought I'd try. After lunch I came here, then I motored to Kilteragh by four and saw Baby for a moment and had tea and wrote the play by 7.30 said goodnight to Baby and dined here. After dinner I descended on the poet and read him the play and when all the good passages have been deleted by him and Lady Gregory it is going to be acted at the Abbey Theatre on April 29th and 30th and May 1st. Plays never run more than three days there I think.

I'll send you the play as it stands now when I get it typed. I mixed up the idea that I had forgotten with another idea that we both remember well. The chief idea was only one for a picture and I forgot to draw it, though it would have been exceedingly simple. An Arts Club lady seeing me at that Club with Yeats and having mislaid in England the man who was to have lectured them on 'The Drama' tonight asked Yeats to ask me to.

I think I'll do it for her, I'm totally ignorant of the entire subject but small things like that ought not to stop any enterprise. I haven't thought about it yet, but I suppose ideas will come as of old when I see them gaping at me – if I do it, I've not made up my mind. I'd better go and tell the lady one way or another. It's 11.40 a.m. now.

Your ever

Loving

PONY.

The old idea was a picture (which he did in fact draw) of the great golden gate of heaven, set in green marble with a burglar condemned for his sins to try eternally to break in. This

1. Eva Hamilton was a neighbour and contemporary of Dunsany, one of six daughters. She painted and they agreed that whichever of them was the first to become famous should give the other dinner; but the dinner was never eaten.

furnished the set and Dunsany introduced another burglar so that they could talk to one another. One opens an endless supply of beer bottles that are always empty. The other attacks the gate with his jemmy. When it yields at the end of the first and only act, he discovers only 'Stars. Blooming Great Stars.' It is a slight comedy but there is a tinge of bitterness in the final line as 'cruel and violent' laughter echoes round them: 'That's like them. That's very like them. Yes they'd do that.'

Dunsany accepted the invitation to lecture though he did not in fact do so in the end. He had become a dramatist within hours of the suggestion and he was always grateful to Yeats for nudging him into the theatre. This first dramatic work was called *The Glittering Gate*. He had never thought of writing for the theatre before, but plunged ahead confidently. Technical problems did not alarm him. A few years later a friend said he should study such things and he bought a book suitably entitled *Dramatic Technique*. On the first page, laying down fundamental principles it declared 'All from Aeschylus to Dunsany . . .' and he then decided that if he was an example he need not also be a student and let the matter drop for good. So in one afternoon Dunsany had become officially involved with the theatre and the Irish Renaissance.

At first he, and Beatrice when she returned, adored Yeats. He was after all 'The Great Irish Poet' and with his magnificent voice, looks and flair for the dramatic fully lived up to the part. His conversation was impressive, his attention flattering. Later doubts and reservations crept in.

Lady Gregory, who was thirteen years Yeats' senior and had been his close companion now for over ten years, was never so popular. She has been described as a cross between Queen Victoria and the Galloping Major and was referred to by the Dunsanys as 'The Bad Old Woman in Black' from the title of one of his own stories. The clever Lady Gregory and the rich Miss Horniman used Yeats as the rope in a tug-of-war for control of the Abbey Theatre until Miss Horniman took her money and went away in 1910. Dunsany found her 'a perky old governess' but did not see her often.

Synge's *Playboy of the Western World* had been put on at the Abbey two years before and caused immense scandal, indeed riots. The Nationalists were against Synge, the play was found to exhibit the Irish character in an unflattering light and eventually someone mentioned the word 'shift' which, a member of the audience explained later, a lady would blush to use even when alone.

The Dunsanys went to the first night in London, where a group of Irish had gathered to boo. This provoked wild counter-cheers from the English, who were not however quite sure what it was all about. Dunsany commented on the grasping of inessentials that caused the riots: 'It was rather as though you offered a plate of roast beef with all necessary vegetables and condiments to someone not quite familiar with them and as though he started his meal on the mustard, and were sick.' The Abbey was shaken and over the next years when they became more objective the Dunsanys considered that Yeats had thought that to have an Anglo-Irish peer involved would give it a healthy injection of respectability. He used to speak of the financial troubles, and though he did not ask directly for money Dunsany gave him £300. All this does not deny a real friendship and respect for each other's talent; nor was the £300 badly spent. Indeed Yeats wrote to his father in April from Dunsany '. . . Dunsany is a man of genius I think . . . I want to get him into "the movement".' Dunsany's letter to Beatrice two days later, though treating the whole affair lightly and already showing a determination not to be patronised by Yeats, betrays a hint of excitement in the last line.

March 26.

My Darling Mink,
Here is a letter from Baby to say 'Come back mother'. I gave him a pencil to write with but he dipped it in the ink-pot. He came and asked to be allowed to write to you.

I also enclose the play that I wrote on the 2nd and which as I told you is to be acted April 29th and 30th and May 1st. I don't think it is going to be so badly mauled about after all. Yeats wants me to make Jim a trifle more brutal, a single sentence might do that, and then recognition is to take place a little slower on page 2. This I shall do myself. I stuck out rather against suggested alterations and Yeats came to agree. I'll let you know how things go.

I go back today and Baby tomorrow.

I have been among great men,

Ever Your Loving
PONY.

I'll be glad to see you again, Mink.

Kildare Street Club,
Dublin.

My Darling Mink,

I wrote a little more dialogue for my play yesterday as Yeats told me that I had left one of the characters silent for too long. So I'll probably send it you tomorrow.

By the way I didn't have to speak on the Drama at the Arts Club after all. There died yesterday morning Synge, and Yeats came down to the Arts Club and spoke of him, I in the chair. He was quite young and a great gain to Ireland and a great loss. He was engaged to be married.

I admire Yeats more and more. A.E. should stand in huge metropolitan ways and prophesy downfalls and the ruin of Kings till the dusty grey winds wept; and Yeats should sing into being fantastic towns with Apollonian song.

I can see them both doing it, A.E. chanting with the wind in the ends of his beard and Yeats waving his right hand and singing more softly, his jet hair drooped to his left eyebrow. Mr. Lopes doesn't think April very suitable for Wilts. Good! So I won't go . . .

Dunsany Castle.

My Darling Mink,

I had thought of a little larger house, also Hans is a trifle out of the way, but we can discuss all this when you come. The point is *don't stop two days in London* or one day either for any object so utterly trivial as looking for a house – anyone living there can do this for you, they often have.

If you are tired you must of course consider your health but chasing housekeepers returned from their bank holiday is a silly occupation.

If we can't get what we want we can wire and get Hans. Now I come to think of it the less fashionable houses like that are often finely built and pleasant.

Besides if you stop you may miss my play for I am not certain yet what dates in April it is to be. Yeats and Lady Gregory have not altered a word of my play. I added three bits at his request and one of these was not wanted after all, on the advice of a stage-manager. I think nothing of the play but they speak highly of it.

Of course, break the journey if you are tired or apt to be but do not break it for houses or for any other trivial need that may arise such as hats, clothes, seeing a friend, nail-brushes, soap for Baby, playing bridge with your father or any other similar things that may seem essential.

. . . Post going.

Ever your loving
PONY.

The first night at the Abbey was on April 30th. One of the burglars was played by a hunchback, which added a sinister effect. It was a success, but not a sensation. The *Dublin Express* reported that 'the play caused great laughter and is certainly one of the most unique short things produced for some time'. A week later the *Athenaeum*, a literary magazine, mentioned 'the ironic humour' of the dialogue and thought 'the author in the quaint fantasy shows not a little dramatic skill'. The faintness of the praise was, presumably, supported, even concealed by the excitement before the production and the fulsome compliments of friends and professionals after it. The total effect was enough to encourage Dunsany to try again. *The Glittering Gate* is typical of his plays in that there is a striking scene and only one problem to be resolved, a form which tends to a paucity of action, more or less cunningly spun out. Yeats's advice on technique was, 'Surprise is what is necessary. Surprise, and then more surprise, and that is all.' Dunsany applied this to his setting, and to the language, but seldom to the plot.

In the autumn it was put on at Manchester where it received a cool press and one hiss and in Belfast next year it was received with moderate reviews and one startlingly extreme attack by a man who had 'never sat out a more unpleasing production'. His objection seems to have been religious. In a season of Irish plays at the Royal Court in London it was better received by the audience than the critics, though as usual these ranged from one finding it a 'strange and horrible little play' to another a 'beautiful little play, not likely to be forgotten by anyone who saw it.' Nor was this the end of its career. Dunsany's first dramatic effort, written in a few hours at the suggestion of a friend was to have production after production yet.

With his plays instigated by Yeats and presented by the Abbey Theatre, Dunsany inevitably appeared to the world as another of the group which had been hailed as an Irish Renaissance. The group itself was willing to welcome him, but less certain of his suitability for membership. If his tales were not about Irish Gods and ancient Irish days, they were tolerably similar, and might become more so. Perhaps he was not of them yet, but he seemed on the edge of the circle likely to plunge in totally at any time. He never did. There were small reasons. The distance from Dunsany to Dublin still made the journey something of an expedition. Politically he was not even neutral which had been bad enough to get Synge into trouble, but violently on the wrong side, denouncing Home Rule as a lot of nonsense. Nor had he any particular interest in Irish literature, legend or language; it is not surprising that neither he nor Beatrice ever tried to read *Ulysses*. The books that influenced him had been part of a traditional English education. George Moore had been a middle-aged man when he broke in on Lord Howard de Walden crying 'Howard, Howard, I've found the most wonderful book. Have you ever read the Bible?' If some of the others had glanced at it, none had been decisively influenced as Dunsany had.

He had not the character to fit easily into any group particularly in a subordinate position. But above all his way of life excluded him and it did not occur to him ever to modify it. A great deal of the year he spent shooting grouse in Scotland or partridge in Yorkshire; he enjoyed some weeks in London and was certainly not going to cut down his visits to Dunstall. So that much of the time he was simply not there and when he was his pattern of life was that of a sporting peer with the company of those that fitted this pattern. When he mused aloud, as a tease, 'I really must take Yeats to the Kildare Street Club,' he received, as he expected, horrified shouts, 'Oh but you wouldn't, you couldn't,' etc. There was a gap between his two types of friend. In fact most of the literary lot were only acquaintances, and, though some, like A.E. and Gogarty, became more, it was never his circle, or the centre of his social or creative life.

Stately, plump Oliver Gogarty first made an impression on Dunsany incongruously firing arrows like a mature clothed cupid. A friend of Colonel Hammond, the agent at Dunsany, he was only pursuing a passing hobby at the Castle. Gogarty recorded an earlier meeting, at a hunt ball at Dunsany.

. . . while it was in full swing I wandered through the passages searching for some place where I might sit in quiet and get, if necessary, the spirit of the thing, without the action; for I am strangely averse to group enjoyments of any kind. At last I found a settee in a corridor on one end of which a tall youth was seated biting a fingernail. His hair was fair, his forehead extraordinarily high, noble and unfurrowed. His mouth which a light moustache left unconcealed, was imperious with a clear chin line under a cold beauty of eyes and brow. He looked as if he belonged to a race aloof, exempt from the pathos of the common concerns of mankind.

I took a seat beside him for there was none other to be had . . . I had quoted almost all Herrick's *Hesperides* and was about to start on his *Nook Numbers*, when someone drew my audience away.[1]

Their friendship lasted till death, still over forty years away for both, and inspired several poems to one another. Not only a surgeon but also a busybody, a gossip, almost a troublemaker, Gogarty was so kind, so quick and so amusing that Dunsany forgave all, even listening to his off-colour stories whereas, when Sir Shane Leslie tried some, Dunsany brought out a book and sat ostentatiously reading in the drawing-room. Gogarty remained on good personal terms with almost everyone almost all the time, no easy feat over the next twenty years in Dublin.

In two days in February Dunsany had completed a new play *King Argimenes and the Unknown Warrior*. When he had written another, *The Gods of the Mountain*, he sent a copy of the first to Sir Herbert Tree and the second to Mr Herbert Trench who ran the Haymarket. Impatiently waiting for the reply that could bring the London success he sought he wrote at Dunsany:

> I sit all day upon a bench
> And mutter like the sea
> Still not a word from Mr. Trench
> And not a word from Tree.

Beatrice sporadically kept a diary, not for anyone to read, not even particularly herself. When in Australia her mother had given her a big blank book (subsequently lost) to record 'new things', and she had formed the habit. Dunsany did not look at it.

March 28th, 1910. Dunsany Castle.
I think I will begin a diary again after five years interval. Lady Gregory and Mr W. B. Yeats have been staying here and left

1. An unpublished essay on Lord Dunsany by Dr Gogarty.

today. He is the most charming and wisest of people – very entertaining full of learning and with most courteous manners – he is
also handsome with a very nice voice. Lady Gregory is a wonderful
old lady but she is obviously aware of the fact – it is doubtless very
clever to begin writing books and plays (good ones too) quite late in
life and to talk well too – but she has not Yeats' gift of helping her
listener out and I am afraid is touched with the snobbishness which
consists in gibing at Royalty while making it very clear that those
are the circles she could move in if she wasn't so far above them.
But it is enormously to her credit that she can overcome her somewhat arbitrary character to the extent of making a home for Y for
nearly half the year and running the Abbey Theatre with him and
submitting to his criticism of her plays – she admitted to me that
she did not always like it from someone so much younger. This
sounds as if I did not like her – I do and it is only that she has to
compete with W.B.Y. They were both most interested in E's new
play and evidently believe that that is his line in the future – indeed
it was Mr Y who originally suggested to him to dramatise his story
of the Highwayman.[1] They will take it for the Abbey. They said that
I was a very good dramatic critic – but I fear their motive in so
saying is transparently that they wish me to encourage E's new
departure. Y said an American lady came over to write a thesis on
the Irish Theatre – she was what he called 'a living refutation of
history' as after getting everyone's account she found no two tallied
sufficiently to give even a vague notion. Apropos of that he told me
the story of Flaubert and another who began to write a French
history. They were disturbed by rumours that the stable boy was in
love with the kitchen maid. A month's close investigation failed to
reveal if this was the case, so they decided to give up the history!

Beatrice saw her relations when she could. When her sister
Mary returned in April, still a little lame and rheumatic, she
went over to Pakenham Hall[2] for one night and surprised her
eldest nephew Edward[3] by giggling with his mother in a
school-room manner. When the Dunsanys crossed to London
at the end of the month she called on her father and discussed

1. *The Highwayman* was dramatised but never staged; but perhaps Beatrice
does not differentiate between burglars and highwaymen and refers to
The Glittering Gate.
2. As the house was then called. The original Irish name 'Tullynally' is
now used.
3. Viscount Silchester (1902–61), later Lord Longford, succeeded by his
brother, Frank.

trees. He had decided that there was no point in planting any
as socialist legislation might go to any lengths; she argued that
someone would be there when they grew and might be pleased
to see them, adding in the safety of her diary that that was
what he actually did in any case. Her parents were at one in
their inevitable view of the Liberal government. The Dunsanys
went to an immense dinner at Claridge's full of writers and
Ministers and American women and Beatrice felt later that
her mother would have liked her to leave the room when Lloyd
George appeared, she was so distressed to hear that he had
been there. In fact Beatrice remained and rather admired the
Chancellor of the Exchequer for escaping neatly from one of
the American women, who asked exactly what he was going
to do, to which he replied, 'Really I wish I knew. What would
you do?' Anthony Hope[1] was at her table talking exactly like
one of his own characters. Beatrice retained the same Conservative political views in a quieter form than her husband or
parents, but did not feel much enthusiasm or distaste for any
politicians, who all seemed to her to be more or less well-
meaning mistaken men, obliged gradually to forsake their
ideals for expediency. The vision of Dunsany as a Member of
Parliament was already a curious half-forgotten fancy from
the past. When they went to stay at Wingfield House in Wiltshire, from which they had once electioneered, pleasant friendly
people came to greet them and say that Dunsany would have
won the seat where no one else could have; but Beatrice only
felt the more relieved that she was no longer trying to catch
their votes.

Dunsany felt the same. He wrote a story that year, *The Day
of the Poll*, which shows in a dialogue between a poet and a voter,
whom he kidnaps, how much more he felt himself to be the
former than even the latter, let alone a political candidate.

And for long the voter talked of those imperial traditions that our
forefathers had made for us and which he should uphold with his
vote, or else it was of a people oppressed with a feudal system that
was out of date and effete and should be ended or mended. But the
poet pointed out to him small distant wandering ships on the sunlit

1. The Author of *The Prisoner of Zenda*, *Prince Rupert of Hentzau*, *The Dolly
Dialogues*, etc.

strip of sea and the birds far down below them, and the houses below the birds with the little columns of smoke that could not find the downs . . . And as he spoke and as the sea-wind blew on that high and lonely place there began to slip away from the voter's mind meaningless phrases that had crowded it long – thumping majority – victory in the fight – terminological inexactitudes – and the smell of paraffin lamps dangling in heated schoolrooms and quotations taken from ancient speeches because the words were long. They fell away, though slowly, and slowly the voter saw a wider world and the wonder of the sea.

He too was greatly relieved that he need never again get within sniffing distance of a paraffin lamp. When that summer Aubrey Herbert recounted at dinner how he had made an eloquent speech in favour of Home Rule, recollected himself in the middle and attempted to save the day by explaining that that was what some misguided men might think, it was an anecdote from another world.

In London, Dunsany always went to the theatre enthusiastically, though he was too big to be able to fit easily into the seats, a fact he found increasingly discouraging as he continued to grow larger but became no more tolerant of discomfort. Shakespeare was supreme. He thought that modern dress made Barry Jackson's *Hamlet* more immediate and enjoyed some real rabbits in a production of *Midsummer Night's Dream*, but relied on reading for a closer knowledge. When he liked something he went often. This year he was asked to write something on the 200th performance of Maeterlinck's *Blue Bird*, which was very much in his vein of fantasy, and he went three times.

The article was for the weekly, *The Saturday Review*, whose editor Mr Hodge bred dragon-flies and went to *The Ring* at Covent Garden with Dunsany, after which shared experience they were friends. Beatrice liked him too:

When one says some triviality that strikes him, instead of merely commenting or rushing on like many people he goes back to it again and again. When he dined here the other night I happened to say that I disagree with people who sigh over modern Rome – that I found a certain charm in the way it remained the centre of the world in different ways for so many ages, for instance, that the Pantheon should always be a Church of the reigning religion whatever it might be, and that people were wrong to blame the modern Italians for continuing to make history instead of leaving Rome a mere museum of the past like other dead cities. Today he began at once on the same subject and quite argued me out of my view.

Beatrice often records conversations or random remarks that pleased her: A woman at the Royal Academy who wanted to 'just take a bird's-eye view', Sime describing Time as 'an old grey rat whose teeth are blunt with biting the wrong end of things' or a passage in the Commons when, during a Minister's speech, Ivor Guest muttered 'Rot', whereupon a supporter of the Minister turned and said: 'You call that rot, Sir, rot, Sir? I call you clown, Sir, clown, Sir!' If there was someone in London whom they thought it would be nice to meet, they asked him to dinner. Only four men had climbed the five inner chambers of the Great Pyramid; Dunsany was one of them; another an American, who was passing through England, turned out to be simple and interesting and did not boast about his feats.

Dunsany met Mr Trench, who controlled the Haymarket and had not sent a word when Dunsany was waiting in Ireland. Now he asked for a new play; it was finished in two days. When Dunsany read *The Gods of the Mountain* to Yeats and Mrs Bland after luncheon at Cadogan Square everyone was delighted and Beatrice thought it a beautiful play and the best he had done. Mrs Bland, who wrote under the name E. Nesbitt, had not met Yeats before and thought him like a very handsome raven. She was an old friend and admirer of Dunsany, who said she was his second reader, the artist Spencer Pryse being the first. Admiring *The Gods of Pegana*, she had written asking for a contribution to her magazine *Neolith*, which Dunsany was delighted to supply. In a letter she asked frankly 'Do I address you correctly on this envelope? I am inexperienced in my correspondence with Lords.' She stayed at Dunsany and together they enjoyed building houses in the drawing-room, turning chairs upside-down and decorating the results with candlesticks, dominoes, ash-trays and chessmen. They also shared an energetic liking for charades and paper-games.

Less than a week later on June 4th, Dunsany wrote another play between six and nine in the evening and then hurried out to read extracts from his own work to the Irish Literary Society. Two days later Beatrice saw his first play, *The Glittering*

Gate at the Court Theatre, where the audience was very good and very appreciative though it took them a minute or two to get over the surprise at the end, when the heavens contain only stars.

In September Dunsany published a collection of sixteen stories under the title *A Dreamer's Tales* with nine illustrations by S. H. Sime, six shillings net. His reviews were growing steadily longer and less patronising. Most found the *Tales* charming and claimed to have long admired his other books, though there was some objection that there was too much decoration. *The Hashish Man* drew a fan-letter from Aleister Crowley, the Great Beast and black magician, who praised it fulsomely but with one reservation: 'I see you only know it (hashish) by hearsay not by experience. You have not confused time and space as the true eater does.'[1]

He enclosed some erotic magazines. If he hoped to lead the young author into a maze of nameless vice and unwholesome delights, he did not know his man. Dunsany was pleased by the admiration, replied that the strongest drug he took was tea, and left it at that.

The stories have a little more plot but are often concerned with familiar themes like the fall of cities or the eventual power of time and are still dominated by language with little humour and few humans.

The season had been full of incident and success. For the first time they found that wherever they went people were familiar with Dunsany's work. It felt like a turning point, or at least as if with one more heave he would be established in London as he longed to be. His reputation had also started to grow beyond Britain. That summer he met the director of the Moscow Arts Theatre who was an admirer and eventually translated and produced *The Gods* and *The Golden Doom* in Moscow. Called Michael Lykiardopulos, he was charming and discussed suicide over tea with Beatrice:

M.L. We drink ammonia.
B.   Isn't that very painful?

1. Quoted from memory by Lady Dunsany.

M.L. Yes, but we are not allowed firearms and poison is very difficult to get without a lot of formalities.

B. Couldn't you drown yourselves?

M.L. In Russia the rivers are frozen over for six months in the year.

B. Couldn't you wait?

M.L. No, we could not wait.

Autumn in Ireland was the same pleasant mixture of work and play.

October 20th 1910.   Dunsany Castle.

Mr Sime stayed here for a week and left last Monday 17th. He is *very* nice most interesting and amusing and the nice kind of guest who likes doing and seeing anything and is perfectly happy sketching or reading or talking when there is nothing to see or do. He started life as a miner but the only trace left is in his features which are rough looking – his head is magnificent, his manners perfect, his conversation that of a scholar and a philosopher, his interests and knowledge vast and varied. Mr Russell [A.E.] came for Sunday and the two made great friends and sat up nearly all night together. A.E. is like Isaiah to look at. He recited one or two of his poems in a sort of slow monotone, just as the old harpers must have sung or rather intoned to their harps – it was very simple and very effective – it takes a poet to write of trams at night as 'the high built glittering galleons of the street' which was in one of the poems he recited. It is so like Uncle Horace to select two poets (A.E. and Miss Mitchell who also stayed here) to run his farmers' agricultural paper! And they do it well. Eddie called it digging with a razor.

The young Gregorys [Lady Gregory's son and daughter-in-law] were here too and I took her for a drive and she gave me her version of Yeats and I always rather wondered what it might be. Apparently Coole was left to Mr Robert Gregory but Lady Gregory continued to live there and run it and Mr G. accepted the position and now I think regrets it but is too fond of Lady G. to protest. But Lady G. did say when she married that Yeats would cease to live there most of the year and he has not ceased and until now has even had the Master of the House's room. That at least she has struck at, but of course their living a good deal in Paris to paint at first must have made it impossible for her now to alter the position. I know there is no reason why a great mind should mean a great soul but she related one or two petty meannesses of his which I should have thought beneath him. Of course a genius often is without the sense of honour or the rules which guide ordinary men, but he generally has a large nature to make up – and Yeats' talk is so wise! For example Lady

Gregory stage-managed *Blanco Posnet* entirely last year and made it the success it was. Y. never saw it acted until the last dress rehearsal. Then, realising that all the English and Foreign critics had collected and that there was a stir, he asked her to let him take the rehearsal, saying he wished the reporters to think that he had stage-managed it, and she is so used to giving way to him that she agreed. Mrs G. says that he does not mind what Lady G's opinion of him is as he knows she will forgive him anything in the end, and that he knows the young Gregorys, the real owners, hate his presence and has no shame about staying on. Even allowing for much bias on her part there is a sordidness and a pettiness shown by him which surprises one – and I must say that I had never detected anything of the kind – I never thought he had the straight-forward simplicity and generous appreciation of other writers that A.E. shows, but I never thought him mean.

Mr Gregory is nice, quiet and I should say easily ruled – he frequently contributes a witty remark. By the way he said that the Bible has been published as 'The Collected Works of God'. She is very nice and very clever with an attractive rather melancholy face. One of the party, A.E., I think, suggested inventing a painter whom they were all to talk of as the greatest modern painter and see how far they could persuade the world of his existence and influence. The others took it up with enthusiasm – Mr Sime suggested Monso as a name and it was proposed that they should say of any gallery 'Such a pity that in such a good collection they should have been unable to obtain one of Monso's' or talk of his influence on this or that painter. A.E. wanted a legendary American who had bought almost all his work and would not let anyone see it – and they all agreed that no artist would dare profess ignorance.

The Abbey Theatre produced *Argimenes* at the beginning of 1911. Set 'a long time ago' in the East the play starts with an ex-king as a slave and follows his ascent as he finds a sword in the earth, organises a revolution and ends back on the throne. It has fine language, vigorous action and enjoyable details such as Argimenes as a slave hoping to get a piece of the Royal dog to eat if it dies, but Argimenes as king having the dog buried with its master. As often this kind of incident encourages the audience to look around for a parable or theme such as the corruption of power or the nature of oppression but none is apparent.

Yeats helped the production and Gogarty, who was in a position to notice, thought:

It would be a mistake to think that the rivalry between Dunsany and Yeats was a literary one. Far from it. Yeats had no rival to fear among contemporary poets. It was not so much rivalry on Yeats' part (shocking to say it before it can be explained) as it was envy. Yeats, though his descent was from parsons, dearly loved a lord. He was at heart an aristocrat, and it must always have been a disappointment to him that he was not born one. Not by taking thought could he trace his descent from the year 1181 . . . This then was at the bottom the cause of the failure of friendship between Dunsany and Yeats. Dunsany sensed some sort of opposition, real and imaginary for some of the forms it was reputed to have taken were probably part of an over sensitive suspicion.'[1]

There was an unlucky incident. Yeats kept a diary, which he often had on him and when at Dunsany he read out a remark Lady Gregory had made about his staying there. 'It is good for you to stay with simple well-bred people.' On another occasion Lady Gregory, not knowing they had heard the quotation and therefore knew it to be about themselves, said to the Dunsany's 'I see I said to him "It is good for you to stay with simple well-bred people, they need not be clever". ' Worse was to follow:

January 27th, 1911.
Eddie, Georgie and I went to Eddie's new play at the Abbey *King Argimenes and the Unknown Warrior.* The first act is really magnificent and the audience never even rustled – and the second is very good too – O'Donovan as Argimenes was perfect. They shouted for E at the end and it was a long time before he went up as we didn't know how much ought to take an author on to the stage. At last Mr Robinson (the manager) rushed round calling almost hysterically 'For goodness sake Lady Dunsany make him go up' and then he went round and made his bow and it really was a triumphant success. Neither Yeats nor Lady Gregory were there – is it conceivable that they are jealous or that they guess that E. realises exactly how much Lady G. took from *Argimenes* for her last new play? He read it to her a year ago and she loved it and wrote to me some days later mentioning that 'the play of slaves and kings is much in my mind'. It was, for leaving her harmless characteristic and sometimes really funny Irish Comedies, she suddenly wrote *The Deliverer* with an Oriental background, slaves, an overseer and

1. An unpublished essay on Dunsany (see above).

even ending in the last act with a remark about 'the King's cats' –
Eddie's ending with 'the King's dog'. Then she produced it the
week before *Argimenes*. Of course they talked Kiltartan dialect and
it was supposed to veil Parnell – but still she is a bad old woman. I
said to E. that he must read them no more plays, but he said it
would not matter about Yeats – 'If you plant a cowslip in your
garden Pegasus won't eat it, though a slug might' he said. He isn't
half angry enough within. He feels gratitude that they suggested
play-writing to him – they are not troubled with gratitude in any
case as he gave them £300 for the theatre and I should think it is
about the only first night they have missed. Georgie says that I am
the only woman she knows with a detached impartial judgement
and that is why I am the only one whose opinion she values – and I
think that I often appreciate people's motives and tolerate accordingly (they interest me) but this is a slight to Eddie and it would be
inhuman not to resent it. And I cannot help being viciously pleased
that *The Deliverer* was a failure (I shall despise myself for this later –
these things matter so little – but I care so seldom that I will record
it when I do) whereas even A.E. who 'cannot lie in literary matters'
said how much he liked *Argimenes*.

I objected to E's use of vague generalities. 'But truth isn't a bird
that perches on one tree only' he remonstrated ... Eddie gets
wonderful letters from many unknown admirers – several a week.
It is the most perfect reward. Some day our families may realise
that he is an acknowledged great writer – will it surprise them then
if we are not blindly grateful for late interest? Of course he has the
supersensitiveness of the artist – I understand that one cannot judge
a younger relative by any standard other than that of early teething
troubles – or in the case of a son-in-law look on him as anything but
one's daughter's husband. Now I fancy they wonder why we don't
tell them things and send them the books. But one can't, one can't
– they should have been interested six years ago. I could now, for I
don't expect anything but a genuine, if unappreciative, affection
and that would satisfy me though it might not elate – but Eddie
can't. Indeed, how should he? I understand that too, though I don't
feel it.

Plagiarism is never easy to prove. The case against *The
Deliverer* is well put by Beatrice and whatever the extent to
which Lady Gregory used *Argimenes*, the Dunsanys were not
pleased and their relationship with her and Yeats deteriorated
further.

In later years when Dunsany heard that Lady Gregory was

claiming that she had saved the great poet's life by feeding him on Bovril, he dismissed it tersely as rubbish; but this may have been because he disliked Bovril.

January 28th 1911.   Dunsany Castle.

. . . I went up to see the play again and came back with Eddie. To my amusement even more than my irritation Yeats came and sat near me and during the interval talked with unnecessary loudness and enthusiasm to Eddie of certain slight alterations he (Y) was suggesting for the second act . . . When it was over and E went to the Green Room Yeats continued talking on the same subject to me in the hall – I could not help thinking it a pity that everybody should think that he had superintended it, for the hall was full of men smoking silently and one must listen to Y when he is there, so I asked in a slightly raised voice if he had arrived from England that day, and was interested to note that in his reply he adroitly switched the conversation off *Argimenes* on to his own *Deirdre* where he felt safer perhaps.

Even George Moore acknowledged to Colonel Hammond that there were 'fine bits' though of course to E he made a point of calling it 'slightly slight'. And Mr Herbert Trench has taken *The Gods of the Mountain* for the Haymarket – and that is a play without inequality – it was a glorious day when his letter came about a week ago.

Georgie Buller was staying on the glorious day and remarked that they did not seem excited enough. So Dunsany jumped over the sofa on which she was sitting and asked 'How is that?' They had been willing to accept whatever terms were offered (£10), but when asked the Authors' Society advised grudgingly that they did not suppose they would make much, or cared if they did, but that it was always foolish to sell anything outright; so they leased it for that sum. Sir Herbert Tree did not take *Argimenes*.

On February 19th Yeats wrote from the S.S. *Zeeland*, which was taking him to Boston where the Abbey Theatre were opening what was to be a strong tour of the United States, with *The Playboy* still leading to threats, missiles and even arrests. He wanted Dunsany's permission for his sister to publish selections from his writing. 'You will be there with Lady Gregory and J. M. Synge, and Douglas Hyde and A.E. and the rest of us. It is my way of claiming you for Ireland.' It was a claim that had to be made, that did not go without saying even at this moment when he was most identified with Ireland and the Abbey; and it was a claim Yeats wished to make. Dunsany was never closer to the Irish movement than in these months.

Permission happily granted, the book appeared at the end of 1912[1] and in the foreword Yeats wrote on Dunsany's apparent irrelevance to life. 'Had I read the *Fall of Babbulkund* or *Idle Days on the Yann* when a boy I had perhaps been changed for better or worse and looked to that first reading as the creation of my world; for when we are young the less circumstantial the further from common life a book is, the more does it touch our hearts and make us dream. We are idle, unhappy and exorbitant, and like the young Blake admit no city beau.iful that is not paved with gold and silver.'

June 14th 1911.
Success is pleasant. *The Gods of the Mountain* came on at the Haymarket on June 1st – Trench was undecided as to when he'd put it on till about a fortnight ago and very dubious as to its success all the time. He thought it over the heads of the audience and the lighting and staging were difficult and expensive for such a short play. It was a huge success – after a very few days it was promoted to coming after instead of before *Lady Patricia* and it filled the theatre which was half empty during Lady P's run alone. Eddie found only one empty stall last night and that he filled. It was not very full the first night but the audience delighted in it and it had glowing reviews next day. Mrs Patrick Campbell sat in the box with us and was charming about it though her play had to be shortened for it. Well as I know the play and quite apart from nervousness, it gives me a thrill to see and hear it each time – it is full of beauty and the unjustly maligned public have seen it. And we talked about it to nobody before and therefore to hear everyone talking about it has the extra joy of novelty. And the pit is full too – and people write charming letters, people we don't know but like the more for it.

Eddie hasn't had long to wait for recognition – constantly we

1. Yeats selected – *The Gods of the Mountain*
     The first act of *King Argimenes and the Unknown Warrior*
     The Fall of Babbulkund
     The Sphinx at Gizeh
     Idle Days on the Yann
     A Miracle
     The Castle of Time

hear now of new people, strange to us, who have the books – and to think how slowly the first one sold and how nobody ever seemed to know even that he wrote! Well there is an end to that now, and to the peace which goes with obscurity, at present we are still new enough to it all to be gratified when people ask for criticism of their verses, or interviews or articles for their magazines.

On the first night of Dunsany's first attempt on the West End, he told no one except John Hawksley, his brother-in-law Lord Longford and a cousin, Captain de Burgh. It ran about forty-five minutes as a curtain-raiser to the unsuccessful *Lady Patricia*.

The Gods of the Mountain, set in the East, concerned some beggars who passed themselves off as gods, the seven green gods, with some success until the Gods themselves come from the mountain to take revenge, turning the beggars to stone. Then any doubters are silenced and the petrified beggars are worshipped indeed. Gods in Dunsany's plays are invincible and terrible, while in his early books they are often ineffective and vulnerable; perhaps this was because, from the nature of things, the plays had to concern themselves mainly with humans, with whom the Gods are contrasted. The reviews were almost unanimous in praise of production, acting and play. *The Times* found 'humour, rough and sly, and irony and wisdom and the excitement of uncertainty, and horror'. It was 'a decorative nightmare', 'a thing of pleasant and suggestive charms' and again and again 'successful' 'well received'. That the author is a peer is mentioned several times but Dunsany had no need to cavil at such a detail. Greeted as a promising playwright, his new fame bounding forward to promote his books, full of ideas for further work, even fashion helping him with a sudden glance at *Kismet* and the East – after a short struggle he seemed to be pausing on the threshold of a success to which no limit need be set. Beatrice's family went and enjoyed it. On his opening night Mrs Patrick Campbell had taken one look at the empty seats for her play and boomed 'This is not to be borne'. Nor was it; her play came off, the replacement was no more successful, but *The Gods* ran for three months – a successful run then – and more seats were jammed into the stalls to accommodate the crush.

Frank Harris wrote an impression[1] of the author:

'The first time I saw Dunsany was the first night of *The Gods of The Mountain* in the early summer of 1911 : a sympathetic appearance, very tall, over six feet, very slight with a boyish face, rather like Dowson's but with power in the strong chin and long jaw. The nose too slightly beaked – a suggestion of the Roman or aristocratic type, but combined with the sensitive lips and thoughtful eyes of the poet; the manner and voice too were reassuring. He was more courteous, amiable, than an Englishman ever is, with a boyish frankness and joy in praise and superb Celtic blue eyes that were reflective and roguish, piercing or caressing – all in a minute – speed was here and strength and joy in living.

Harris, writing after the war, knew Dunsany was a poet and playwright, which doubtless aided his natural observation to spot those 'sensitive lips and thoughtful eyes'. Less keen and informed scrutiny still tended to see in the same figure the Eton and Sandhurst peer who was an excellent shot. Harris scarcely knew Dunsany, though he seems to have been eager to do so. Dunsany called on him in the South of France, and, finding him asleep, left a note. Harris apparently woke and pursued him some distance in his pyjamas. However he was acute if inaccurate and though it may have been carelessness to use the word 'boyish' twice in one paragraph, it was an emphasis on which all could agree.

The coronation of George V was on June 22nd. Just before they set off from Cadogan Place, Dunsany discovered that his coronet had been left behind. Panic ensued. He refused to go. Beatrice persuaded him to set out. As they passed through Belgrave Square he remembered that Lord Howard de Walden had gone to Scotland, where presumably he was not using his coronet. He dashed into Lord Howard's large house in the corner and found that it was full of Japanese officers. The distraught and ermined peer, head and shoulders taller than the visiting military, was much relieved to catch sight of an English butler and within five minutes had returned triumphantly with the borrowed coronet. They just reached Westminster Abbey in time to be allowed in. Beatrice was at the end of her row so she could see the actual crowning, annointing and robing. Moved by the peace and simple

1. Contemporary Portraits, 1919.

dignity of the service, and thinking of the political crisis that questioned the future role of these same Lords she wondered if there could ever be another coronation that was not mere pageantry.

The next day they found that Yeats and Lady Gregory spurred by the success of *The Gods of the Mountain* were rushing on a production of *King Argimenes* at the Court Theatre. Some of the script had been lost and Dunsany supplied it as best he could from memory. The clothes and scenery had been ordered a week before the first night, when all had agreed previously that it must be staged splendidly. Beatrice is severe: 'It is difficult to be angry when one has won, but I am very nearly very angry with Yeats and Lady Gregory. They have lied ... we can afford to be generous, but it is paltry of them. We went to a tea-party she gave one day – very pleasant it was too – in Sir Hugh Lane's beautiful house but, we have been somewhat disillusioned about her.' In the event the play looked impressive with one Queen in scarlet and everything else in blacks, whites and greys. Though a muddle as to whether some off-stage chanting was supposed to be triumphant or grief-stricken caused Dunsany to hide his face and mutter 'This is awful', Mrs Bland spoke for the rest of the audience when she whispered 'He needn't worry. It is perfectly beautiful'. *The Times* found that 'For the first quarter of an hour Lord Dunsany's imaginative little drama seemed likely to be a small masterpiece. It is unfortunate that the promise of the beginning is not kept up to the end, but there is much that is interesting in the piece and a good deal that is striking'. The *Manchester Guardian* thought 'the piece wobbles curiously between poetry and realism' but otherwise enjoyed itself.

Like the successive waves of an incoming tide, each year carried Dunsany's career a little forward. Each winter he retired to Ireland and, if he spent most of his time on the bog with a gun, he did not often fail to produce a new work for the next season's assault on the capital. The Dunsanys were now sufficiently familiar with the quirks and foibles of the great men of Irish literature to relish Dr Gogarty's gossip. He came to stay and told them how the applause for a story by Douglas Hyde seemed to pain Yeats, 'He kept putting his hand to the back of his head as if a bee were annoying him. That play

L.D.   F won't be acted again at the Abbey.' George Moore was also fair game. Gogarty heard that the sociable author was ill and arranged for him to be asked to eight dinner-parties in a week, with the guarantee that poor Moore would much regret that he was unable to accept any of the kind invitations. When his secretary got married she did not dare tell him and he never found out, though her husband came regularly to collect her, pushing a pram. The actual birth caused so prolonged an absence that Moore grew anxious about her and asked Gogarty to motor him into the country to see her. 'But I was warned and you wouldn't believe what trouble the tyres gave us that day. We never got there.' Another time A.E. charmed them by reciting his version of Irish history. Beginning with the small holdings of the nineteenth and twentieth centuries, which came into the hands of large owners, he took in the eighteenth century where the first glimmerings of self-government appear, religious troubles and wars follow until the last Englishman, Strongbow, leaves the country, culture begins, religious intolerance ceases with the disappearance of Patrick, about A.D. 400 and the great days of the heroes and the gods approach. It is then discovered that the publisher has bound the book back to front.

Relations with the Lord-Lieutenant of Ireland, Lord Aberdeen,[1] were delicate. He wished to placate the Irish people and to this end had supported some land laws, which the landlords naturally, and with some reason, found iniquitous. He had also cold-shouldered them socially, where they were used to being lavishly entertained. Rumour had it that he was skimping in order to have the funds to rebuild his house in Scotland; he became the victim of a social boycott. So when a Captain Forbes, who had been staying at Dunsany and was on Lord Aberdeen's staff, persuaded them to stay at the Castle in Dublin for a weekend at the end of January, their Unionist acquaintance was mildly scandalised. The Lord Lieutenant, now apparently eager to be friends with everybody, asked Beatrice why people refused his invitations. She thought him a silly old man, and recorded 'Well we had stretched a point and come, and I was well able to give him many eloquent reasons,

1. 1847–1934. A Liberal, he had been Governor-General of Canada, 1893–98, and was created the first marquis in 1916.

but thought it made for peace if I was merely sympathetic and non-committal.' Later Republicans too were to have their problems. When Timothy Healy[1] was Governor-General, Miss Mitchell, A.E.'s secretary, said she would not curtsey. 'There are two ways,' Dunsany replied, 'to greet the representative of the King. You can throw a bomb or you can bow. Miss Mitchell, have you a bomb?'

On March 2nd Lady Dunsany had a bad fall hunting. She did not see a doctor and her back hurt for many years. Also that year she had an operation and when convalescing comments, 'I can't explain my case to everyone and they must put it down to natural bad manners if they wish when I keep my feet on the sofa ... I thought I couldn't be surprised by anything that people do now, but really I was a bit amazed to hear that Ruby Peto has several friends in her room while her treatment (same as mine) is going on. Of course she is a "Soul" and I think they don't acknowledge the existence of any part of them except their souls.'

Reggie used to come for his leaves from the navy to hunt and Beatrice got on well with him though the brothers were still incompatible, Reggie with a brooding, aggressive silence, Dunsany loquacious and ready for opposition, both, when some trivial argument arose, obstinate and violent. Dunsany's temper came and went leaving no after effects, Reggie was more lastingly disturbed.

In the spring they went to the Jerseys' villa near Cannes. Dunsany disliked the beach and avoided it. Sun-bathing was not yet fashionable. He spoke confident inaccurate French and met a friendly native, who suggested they go big game shooting in Africa, to which he assented in principle. Beatrice spoke good French and German and a little Italian.

In the autumn the poet Padraic Colum had stayed at Dunsany and Beatrice noted: 'I believe he started life as a cattle drover. He has a fine head and is a very nice little man. We had a heated argument at dinner ... Eddie, brilliant talker though he is, is so medieval in his views that it is difficult for him and an advanced nationalist to argue ... I think my parents' hair would stand on end if they knew we had guests of

1. 1855–1931. A Parnellite MP until the O'Shea divorce case, later in general sympathy with Sinn Fein. A tactful Governor-General 1922–28.

that kind.' Now he suggested collaborating with Dunsany on a play, perhaps about Alexander the Great. It was agreed and they read Plutarch to each other. But you had to be a fast worker to collaborate with Dunsany and while Colum was busy, he wrote three and a half acts by himself in less than two months. Then he felt rather sad that only half the glory could be his; less than half perhaps, for the old spectre of the dilettante peer returned and he began to fear that people would think Colum had really written it all and then that he had probably written Dunsany's other plays as well. Still, as Beatrice wrote, 'Of course one can't even imply that Mr C. ought to drop out'. Nor had he anything else to offer London.

While he was completing *Alexander*, sitting in the park near the bank of the Serpentine, Dunsany saw a boat capsize and a man fall in. With a passing policeman he dived to the rescue, but the man, who turned out to be a footman to Lord Morley, never surfaced even once. Dunsany's customary large felt hat stayed on his head throughout. He was awarded the medal of The Royal Humane Society. On the next day the ticket-collector told Beatrice that it was the finest thing he ever saw; she thought he had recognised her and was being polite, but then realised that he was simply bursting with excitement. Dunsany was also accosted on the subject by someone who had seen the event, a small boy.

'Are you the man who dived in yesterday?'

'Yes.'

'Is that the suit you were wearing?'

'No.'

'Oh. I suppose it's drying.'

Three weeks later Colum generously offered to stand down and though they refused at first, when he had come round and heard the play, he insisted that none of it was his. So now Dunsany had a full-length play under his name alone. *Alexander* charts the rise and fall of its eponymous hero, who becomes increasingly unpleasant and arrogant. It is a simple plot to spin out over three acts, not unlike Marlowe's *Tamburlaine*, and is partly sustained by the Queen of the Amazons, who loves Alexander and is the first woman of any importance in a play by Dunsany. Martin Harvey, a successful actor-manager who was later knighted, was enthusiastic but wanted several alterations, particularly to the end, so that he should hold the stage alone at the final curtain. Dunsany did not like this tampering with Art, and after a certain amount of bickering removed the play at the end of 1912. Beatrice sympathised, but felt that 'he [Harvey] was keen and would have done the main part well, and it is such a big expensive play to manage that we may find ourselves mistaken. But even so *Alexander* must succeed some day.' She was right both times. *Alexander* did have a success, but not for twenty-five years and then at a festival, and only for a few performances. So they were mistaken and Dunsany had no big new play that year.

On the day that Colum bowed out, Beatrice also recorded a problem of etiquette and shows by implication how Dunsany's career was progressing:

... The Gordon Craigs came to tea and I introduced them to others who came in as Mr Craig and Mrs Craig. E said that I should have put in the Gordon as that would explain the existence of his long hair and her wild eyes in the room – but I said if they were in my house then it was enough for my guests and I don't approve of 'explaining lions' – but as we were each of us immediately converted to the other view, an unusual occurrence in any discussion, I do not know which was right. I think in the case of a European reputation like G. Craig's I ought to have introduced him fully especially as he wishes to proselytise and had come here to try with E. But I don't know what Mr Craig does want – he disapproves of the modern theatre, so do many people and he wants £40,000 to start a school in Paris to receive suggestions anything vaguer or more visionary it would be hard to find. He approved of E's having written *Alexander* but said that was enough and held up his hands in horror at the idea of him wishing to have it acted. However he [Dunsany] invited Lord Howard de Walden to meet him here for which he was very keen and as Lord H. left the final rehearsal of his and Holbrooke's opera *Children of Dom*, to come, the desire must have been mutual.

Dunsany gave the first £100 (Lord Howard de Walden gave £5000) to Craig's school the following year and was with Yeats on an international committee but the war seems to have swept away these intentions. The year before Yeats had asked if some screens designed by Craig could be used for *King Argimenes* at the Court. Craig replied: 'I don't understand a word of what you write about Dunsany. Who is he – and why do you write me of him? It sounds a nice name anyhow. And what will *he* do with my screens, grace or disgrace them? The thought that his work (if he be a carpenter) should go into my screens is pleasant enough – but Lord he might be someone else – one never knows.' The screens were not used.

The Book of Wonder, published in November 1912 was thought by the critics to be Dunsany's best collection of stories yet and Sime is back in favour. 'Are you a Dunsanyite? That is one of the questions of the moment' said the *Daily Citizen*, which implies an increase in renown. For ten of the fourteen stories the Sime–Dunsany partnership had gone into reverse. Sime had been complaining that editors offered him unsuitable subjects so Dunsany proposed that Sime draw the pictures first and he, Dunsany, would 'write stories explaining them, which may add a little to their mystery?' When he asked later whether one explanation was correct Sime replied 'It sounds extremely probable.' The unaltered tone and lack of strain are a tribute to the unity of the partnership. As the title implies, the stories are all fanciful, perhaps the nearest Dunsany came to writing fairy stories, as people often thought he did. But the last sentence of *The Hoard of the Gibbelins* runs 'And, without saying a word, *or even smiling*, they neatly hanged him on the outer wall – and the tale is one of those that have not a happy ending.' Happy endings are almost obligatory for fairy stories and though Dunsany deals with monsters, treasure and magic, he does not quite include fairies or sets of brothers of which the third is the hero – his tales never have quite the correct formal qualities or personalities to become orthodox fairy stories. Also he includes more comic and realistic detail; the victim whom the Gibbelins hanged was a burglar and though it is true he overcame a traditional dragon he did so by pointing out that dragons never won and it would do much better to carry him to his destination; indeed he was right, for the dragon was alive and free at the end of the story.

Some years before a roadworker named Francis Ledwidge, who had met Dunsany through A.E., had sent him an old copybook containing the poems of four or five years, asking if they were any good. Dunsany thought they were, gave him money, encouragement and introductions, and became as fond and

proud of his protégé as the young poet was of him. Beatrice
thought him: 'a nice youth with a fine straightforward face and
that combination of naturally perfect manners with a village
education and accent that is found in Irish peasants, though by
no means universally there, and certainly nowhere else. He seems
a real poet, no imitations or affectations.' Ledwidge used often
to bicycle fifteen miles to Dunsany, where he was simple and
relaxed. He wrote a poem to an Old Quill of Lord Dunsany,
but mostly he dealt more directly with nature and Dunsany
explains in an introduction how he could admire Ledwidge
and yet write in his own style: 'Of pure poetry there are two
kinds, that which mirrors the beauty of the world in which our
bodies are, and that which builds the more mysterious kingdoms where geography ends and fairyland begins, with gods
and heroes at war, and the sirens singing still, and Alph going
down to the darkness of Xanadu. Mr Ledwidge gives us the
first kind.'

His behaviour was not always perfect. He told an improbable
story about a cheque unhappily left at home and borrowed £5
off A.E. who wrote to Dunsany: 'You are in a way his literary
god-father and adviser and councillor, and mother and father
of his soul, and it is perhaps just as well you should know his
little ways.' Such incidents might call for a few harsh words but
there was never a lasting quarrel. A.E. himself always tried to
think well of everyone, and generally succeeded. George Moore,
had just upset his friends by telling a series of anecdotes in his
reminiscences and naming the protagonists. 'Moore is like a
friendly porcupine,' said A.E., 'rubbing himself against your
legs, unconscious that his quills are sharp.' 'All very well for
you,' said one of the punctured, 'he strokes you but he backs
into us.'

In the new year Beatrice is so hot in defence of Dunsany's
rights that she is uncharacteristically harsh:

February 3, 1913.   Dunsany Castle.
I never wrote about *The Golden Doom* and if it wasn't that I must
record its great success I should hesitate to even now for it is disappointing to record pettiness in people. It went splendidly – the
curtain fell and went up again and again (eight times) with constant
shouts of author from all parts of the house (and we had no personal
friends there except Georgie and Mr Pryse) and at last Mr Pryse

came running from the back saying 'You *must* go on, they are all wanting you', other people began looking about and we heard them wondering where he was. So he got up and had to go through the stage box where Lord Howard de Walden who is part owner, was sitting, who stopped him going on. I was very cross but thought it was only because Lord H's own things were always a failure though he packed the house and so he didn't know that there was ever a genuine call. However though *The Golden Doom* had much better reviews than either of the other plays with it (and indeed the long one *The Younger Generation* was the dullest affair) they took it off after twenty-nine performances. Of course left to itself *The Younger Generation* has collapsed now.

Lord Howard was shy but not mean. Beatrice seems to have seen him as the man that they were forever establishing Dunsany was not – a dilettante peer who had the money to support his untalented plays.

The Golden Doom takes place before the fall of Babylon in front of the King's Great Door in Zerichon, on which a child writes an obscure verse. Priests and soothsayers interpret it as a premonition of doom and the king leaves his crown and sceptre as an offering. The children return, take the hoop and stick which they had prayed for, and the miraculous disappearance of the crown is taken to show the Gods are appeased. 'A pretty poetical conceit' thought the *Daily Express*, but the *Daily Telegraph* found a 'seething satire on priestcraft'. It struck a new note and 'pretty' 'fragile' 'delicate' replaced 'eerie' and 'horrid' as the most popular adjectives to describe it. *The Times* was, as always, less enthusiastic than most: 'while its dainty part pleases us greatly, its super-solemnity provokes us to smile'. A slight one-acter was no substitute for *Alexander*, but was better than nothing.

Dunsany always liked children and those that could stand the pace liked him. He ignored differences in size or strength and continually beat them at games. This boisterous roughness was disapproved of by nannies who muttered 'That Lord Dunsany' as they mended torn clothes and dried tears, and his trick of hiding behind a yew hedge and roaring like a lion with unusually powerful lungs frightened some children more pleasurably than others. One niece, Imogen Rhys, remembers him throwing a little girl into the rhododendrons at Osterley and destroying her muslin hat. He replaced it three days later. Also she had to watch in polite silence when he came to nursery tea and devoured all the strawberries, which were a special treat.

At Arden Lady Mexborough's[1] son Jock, aged five, summed up his feelings, 'I *like* Lord Dunsany, but I *don't* like his ways.' These ways included a game of hide-and-seek during which a small girl, Betty, emerged crying from under a seat at the bottom of the garden, a hiding-place that had been wet and covered with slugs. Another time, playing sardines, he used a favourite trick – hiding in the bathroom with the door properly unlocked but the taps on full blast so that, thinking a bath was in progress, no one entered. Unfortunately he used all the hot water and the children were blamed. They were deeply impressed by his killing wasps by clapping his bare hands. Disasters are more memorable than successes; some games presumably ended happily.

The Pakenhams, the children of Beatrice's sister Mary, were his especial favourites and they were alternately thrilled, shocked and frightened by the spirit of mayhem which he introduced. He seemed to be on their side against the grown-ups and he did outrageous things which they would not have dared to do themselves. At Christmas they looked forward eagerly to his parcels which contained large books of fairy-tales illustrated by Arthur Rackham and Edmund Dulac, each one containing a comic inscription in his enormous writing. He also invented kingdoms and a system of orders for them – Titular Despot of Frankieland (Frank), Queen of Lesser-maryland (Mary) and so on. He spent much effort designing uniforms for their regiments and writing out with appropriate seals attached documents running

I, Uncle Eddie of my own free will, and neither by nor with the consent of Parliament, but solely of my just avuncular right, as properly established in law, do hereby herewith and hereon promote, advance, ameliorate and set up my right colloguous niece the

1. The Hon Margaret Knatchbull-Hugesson (1883–1957) m. 1905 Hon John Savile, later 6th Earl of Mexborough, of Arden Hall, Helmsley, Yorks. They had a son and four daughters.

Queen of Pansieland etc. etc. etc. . . . Given under my hand and seal this day at my highly desirable residence in Pont Street, the day being fine just now, but it looks like rain.

EDWARD the Uncle.

He made them models and medals as well. They liked it and they liked being read *Golden Tales of Samarkand*; but they thought him very odd.

The French marquis, who had met Dunsany at Cannes and suggested that they go to Africa together, had meant what he said and at the end of January, 1913, Dunsany, delighted at the prospect of adventure, set off for Algeria to shoot gazelles. However, things did not go well. There was no sport but guinea-fowl. Moreover the marquis had a mistress, which Dunsany could accept, but he wanted Beatrice to come out as a chaperone, which was going too far. So they parted, and Dunsany sent for Beatrice.

Beatrice, enjoying hunting in Ireland, was not over-enthusiastic about being summoned to the wilds, but dutifully made her way to Biskra. From there they made their way across the desert to Bon Saada, which took two weeks. This was Dunsany's first big game expedition and his first meeting with his guide, Smail. Beatrice thought Smail not quite straight, as he was paid to provide everything, but found a saddle only for Dunsany, while she had to ride perched high on a rolled-up mattress, from which she took 'no end of a toss'. They met nomads with guns and charming manners, shepherds playing flutes to their sheep, wonderful wild flowers and huge dry rivers. She painted the flowers, noting how well they were adapted for survival with thick stems to suck up every available drop of moisture and prickles sharp enough to deter all but the hungriest predator. The desert looked blue in the distance. Dunsany soon found gazelles to kill and eat. They enjoyed themselves very much.

When they returned it was still spring and they had time for some cheerful social life in Ireland. When George Moore came for a night, Beatrice found him 'most witty and I must say I started with a strong prejudice against him and a great contempt for his character and habit of betraying all confidences, but found him extremely pleasant. "Now I don't mean any

harm, I am saying this to amuse you," is the preface to some
scandalous talk about some friend. The comment "he has no
enemies and his friends don't like him," was apt.' He told them
he planned to write a play on the theory that Christ was an
ironic mystic, who, after escaping from his tomb, went into a
monastery. There he later met St Paul and found that a whole
religion had been founded on a lie. St Paul will not allow
him to interfere. 'I hope I shall write it with all reverence,'
he said gravely, 'I have the greatest respect for – an ironic
mystic.' The theme appeared as a novel, *The Brook Kerith*, in
1916.

Naturally Gogarty came over brimming with anecdotes.
One concerned Professor Tyrrel of Trinity College, Dublin,
who was lying ill in bed when he heard that his colleague,
Professor Dowden, was dead. 'All my life,' he told his wife,
'Dowden has been held up to me as a model because he
abstained from alcoholic drinks. And he's dead. Bring me
another bottle.' The deeply Irish character of the story lies in
the word 'another'. When Dunsany complained of typewriters
and the mess they made of manuscripts, Gogarty replied that
some lines of his had been printed without the verb, but he did
not mind as his verse was always obscure, and it was still more
obscure that way. Dunsany suggested going into a monastery
'for the repose of the body'. In August *The Lost Silk Hat* was
put on in Manchester. The plot is slight: a young man has
left his hat behind, and unwilling to face the girl who has just
spurned his proposal, he tries to persuade a series of passers-
by to help him. Eventually he gets it himself and we assume a
reconciliation. The critics found it 'trifling', 'frothy', 'decidedly
humorous' and 'fanciful' but it was not played in London until
after the war, when it also appeared in China. Another geographical surprise was a not very successful production in
Russia in 1915. He had no new play in London for the first
time for four years.

In October Dunsany went once more to Africa to shoot.
This was a bigger expedition to the East instead of the North
in search of more dangerous game. Beatrice preferred to
remain in Ireland, not because she did not care to cope with
lions and elephants, but because she wanted to spend as much
time as possible with Randal in the years before he went to

school, an event she dreaded. Earlier in the year Dunsany had planned to spend several weeks abroad without Beatrice for the first time since their marriage; now he was to do so. It is hard to judge whether his restlessness had any connection with his failure to produce a play which would be an undeniable all-conquering, full-length hit. If the last two years had been a little disappointing as far as the stage was concerned, *The Book of Wonder* had been a success; moreover he had always had a longing to escape civilisation and search in unknown deserts like an Old Testament prophet, and if he felt that this yearning rather suited a Creator of Beauty, that does not mean to say that it was in any way insincere. His heroes of all dates are often wanderers and constantly express their wish to be somewhere else: 'of late there had seized me in London a quite unreasonable longing for large woods and waste spaces'.[1] 'He was so far from civilisation then, that at evening he used to take out a white linen collar, all starched, and look at it. I imagine that he gazed on it wistfully, thinking of London bathrooms.'[2] 'When the hills called I used to go to them by road, riding a bicycle. If you go by train you miss the gradual approach, you do not cast off London like an old forgiven sin, nor pass by little villages on the way that must have some rumour of the hills.'[3] This last is a description of bicycling down to see his mother at Dunstall, a distance of twenty-one miles.

He wrote almost daily. From Marseilles he announced, 'I am here. No other news,' but in fact added an account of how the little waves had spun his little ship about, making his sense reel, until he swallowed some pills. He had left his glasses behind. His spirits remained excellent across Europe, as he enjoyed the sights:

... I did not see our entering into the Bay of Naples, but being awakened by the fog-horn when we were quite close in I went out to look at Vesuvius between six and seven and saw him mainly sending off grey smoke, no more than a smokey hill, and then dawn came up very suddenly behind him, or more likely we turned so

1. *The Last Book of Wonder.*   2. *The Man Who Ate the Phoenix.*
3. *A Dreamer's Tales.*

that the smoke was between us and the dawn and so glory came down upon Vesuvius.

I have just found out that Major Uribi, my antagonist at chess, is not a yellow man after all, in spite of his name, in spite of his stature and above all his neatly brushed black hair, which are all of the rising sun, he comes instead from the country of Ecuador. This accounts for one or two of his mistakes last night, the uncanny people of the inland sea don't seem to make them.

... I think I must write a tale some day to be called *Doomed Cities* telling of all the doomed cities I have known, saying how Pompeii wears the air of doom least of them all, for nature held up her hand as it were there saying Hush and all ceased in midmost life escaping the wear of the long lost war with Time in which he triumphed over Tingad over Ammino and over Carthage twice, sparing Thebes only for the sake of his brother Death (whose city it was) and saying how of all doomed cities London wears the air most, because her doom is not fallen but foretold by manifold signs. And then you shall read of Pompeii.

Major Uribi is buoyed up by the hope of beating me always next time, but we have had four games so far and it has not come off yet. I haven't played any of the others but he does and beats them. We post letters on board tonight.

Ever your loving
PONY.

On October 16 he reached the Red Sea.

Last night we went strangely between woods and desert going down the canal and all today we have moved between chocolate mountains. Tired today with arguing with a foolish lady that Bacon wrote *Novum Organum*, and Shakespeare *Hamlet*, and *proving* at great length with her own proofs that Lord Salisbury wrote *Maud*. I at last met a chess-player, a Colonel Ward, who really can play chess. He replied to my favourite opening with a variation I had never seen before which greatly embarrassed me before I knew where I was, and we had a desperate game; and I won. I have played three others beside him, but only to justify myself in talking about chess. He is really a good player. This letter may not be a long one for it is beginning to get hot. I bought two suits of clothes in Suez at twelve shillings each. I also bought three cigarette cases, *as I had only two*, but they were very beautiful indeed. Japanese gold work on iron, and (on one of them) on silver. They are really lovely. One was only £3 and the other twenty eight shillings so I offered £4 and secured them.

Oct. 17 2 p.m.

There's a following wind!

8 p.m.

No news.

Oct. 17.

Today there's a breeze hot but most welcome; and some Sudanese mountains are coming into sight faintly like blown dust.

Port Sudan.

A sandy place full of huge fossils and mountains in the distance lifting out of mists. I hope you're enjoying yourself.

Ever your loving

PONY.

In Port Sudan he went out at night with a lantern to try to spear fish. An Arab rowed them through the shadows of the wharves over the silently steaming sea. 'I saw a huge one but missed it.' The heat was becoming oppressive. Chess dominated his day. He was nervous about the Captain, 'sure to be an awfully tough nut', but, after a shaky start, beat him. The second-class thrashed the first in a four board chess match, 'and I alone escape to tell thee.' Colonel Ward insisted on another game and though he reportedly played extremely well, lost again. The first-class revenged their humiliation and Dunsany, who played a long and thoroughly dull game, what with the heat and no rival, finally announced that he had had enough and that that was the last game he would play in the tropics. He had not lost or drawn.

The cigarette-cases turned out to have been overpriced. 'You wouldn't see what was wrong, nor did I, but paint had been used too freely. Still they are lovely.' On the last days of the voyage he made a new acquaintance:

'. . . Do you remember Major Pope Hennessy's extraordinary tale of a man wanted for murder who dwelt in Africa just on the German border, who rose from the ranks to be a major during the war, won the DSO and always hanged his prisoners, who in Klondyke once had a quarrel at cards and went next morning to his comrade's tent shouting 'Dick' till Dick put his head out, which the future major, game ranger and DSO cut off with an ice-axe? Well he is on board. I've had long talks with him. He is pleasant and very rugged of face and neck, many bitter winds must have blown at him. For some while he lived in Utah as a Mormon . . .'

On dry land at last he caught one of several uncertain trains:

Uganda Railway
Beyond Ulu
Oct. 28th.

My Darling Mink,

We, the 1.30 from Kulindi have caught up the 12.00 noon from Mombassa owing to an accident to the train in front, so the two trains have joined up both engines pulling. Last night our colleague train hit a giraffe who smashed a good deal of their footboard and bent some iron bars.

We left Ulu with the brakes still on under our compartments; as there is no communication cord we just had to leave things as they were but luckily the brakes have just come off. We left Mombassa last night through rubber plantation and coconut forests, some huge blue water-lilies and all manner of flowers, the sunset came and the pale stars and the splendid triumphing sparks of the wood fire of our engine which remained the only beautiful things to be seen in the black night. We dined among flying ants in the station at Voi and afterwards wrapped in a rug or so, I lay down on the seats in the train . . .

Nairobi Oct. 29.

Raggie met me at the station, he seems a very pleasant fellow but especially a sound one. We start today. Also met Percival.

Ever Your loving

PONY.

A cable had come about engaging 'Reggie Hall' but had arrived 'Raggie' and lost the 'Hall' so he was referred to as Raggie.

Oct. 29 5 p.m.

. . . Last night I dined with Percival, a charming fellow; and the man whom the police of so many countries have wanted (he of the ice-axe). He told me at dinner that he had eighteen wives. Our talk was mainly of lions.

. . . I think he (Raggie) will run our trip very well. He was in the navy though I think he retired as a sub-lieutenant, but in Peru they say he was an admiral . . . Nairobi is a rubbish heap on which they intend to build a capital and have just begun . . . I asked Percival what kind of folk they were on the boat. 'Oh I don't know what kind,' said Percival. 'Hell's full of them . . .'

Raggie organised seventy-two Africans, who walked through the bush behind Dunsany with boxes on their heads. Dunsany rode. Though there was little game, he was enjoying himself. He saw 'a forest that climbs a cliff across a little stream and falls in hundreds of white beards . . . These graceful things Hall tells me are parasitic.' The tracks of the elephants lay 'a few yards back from the precipice so that they would not show on the skyline and none should see the huge black shapes slipping silently by in the night upon hundred mile journeys . . .'

The first time he used his rifle ('horribly new'), he was watched by everyone. Fortunately he got two jackals with two cartridges from rather over a hundred yards and felt with relief that it did not matter so much if he missed after that. In fact he got a wart-hog 'with the ugliest face in Africa' that evening. If his letters seem full of boasting, it must be remembered that he had nothing except his own feats and observations to record, that he was indeed a remarkable shot and chess-player, that he was writing privately to his wife, and that in any case he did not particularly relish modesty.

It rained a lot. He got a zebra and met an Irish doctor who shot leopards from his bedroom window, and travelled with an alleged niece after whom Dunsany placed a bracketed question-mark. He was so far from such behaviour that it is a surprise when he suspects it in others, however reasonably. A wounded buck was lost twice and crossed a river before he finally caught up and dispatched it. 'There was loud talking round the fire that night from men well filled with meat.' It was now a month since he had left England and almost two weeks since he had landed. He had shot creditably and liked the country, which he celebrated in sporadic bursts of prose: 'Africa by day is parcelled out amongst settlers, tribes and empires but at night-fall it all passes into the possession of One, on whose forest we trespassed, whose voice we heard, a few low growls at first and then the proclamation of his presence, the lion's tremendous roar, then silence for a moment even among the frogs, then the whining hungry cry of his horrible mate . . .' But that was the problem. 'No lion' and 'Still no lion' appear regularly in his letters. Then lions have been seen. At last on November 14: 'At first we could not see him, then met him at ten yards, very angry, turning round and roaring in defence of his kill. Much divided in his mind between hunger for zebra-meat (he was very old and lean) anger against man-meat, and his own safety he dodged about and then ran round us and I broke his back with a lucky shot at about twenty yards ... Eleven feet from nose to tail and a fine mane ...' That evening there were 'Seventy yelling natives round me at the camp-fire all wanting to shake hands, dancing the lion dance and singing his song.'

So Dunsany crowned a successful trip; now he wanted to go home. On November 27 he began a series of rambling, repetitive, depressed letters getting unusually near to introspection.

My darling Mink,
We've been in a bad bit of climate and the heat has almost got hold of me. Still I'll struggle rather than upset Hall's plans. But if I can no longer shoot I'll have to give it up. In any case I'm beginning to get tired of destroying.

Hall's temper is permanently awful, he is a very good hunter for all that and a splendid worker. We never quarrel because it would be silly to be offended at one moment when one was not at another unless of course one quarrelled all day long.

I'm afraid I've been cross with you Minkie, I'll try not to be any more, it is a bore when people are cross always—not that I minded until yesterday when I began to get ill, incidentally we had our longest march ...

Dec. 1. 3 p.m.

I still feel the same. What had I better do I wonder. Chuck it for a German steamer about Dec. 15 or struggle on. What's the use of struggling on though, feeling ill too often. I've nothing to gain by it for you said bring about twenty heads and I've got over fifty ... I'm influenced most by the wish to see you again. I wonder what you'd advise. I've been here for nearly six weeks now ... there's little left but my resolution. Why shouldn't I use it? and tell Hall.

4 p.m.

I've told Hall ... I don't like to be beaten even by the sun by him whom our ancestors worshipped. I'd go on in spite of him if there was anything to go on for. I'd like to have got a buffalo ... I shall come back much fitter for this trip. Two cold days would cure me but I can't get them ... This is my bag: 3 Jackals, 4 Congoni, 4 Wart-hog, 3 Stainbuck, 6 Zebras, 1 Waterbuck, 1 Rhinocerus,

L.D.

G

8 Impala, 5 Thompson's Gazelles, 5 Grant's Gazelles, 4 Hyena,
1 Lion, 1 Dik Dik, 4 Oryx, 1 Gerrynock, 2 Queen Stoats, 1 Hare,
1 Snake, 2 Great Bustard, 2 Lesser Bustard, 5 Guinea Fowl, 9 Spear
Fowl, 2 Partridges, 10 Quail, 1 Snipe, 4 Pigeons, 9 Red-legged
Plover, 1 Grey-legged Plover and 2 various birds. Total 55 beasts
and 47 birds. Total 102.

Dec. 2.

I'm not fit enough to go on, under this sun I mean. I'd come again
though (fresh from England) if we ever find room for more heads
as it's a good life and I could keep the *Wide World* magazine running
for a year on things I've seen and done.

Ever your loving
PONY.

Things got worse before they got better.

Dec. 2.

. . . I've just this moment heard we can't start tomorrow. The man
who we hope will arrive today must have a day's rest.

1.30

I will be so glad to see you, you were quite right of course it is much
too long, why didn't I do as you said. I'll see you again all right I
trust: but when I feel ill I sometimes think I won't and really seeing
you is all I think of.

I stopped writing this morning because I was too depressed and
really one needn't record one's feelings then. I'm no better now but
I must remember the truth my experience has found – that the
lowest pits of the spirit are near the mountains, this is especially true
of we Irishmen and of a genius too. Funny if my genius (though I
haven't bothered about this) were cast away in the desolate places
among people who were unaware of its existence, not that my life is
any more valuable to me than any other man's to him, but I was
thinking of men in Bogota, Germany, Russia, Ealing! to whose
children I might be some loss if lost here as I don't intend to be –
yes I distinctly feel the feet of my spirit as I write treading painfully
once more the lower slopes of those mountains, far down and weary
but my spirit doesn't stay long on the lower slopes once she gets foot
on them. Remember how very glad I shall be to see you again my
dearest Minkie.

2.45

Down in the pits again. Yet I must see you again Mink and I must
make up my mind to do it.

4 p.m.

I'll have another talk with you again. I think it cheers me up. You have been a good Mink to me, how I wish you were here, you'd make me feel so much better and tell me how much fitter I am. And you'd make Hall start tomorrow (if the men come) and go the coolest way. He's no good whatever to a sick man. I'm so sorry that when I was with you I was so often cross, I'll try to make you happier Mink and you must remind me that I said so in writing which you may show. And if I don't come back (though I shouldn't say that for I'm not very sick) then I want you always to make yourself as happy as you can for my sake because I owe this to you and wish you to pay this debt for me if I can't. But I will Minkie, in person Amen.

Isn't this a dreary letter? But you will know from it if I snuff out that I do not *compare* all else I should lose with losing you, my Mink. Furthermore I trust not to snuff out and don't see why I should. So that's all right.

And it was. From that moment on he steadily returns to his old self.

6.15.

Ever so much better now Mink. Yet lament for me with a lesser lamentation that several lions were seen close to the camp this morning, I actually heard them and Hall went out with Flood and had I been there I had one for sure . . .

Dec. 4.

Lord Claud Hamilton has just appeared and camped. Hall is in a very bad temper. Suddenly came a rumour that yet *another* safari has appeared. I tell the rumour to Hall to see what he'll say. He felt it very much. He said 'The bloody place is like the Strand! Oh, Africa's finished' and then walked away. . . .

Dec. 5.

Another long march. Very tired. The others didn't get a lion.

Dec. 6.

I got up from my bed to help chase a lion away from the camp yesterday. Unfortunately I missed him.

Dec. 7.

. . . here's a suggestion for the arrangement for the hall at D [drawing with positions for heads marked] . . . Randal can have a zebra's head in the nursery. We can throw a few hyena skins down by the fireplace in the billiard room.

Dec. 8.

. . . I got an eland; so I must make a new scheme for the hall . . .

Dec. 11

Civilisation! And I felt devoutly thankful. I loved to see oxen
drawing carts, to hear natives singing, to see a house or two,
and gardens! And the red straggly road. I felt thankful to have come
alive out of a wild and wonderful country closing a very successful
trip . . .

Dec. 17.
Woeman-Linie
Hamburg.

A charming boat has delivered me from Africa, instead of discomfort
I find nearly everything better than on the Union Castle.

Later in a story he wrote: 'There is a fascination in the
Sahara, a day there is delightful, a week is pleasant, a fortnight
is a matter of opinion, but it was running into months.'

On board Dunsany completely recovered his tone. In a few
days he reported a game of chess, which was watched not only
by the chess-players on board, but by the officers as well, for
his opponent worked on a boat and they were proud of him.
Indeed, it was an exciting game and he played with 'some
genius', but Dunsany's unbeaten record remained intact.
The passengers were as successful in a tug of war against the
sailors, pulling ten of them over the line with ease. On December
26 he said in a letter '. . . I hope you'll come to London to meet
me. I suppose of course it seems a big journey to you, as it used
to to me, and will again, but while I am actually on my way from
Ngare Ndare to Dunsany it doesn't seem so far to me . . . I lost
a game of chess yesterday, the first since I left England. Never
mind, I'd beaten the same man before for one thing and he's
about as good as me for another' (presumably this was the
sailor).

Beatrice went not only to London but to Dover and met him
on January 4 1914. While Dunsany had been away she had
stayed at her old home, Middleton, and with her sister Markie
at Dynevor in Wales for a few weeks. Then she returned quietly
to Dunsany where she writes of local committees, Randal and
the servants before deciding, 'No it is better to write no diary

than to prose like this.' Even then she occasionally slips in an entry. John Hawksley, who came to stay, was:

so gentle, almost prim, but with a delightfully unexpected twinkle. He was very diffident about the propriety of coming to stay while E. is away, though longing to hunt. He and I agreed that it really isn't any good hoping that E. and Reggie will ever get on for long, they are too much alike. They are really quite fond of each other for an hour, but a long visit is too much for them and neither shows at his best with the other unfortunately.

A Mr Brodie came and regaled her with his experiences on the hunting field. An inexperienced horseman, he was told that his horse would stampede if he touched its withers. Unfortunately he had no idea where these could be found, and so spent the whole day trying not to touch any part of his mount. It had a strong mouth he said, but that was all right because Mr Brodie had strong arms. He survived unscarred. Georgie Buller had been ill and convalesced at Dunsany. She received a letter from a mutual friend, who described Beatrice as 'a delightful mixture of peacefulness, sweetness, insight and spice'. These qualities are apparent in her description of a local dinner-party:

Mr Donnelly is always good company with a most human appreciation of his neighbour's weak points. He listened with sympathetic attention to Mrs Stammer at luncheon as she said enthusiastically 'Stammer is wonderful, never tired, he is just as bright at the end of a long day's hunting as before he starts'. 'I am sure he is, *just* as bright' agreed Mr D. gazing solemnly at S's dull foolish face. 'And he has such a wonderful appetite,' continued Mrs S., 'He'll eat two woodcocks at a sitting. And oysters any number of oysters'. Someone said three dozen oysters was the right number 'Is three dozen oysters the right number, Stammer?' inquired Mr D. anxiously. 'Four dozen is better,' said Stammer with grave greed. And then G. heard Mrs Lucius and Mrs Donnelly discussing how busy they were – they must be wholly unoccupied most of the time, but these folk talk as though they were as importantly busy as Prime Ministers.

'I really haven't time to order dinner now,' said Mrs Donnelly (the cause of this extra work is a new rock garden) and I go upstairs when I know the servants are at dinner for fear the housemaid should waylay me.'

'I know' sympathised Mrs L. G. 'I go to play bridge in other people's houses – then they can't get at me.'

Dunsany returned to a country more than ever concerned with one topic: Home Rule. It seemed inevitable but impossible. Would Ulster secede? Carson[1] and the North might be willing to part from the southern unionists, who included the Dunsanys, but surely the nationalists could not afford to let so rich a fragment go? A friend of Reggie's said that he would chuck up his career in the Navy to go and fight for Ulster in the civil war that would follow the declaration of Home Rule and this was seen as a realistic and honourable decision. As Protestant landowners, the Dunsanys had every reason to fear and oppose an independent Ireland; but they had no need of reasons. Instinctively loyal to the Government of Westminster and the Crown, they saw all those who were not as rebels. Beatrice's views were almost as strong as Dunsany's, though not expressed so loudly. They also agreed that the one bright spot was that it took people's minds off women's suffrage.

Others talked of leaving the neighbourhood and indeed the country, if the Bill passed, but if the local people were about to murder them in their beds, they still appeared amiable enough. In January many Roman Catholics subscribed to the leaving-present of the Protestant clergyman; at a concert given by the United Irishwomen several of the older girls came to Beatrice, the only Protestant, for sympathy and advice because the priest had forbidden them to dance (which they did, though Beatrice was not so foolish as to advise it); a stranger, for whose brother Dunsany had built a cottage, met him on the Dunshaughlin bog, walked with him, picking up his snipe, and left wishing him, 'Prosperity in this world and – (a moment's hesitation) – and prosperity in the next world too, for we may meet, we have the same God after all.' It did not sound like implacable, bigoted hatred. Stories of people who pretended to support what they did not really believe for inadequate, illogical reasons such as fear or simple politeness, made the undeviating Beatrice think them a queer timid race, but there was no dislike on that side either. When Mrs Hinkson, an Irish friend who wrote poetry and volumes of memoirs under

1. Sir Edward Carson, 1854–1935, barrister, Member of Parliament, champion of Ulster and leading opponent of Home Rule.

her maiden name, Katherine Tynan, said how much she loved
England and how beautiful she found it, Beatrice agreed but
said that it was strange to hear an Irish person saying so. She
had been surprised, when she first came over, to find that the
greatest compliment was to be told that she was 'Not a bit
English'. Mrs Hinkson explained that that was the Anglo-
Irish attitude, not the Celtic, and that the English colonists in
Ireland had the same jealousy of England as they had in other
colonies. Beatrice thought it over and found it true.

Because they were friendly, it did not follow that there was
any doubt on either side as to the right of their cause, or any
unwillingness to act. When the Dunsanys returned to Ireland
in May after an absence of two months they found the customs
far more meticulous than usual, as there had been some gun-
running. They had met an acquaintance, who was also a
policeman, on the boat, and been told that it was all finished
now, but they had some trouble with a rifle that Dunsany
needed for rabbits. Finally with much fuss and formality it
was allowed in. So were two wicker hampers which contained
the barrels for twenty rifles. The stocks, said Lord Northland,
who had been Dunsany's best man, was now a colonel in the
Ulster army, and had talked Dunsany into his first and last
appearance as a smuggler, could be made anywhere. Beatrice
had thought it wrong to break the law and in this case rash
as well, but for once she failed to persuade Dunsany. He did it
to oblige a friend and for the excitement of the thing rather
than from political convictions, but could not have agreed if
these had not coincided.

The two months had been spent in London and Paris, gay,
carefree and leisurely. At the end of April *Le Petit Théatre
Anglais* acted a new play by Dunsany for a few performances.
Called *The Tents of the Arabs*, it told in one act how a king who
resembles a camel-driver, agrees to swap occupations with him
for one year. As he is enjoying the simple life and the love of a
good woman, he decides to continue the role for ever. 'There is
perhaps,' Dunsany commented later, 'a little more poetry than
plot in this play and I think that no ingredient that a play may
contain should exceed the plot.' He had never seen the tents of
any Arabs, but found that his only mistake, which he corrected,
was to make them white, where they should have been brown.

The actors had only four days to learn their parts and no dress rehearsal, so it was rather a relief when illuminations in honour of a visit by George V coincided with what was, as a result, a sparsely-attended first night. After that it went well and was generally considered a pleasant though minor work. Beatrice refused to believe a disquieting rumour that all Paris was going to copy Queen Mary's taste in hats. 'After her own country-women have despised and rejected [them] for years it would be nemesis for it to be forced on them via Paris.' But her real scorn was kept for the play that followed *The Tents of the Arabs*: 'How any man can have the face to write such nonsense as *The Music Cure*,[1] I cannot think. Of course I can't believe that Bernard Shaw's reputation will last – he has no original ideas and a cheap verbal originality may be dull when it is no longer topical.'

In London Dunsany went to a dramatisation of *Anna Karenina*, and when he was asked by the Manager to go backstage afterwards he reflected that he was at last becoming a little known in the theatre world of London. However, it turned out that he had been mistaken for H. G. Wells – whom he did not resemble – and the Manager had not liked or dared to withdraw the invitation. Thus he made the acquaintance of the actress Lydia Yavorska, whose real name was Princess Bariatinski, and of Wells, both of whom he admired. The Princess admired him too and asked him to come for a weekend in Brighton, but he declined and asked her to lunch with Beatrice instead.

In June, with the guns safely run, Wells and his wife came to stay at Dunsany, and Sime and a friend of his, a composer called Holbrooke, soon joined them. Mrs Hinkson came over and declared that she had never heard so much heresy in her life, but softened the comment with a quotation about 'knowing many heresies but no heretics'. She was a fat comfortable person less likely to be shocked than to be making mental notes for another volume of memoirs. Once when Beatrice's cousin, Winifred Leigh,[2] fainted at dinner, while Dunsany carried her

1. Published in 1926 by Constable in *Translation and Tomfooleries*.
2. Winifred Jeffreys m. 1912 Major Chauny Leigh (1873-1914) who was Beatrice's first cousin once removed. In 1925 she married Sir Charles Magnay, Bt.

into the drawing-room and Beatrice searched for some brandy, Mrs Hinkson remained motionless at the table, searching for adjectives. 'We know,' said Dunsany, 'what will be appearing in her next book.' Two young cricketers from Trinity were also exposed to heresy, but seemed equally unsinged.

In spite of constant disagreement on almost every topic, the visit was a success. Dunsany admired Wells and he could be tolerant where he admired. Beatrice wrote of Wells:

He *is* amusing and if one had not read his books one would say that he had a pleasant impartiality on all matters of opinion, but he said once that he had his 'religion' and was impartial about others. He looks amazingly young and full of life – his wife pretty, intelligent, faded and adoring . . . When Sime and Wells really got going it was a joy to listen. – S. was out for blood and when W in illustrating a point said 'You and I know we shall die,' S interposed, 'I don't know it.' He did not admit death, generally accepted truths or the necessary limitations and conventions of language as premises to argue from – but Wells was ready for him, as was to be expected from one who has peopled the moon and Mars and the future in such a way that scientists cannot catch him out – 'before I found out the world was serious' as he explained. He challenged S to draw 'an ambitious molecule' ('Cancer' said E.).

The real struggle was not intellectual and waged in the drawing-room, but physical and was first joined on the tennis-court. Wells, like Dunsany, was not fond of losing at any game and thought the Dunsanys would be feeble opposition. A short, fat forty-eight against a tall, lean thirty-six, he lost a hard-fought single to his host. They called in their wives, as Wells had confidence in Mrs Wells's skill, but Beatrice was an excellent player and the home team won again. Then they played stump cricket and Beatrice bowled Wells out immediately. Later he lost at billiards. Perhaps it was as well he finally won a game of tennis against Mrs Hinkson, who was very short-sighted, and her daughter Pamela.

The Wellses left, but the others remained. Strolling in the afternoon, Sime was asked the time by an old woman. 'Later than it has ever been,' he replied. At dinner Holbrooke asked, 'Now is it prejudice or conviction that makes one go against people like Lloyd George and Redmond?'

'Probably prejudice' replied Dunsany, 'but the two men in

question are both such damned ruffians that it is hard to say.'
Holbrooke giggled for the rest of the meal at this criticism.
Dunsany's response shows the broad sweep of his prejudices.
Redmond, though a Nationalist leader, later urged the Irish
to fight the Germans, as Dunsany naturally wished them to,
and lost his position for being too moderate; but Dunsany
made no distinctions between rebels. A hatred for Lloyd
George was almost automatic among men of his stamp.

Holbrooke's reaction does not contradict Beatrice's curious
description of him as 'like a pathetic, good-natured, deaf child'.
After dinner he played the piano beautifully for as long as
anyone wanted, including bits of his own opera, *Dylan*. Sime,
as neutral in politics as Dunsany was extreme, described how
he had divided the wall of his house in Worplesdon with a
chalk line at the last election so that each party could have half.
It had been an easy, enjoyable, civilised house-party.

Less than two weeks later Beatrice and Dunsany were walking
outside in the last of yet another fine summer's evening, when
they heard the sound of drilling. It was the National Volunteers, a supposedly non-political force but in fact dedicated to
the cause of independence and an answer to the Ulster Volunteers, which had been formed in the North. Both were theoretic-
ally unarmed, but there were other gun-runners besides
Dunsany. He was asked to join, and hesitated only because
their politics were not yet apparent and were actually officially
denied. Finally he sent a non-committal refusal, praising the
benefits that must accrue to the health of all concerned. A
future of small armies, hostility and anarchy seemed imminent.
The best hope lay in local incompetence and lack of enthusiasm;
The steward, Cruikshank, was unworried: 'It won't come to
much here. Meath men are never any good.'

The weather remained hot and in the middle of June
Beatrice and Dunsany took Randal to the seaside at Bundoran
in Donegal. After about ten days Dunsany said, 'If I don't
come back this evening, you will know that I have decided to
walk home' and in the evening he did not return. Typically it
had not occurred to him that a tall stranger striding through
the night might be a source of alarm in a country full of spies
and on the verge of civil war. After several rebuffs he fortunately
ran across a vicar who was also a mason. They exchanged

signals and he was whisked to a masonic gathering and eventually given a bed. 'The only time I found being a mason any
good,' he said ungratefully, but he sent the vicar a box of
masonic emblems. The journey was over a hundred miles so
there were two more nights on the road, but he had no difficulty as he got nearer home, which he approached in a canoe
specially sent from Dunsany. The current was too strong on the
Boyne and he finished the last lap in a cart.

After this pastoral interlude Dunsany's adopted poet,
Francis Ledwidge, occupied his attention. He announced that
he could not endure an instant longer the stifling atmosphere
of his village, Slane, where he met with no sympathy or understanding, and he had decided to work his passage to America
as a stoker on a liner. Dunsany believed him, Beatrice did not.
With an unusual touch of malice, she enthused about the idea,
considered the golden opportunities waiting across the Atlantic,
becoming euphoric as his initial fervour seemed to wane. They
left wishing him a successful voyage, which was to start in the
morning. Next day he was not around. There was silent absence
for ten days. 'This time,' said Dunsany, 'he really has gone.'
'No,' said Beatrice, 'he is hiding with his relations in Manchester.'
And so it turned out.

Whether he stayed or not, Dunsany had arranged for the
publication of his first book of verse, *Songs of the Field*. In his
introduction he does not anticipate great sales: 'If one (a poet)
has arisen where I have so long looked for one, amongst the
Irish peasants, it can be little more than a secret that I shall
share with those who read this book because they care for
poetry.' Indeed he rejects the very audience the publisher was
wooing. Herbert Jenkins labelled the book 'The Scavenger
Poet' which was not true but has a romantic swing to it which
'The Ganger Poet' lacks; whereas Dunsany ends, 'I hope that
not too many will be attracted to this book on account of the
author being a peasant, lest he come to be praised by the 'how
interesting!' school; for know that neither in any class, nor in
any country, nor in any age, shall you predict the footfall of
Pegasus, who touches the earth where he pleaseth and is
bridled by whom he will.'

The foreword carries the same message that lies at the back
of several early stories – the poet may be a peasant or a lord,

but he must not expect even recognition, much less fame; which would only be reiterated by one who did want and expect more applause than he was receiving. Yet on the surface his life and career were progressing though there had been a slight check. Several of his short plays had achieved success, and he had hopes that *Alexander* might soon provide him with a full-length hit in London. If he was restless, especially in London, that was an almost permanent adjunct of his energy and enthusiasm; that he had considered joining the National Volunteers suggested that he was. Politically it was nonsense; their interests were diametrically opposed to his, which Beatrice at least grasped swiftly enough. However, if he thought he might find the distraction he still sought in the army, he had not so long to wait. The Dunsanys had been apprehensive and they were not mistaken. But the difficulties they foresaw were postponed by disasters that had not occurred to them.

It was Winifred Leigh who awakened them. There had been a clash between the King's Own Scottish Borderers and the people of Dublin, who had thrown a man into the Liffey. Four Dubliners were killed, twenty soldiers sent to hospital. Yet when asked if they would allow hunting across their land the local people had said yes, of course they would: 'They're the nicest regiment we ever had. They gave the children a lovely Christmas tree.' A characteristic situation, funny but for the blood. Channy Leigh had not been involved but the regiment was confined to barracks and he was possibly in some danger so Beatrice asked Winifred to stay and was not surprised that she was in a perfect fever. But one evening when she burst into tears in the drawing-room and the Dunsanys tried to comfort her, she cried out, 'No, no, it's not that, it's this war that is coming.'

Ireland had filled their horizon. On August 4 Beatrice wrote:

A more bewildering week I have never lived through. A week ago it was civil war we were fearing – talk was of barbed wire entanglements and could the volunteers be trusted to oppose marauders from Dublin or would they join them, and then just before the Home Rule amending bill came back to the H. of C. and the final spark came, Austria goes to war with Serbia. For one brief moment one tried to hope it would stop there . . . now we all seem in for the most ghastly European war – and years ago Eddie was snubbed for calling the Emperor 'a homicidal maniac'. He is.

The Privy Council sanctioned the proclamation of war with Germany at 11 p.m. that evening.

PART TWO

1914 – 1918

THE abrupt arrival of the First World War was shocking but not complicated for the Dunsanys. Their reaction was unwavering. The nominal cause was a wretched one; it was said, perhaps with some truth, that we were not supporting the right side, that a powerful Russia would be even more of a menace than a powerful Germany; there had simply not been enough time to work up any real hatred for the enemy. But war had been forced upon us, as even some socialists admitted in their speeches; and sacrifices were demanded for country and the cause of justice and such sacrifices would be made willingly, almost unthinkingly.

Dunsany was thirty-six, but keen to join up. However he did not want to return to the Coldstream Guards as the officer whom he particularly disliked – and who particularly disliked him – remained. ('He has met his Waterloo' Dunsany was able to say happily later for he was placed in charge of that station throughout the war.) He hoped and expected the National Volunteers would be integrated into the British Army and now joined them as he had thought of doing some weeks before. By the evening of August 7th he was drilling them in the lanes. The Dunsanys were indignant and contemptuous when Uncle Horace admitted that he had hoped that Dunsany would offer to fight but be refused.

Beatrice saw the extent of the disaster, considered it a duty to remain calm, and did so. She promised herself that she would not believe rumours, but found it hard to forget them. England had food for four months, and people said that the war would only last that long, but it did not seem possible that Germany, who had been preparing for years, would submit so quickly and the Russians had to collect their army; and then there would be the settlement, a fruitful source of quarrel. Defeat was not considered. The papers were full of sad little marriages, that had been hurried forward. Private worries mingled with public ones – Reggie was on Captain Beatty's flagship and there was said to be a naval battle going on immediately. Dr Gogarty reassuringly said that a nation did not win when the sentiment of the world was against it. At least the Irish question might be swallowed up and forgotten. The Kaiser had been counting on civil war in Ireland, but it had not come, nor was there any panic. Basic instincts remained intact.

Censorship was efficient and admirable even if the result was that no one knew where their friends or relations were. Reggie wrote a letter to Beatrice headed 'Time, place etc. censored', so at least he was unharmed as yet. Boy scouts guarded the railways, many country houses were offered for hospitals, lectures and classes on first aid were hurriedly arranged. Beatrice noted with irritation that her appendix must be removed, but, though a more considerable business then than now, she recovered quickly in spite of the surgeon rushing in the day after the operation to tell her the famous rumour that the Russian Army was marching through England and had been recognised by the snow on their boots. A silly girl incurred her anger by saying that if she were a man she would join up and in the same breath that there was panic on the south coast. Whether true or false such a rumour was best not repeated, and why boast of deeds you could not perform when you neglected smaller duties within your power? All conversation, all thought, lead back to the war and if Beatrice did not permit herself to day-dream of being a man at the front, she did long to do more than such tepid little things as not using the motor to save petrol. But there was nothing and she could only take comfort in the idea that drilling the volunteers was now of real importance.

On the Sunday after war was declared a hundred volunteers marched on to the cricket ground, where they were harangued by Dunsany. Political differences had separated them in the past. If there was no invasion, these differences could be taken up once more, as children take up cast-off toys they have out-grown. If invasion came and was successful, the old quarrels would die with them. If it came and they repelled it, it would be impossible for them, who had been brothers in arms, ever to have differences again. Dunsany was eloquent, palpably sincere and as ready to die in the defence of Ireland as of England, indeed he made no such distinction. If he belittled

the Irish grievances by the implication that they could easily
be set aside while more serious matters were dealt with, it was
an unconscious, though accurate, reflection of his views. Nor
was his romantic view of the cleansing effects of facing a
common foe unshared. After the speech he gave his section
firing drill, as he was to each afternoon, after the aiming drill
of the morning and before plain drill in the evenings. The
volunteers had still not been recognised officially but that and
equipment must come soon. Meanwhile there was no time to
waste.

A week passed and the Dunsanys went to Slane where two
thousand volunteers were gathered. After an inspection, Lord
Fingall spoke. He told the men with tact and common sense
that they were to accept service under the War Office and they
seemed to be content with that. Next Dunsany spoke with his
customary vigour and was much cheered. Then disaster fell.
Beatrice records

'. . . the MP for North Meath, Mr White, got up and told these
luckless men (all or nearly all longing to do the right thing if allowed)
that they should accept War Office instruction but must remain
under their own leaders. It was sickening. He must know that no
sane man in power could accept a force under these conditions, he
must know that they would be useless, that in case of invasion they
would be mere armed civilians, liable to be hung and their villages
burnt – it can't be that these wretched politicians are going to ruin
the only chance there has been of making a loyal and contented
Ireland. And these poor sheep will follow from habit – it is contemptible that they can believe them. Eddie talked to White after,
argued too, Lord F. keeping the peace with his unequalled tact, 'I
even dirtied my hand,' said E. [by shaking hands with White].

The nationalists were not trying to achieve the loyal, contented country that the Dunsanys wanted, though John
Redmond, the leader of the Irish Party, hoped that Ireland
would gain her freedom fighting for the freedom of other small
countries such as Belgium. But Kitchener, agreeing with
Beatrice, refused the Irish Volunteers under their own officers,
accepted the Ulster organisation under those same terms, and
the burst of Irish loyalty died in resentment. The Irish Volunteers split, the majority following Redmond. As those that were
really eager to fight the Germans grew impatient and joined

up elsewhere, this became a refuge for those that were not really
eager, but did not wish to say so. The minority of more militant
nationalists began to look for arms and support from abroad,
either Germany or America, to pursue their own aims. Neither
group suited a patriotic Englishman.

For Dunsany, with the potentially complex loyalties of the
Anglo-Irish, was never in the faintest doubt as to where those
loyalties lay. He was effectively English, unswervingly loyal to
his King and Country, but also deeply attached to his home and
the lands around it and fond of the local people. He found no
contradiction in this. When it was clear that the volunteers
would come to nothing, he simply reported to Dublin and
accepted the regiment into which they put him. 'Having heard
of the way in which Germans treat civilians, I have consulted
my own safety,' he wrote in a letter. The initial Irish failure to
join the British Army was not a deep blow to him. He had
thought they would, and he still thought they should, but his
basic attitudes were untouched.

Beatrice, an Englishwoman abroad while her country was in
peril, found it more difficult to like where she could not admire.
She struggled to be fair but judged by her own uncompromising
standards and, by these standards, condemned. In England
175,000 volunteered in a single week at the beginning of
September. 750,000 had enlisted by the end of the month and
in all two and a half million were to join up before voluntary
enlistment ended in March 1916. It was the greatest volunteer
army ever raised in any country. Beatrice was appalled by the
need, but thrilled with pride at so magnificent a response and
could not help but compare the Irish to their disadvantage.
She was scrupulous in considering the frustration they had felt
while the Home Rule Bill was delayed and while the British
Army was equipped and the Volunteers were not; but it was
not in her even to consider the idea that some of the Irish
might see themselves as a separate country unconcerned by the
war. Nor could she help adding, 'But still – thank God I belong
to an inarticulate nation which can't talk and so must act. I
have liked the Irish, I try to still.' Again when Dunsany joined
up, she could not refrain from comparison:

'Eddie has volunteered and been attached to the 5th Battalion,

Royal Inniskilling Fusiliers – Eddie, who is too old, not nearly strong enough and utterly unsuited by temperament to the rigidity of a soldier's life in barracks alone – our two English footmen have enlisted in the same regiment – and not one of the Irish country-men about is doing anything. And there almost daily are those terrible lists from France, not one without some friends' names, there is that marvellous retreat from Mons, surely as fine a feat as was every done, these are the men who have fought daily for a month, and that terrible German war staff which has foreseen every detail, except apparently the English resistance which they didn't believe in, there are Cathedrals destroyed and Belgians massacred. And S. Ireland looks on and talks, talks, talks.

Later Beatrice acknowledged the considerable number of Irish that had joined up, 49,000 of whom died.

When Dunsany arrived the sergeant-major told each new officer to give the command, 'Form Fours', and Dunsany's uninhibited lung-power won him the commendation, 'Well, you're all right'. He had after all been in the army before, even if he had disliked it and left at the first opportunity. After an exercise, he told a young subaltern who had failed to keep a rendezvous with his colonel, 'You have got to go and be damned'. The man explained convincingly that it had been no fault of his. Dunsany then spent much energy explaining that he quite understood that, but it had nothing whatever to do with it: 'You have still got to go and be damned'. He knew the ways of the army and was promoted to captain almost immediately, whereas if he had rejoined the Coldstream he would have been a subaltern. Also he was pleased to find several men from the Durham coal mines, in which he had a large interest. They were adept at digging trenches. The hurry to cram everything in prevented the normal monotony of military routine. He learnt some things that were new, like bayonet charges, was aware of others such as aeroplanes and guns with a range of eight miles, but mostly found unchanged practices he had been assured were obsolete. Sometimes he could get down to Dunsany on Saturday nights, perhaps bringing an officer or two to dinner, and all in all, the life rather agreed with him.

Beatrice tried to remain calm and reasonably cheerful even in her diary but she was much alone now in the great grey castle and the news both public and personal was so often distressing; silence seemed to contain threats and even good news turned to melancholy.

November 1914   Dunsany Castle

. . . The personal side grows too bitter – Dick Levinge, whom Eddie long ago called 'the only fool I ever loved' and of whom he wrote 'I am sure he gave his life in the happy reckless way in which he lived it.' Mr Brodie who went down in his submarine and whose joyous keen intelligent personality is of a kind that is a loss to the world. Channy [husband of her cousin, Winifred Leigh] still unheard of, the American Ambassador in Berlin hears he is 'believed to have died in Belgium' but Winifred still clings to hope till War is over, who wouldn't? I can't go on. Besides I should at least be knitting socks.

John Hawksley is Major now – his Battery has been in it since the beginning and recently, after twenty-four hours ceaseless enfilade fire, the Major and two men went off their heads and a subaltern lost his memory.

December 1914   Dunsany Castle

It is the helplessness of everyone to prevent this horror that appals me. Once Eddie wrote in one of his stories: 'A horror and an impotence came over the reason of each. . . .'

The Gogartys dined here on Eddie's weekly night here and we discussed the surprising recovery of William Watson who has been mad for three years. 'It is only that he was comparatively mad before' said Eddie. 'He has not changed but in August the world went mad and now he is comparatively sane.'

Arthur [Villiers] writes cheerfully of eighty consecutive hours in the trenches with heavy snow and hard frost, and so close to the German trenches that fires and hot food and drink were impossible – he said that many men could not get into their boots on the following day from the cold and the cramped position. However at last the French seem to have brought up some reserves and eased the strain on our lines. E. said some old members of the Kildare Street Club had died, and, as he rather grimly remarked, it seems strange for an old man to die nowadays.

Lord Brabourne wrote that in twenty days there were only six casualties in his company, but 187 cases of frostbite.

Mr Anderson of the IACS[1] was sadly aged by his youngest son's death – but he has just heard that his eldest son in the

1. Irish Agricultural Co-operative Society.

same regiment, R. Irish, has done a most gallant thing, fetching in a wounded man, and he looks a different man to-day.

Later – Now Philip the eldest son has died of wounds.

Mary Ponsonby, Tommy's mother, had partly filled the gap when Dunsany's own mother stopped coming to Ireland. Now she foolishly started a quarrel that never properly healed. She wrote a letter saying that she had seen a new book by Dunsany and thought that he should have postponed it till after the war as there were 'plenty of people to write books and plays' but there were 'other occupations now for those of our class and tradition.' It had been completed before the war and Dunsany felt it was a bit much for a civilisation to grudge a soldier the harmless pleasure of publishing a book. 'If she is remembered at all,' he said to Uncle Horace, 'It will be as your sister or my aunt,' which was true. A.E. commented characteristically 'You are offering your life, she wants you to give your immortality.' The new book was *51 Tales*. Though they earned him the title in one paper of 'The Aesop of Erin' They are not really fables or tales, more fantastic anecdotes, frequently including Death as a character. About two pages each, they were found generally amusing or pretty, though occasionally feeble. As often it is difficult not to feel that a little editing would have helped, but if one fails, another is swiftly available. He did not repeat precisely this form of fiction.

The Last Book of Wonder, also written before 1914, was published the following year and contains some of his most successful mixtures of sinister humour. There are titles such as *The Bad Old Woman in Black* and *Why the Milkman Shudders when he Perceives the Dawn* while the plots include a pirate who puts his ship on wheels and so escapes over the Sahara, a host deeply grateful because the uninvited hero insults some ghosts, so that they will never come to dinner again, and the Exiles Club where the ex-kings in the basement turn out to be mere waiters for the members above whom we assume to be ex-Gods. The war suspended any chance of a great success, but two stories reappeared later as radio plays and took their second opportunity.

One Sunday in the middle of April, Uncle Horace brought the Bernard Shaws over to lunch. Beatrice was suspicious of Shaw's character and so opposed to his views that it was charity in her to assume, whether rightly or wrongly, that he did not, could not, mean what he seemed to be saying.

Bernard Shaw is exactly what one would expect, a clever good-tempered witty and malicious old man [he was fifty-eight] whose desire for originality has led him to talk paradoxes all his life till now he is incapable of thinking straight. She is an amiable and rather knavish fool who tries pitifully to be like him – neither has a soul and I should say he liked her and was always kind and encouraged her to be ridiculous because it caused him malicious amusement. I don't think he is really pro-German but he could not bear to be in any majority, and she of course is the clumsy copy. But how clumsy! He *is* funny when, for instance he argues that the Germans are logical to kill the wounded and drown civilians – one can't *help* laughing, but one is glad to give oneself a shake when he has gone . . .'

Dunsany had come down with a new friend from the regiment, Captain Armstrong, whose daughter, Yvonne, was Randal's age and had been staying for three weeks. The parents were apprehensive when their offspring asked them to a surprise play, staged with the help of Mademoiselle, the French governess. Would the old cynic mock their childish efforts? But it was not an invitation that could be gracefully refused. In the event Randal and Yvonne played a passage from *King Argimenes* with accuracy and simplicity, sitting in ragged trousers on ground strewn with leaves, and scored a great success. Then Dunsany played a favourite game, blowing up toy boats on the pond by sending them off with a smouldering fuse aboard. As he used considerable amounts of dynamite which blew the craft right out of the water, the children had to stay on the bridge to watch. The moment the fuses were lit Shaw turned and said wickedly: 'You can move now, he can't stop the fuses.' The children were shocked at the suggestion, remained where they were, and always referred afterwards to 'that Mr. Shaw'.

Two weeks later Dunsany was told that he would shortly be going overseas. The danger was great and obvious. His last leave at Dunsany was an ordeal with the old men who had lived on the estate close to tears as they said good-bye. He accepted the future simply; Beatrice could hardly bear it. That

she had long known it must come was no help. For once her
diary is directly emotional, even bitter:

He had to go this morning back to barracks and then I had to take
Baby to Church and out bicycling and then to see the poor woman
who came to the door recently, just going to have a baby (she's all
right though and her husband couldn't pass the doctor so can't go)
– it filled up the time but I wanted to get away and I've never hated
the lovely Spring weather so much before. And yet I've been lucky
– I know – but he will hate it so – of course he didn't mind these
seven months soldiering as much as I thought a poet must – Tom
[Lord Longford, her brother-in-law] has gone to the Dardanelles
(it was Egypt after all) Mary is much braver than I am I know.
And we think ourselves so clever with our rotten inventions and all
we have done is to keep too many people alive and make it easier
for them to kill and make each other miserable. Of course I know
we can't stop now – either the war or our wretched civilisation –
isn't the despised *Kultur* really a better word for this form of it?
We've got to struggle on and make the best of both. But what a
world.
    He hasn't actually left the country yet.

No date of departure had been set. In the meantime Dunsany was sent to Basingstoke. It has often been observed that
time becomes precious when it is running out; the Dunsanys
found that this was true. For two happy months they lived in a
small house called Hillside, two miles from the town, grateful
for each extra day. Several officers became friends and were
glad to drop in for tea or a bath, two in particular being
Lindsay, a great bull of a man, direct and reliable, and
McWilliam, intelligent, gentle and with something beyond
charm, a gift for inspiring affection. It was a quiet life with
few outings other than trips to Basing Castle to show Randal the
cricket and applaud if someone managed to hit a ball into the
cemetry.
    The Dunsanys were glad to be in England. Ireland was
beautiful and peaceful but not the place for the moment.
England knew she was at war. They saw many of the small
effects for the first time – amateur hay-makers, shop-girls and
soldiers on leave helping out, and lists of those absent on the
doors of village churches. The trade unions might be striking,
the government corrupt and civil war merely postponed; 'but

there was a fine soul under it all. Not that I [Beatrice] ever doubted that. It can never be worth while for this generation – what will be left of it – the next will of course patronise us and tell us what it meant but they cannot know what we know and we shall wonder why we sacrificed so much for their sakes.'

Lord Jersey had died on May 31st 1915. Middleton and Osterley passed to Beatrice's elder brother Villiers (now 8th Earl of Jersey) and her mother set up house in London at 18 Montagu Square. Here she remained till 1939. It was an ordinary house furnished in an ordinary way but Lady Jersey immediately adjusted herself to her altered circumstances. There were several spare bedrooms and enough servants, so that she could continue to be the centre of a large and ever-increasing family circle, a rock in a chaotic world.

. . . What a blank Papa's death would have left, in another year – and now we know we must not repine when the young men are being killed daily by hundreds – and can only be glad that his life ended happily, not for instance like old Uncle Eddie who died from the shock of losing both sons.

The dreaded order finally came. Dunsany's battalion was to go to Gallipoli. At the last possible moment Dunsany himself was transferred to the reserve battalion at Derry. The instant reaction was anger, not only from Dunsany, but from Beatrice and from his friends who were going. 'I knew Best hated me,' he said of his superior officer, 'but I thought he would try and get me killed, I never thought he'd play this trick on me.' When he said good-bye to his platoon one shouted, 'But you're the man we'd have followed anywhere,' while the others cheered; this meant something. It was a bitter, flat disappointment, which probably saved his life. For Gallipoli was a bloody disaster. Captain Armstrong was unhurt but came home with a nervous breakdown. Captain Vernon, who had been an actor and could never quite forget it, was shot dead while trying to carry in a wounded man, himself already wounded. Mr Nelis, whom Beatrice had long felt would never come back from the look in his eyes, never did. Mr McWilliam was badly hurt, but Mr Lindsay searched for him, found him, and he was said to be recovering. Old Major Owen, whom everybody loved, was hit.

This depressing news came to them in September in Derry. At first they had lived in 'the dirtiest most mediaeval inn', then in a small house taken by the month. Life was drab. Dunsany was allowed petrol to get to the barracks each day, but there was none to spare and Beatrice used to bicycle to the works depot. Sphagnum was collected from the bogs, dried and the grass and heather sorted out – 'a most tedious job, but one hears it is the ideal substitute for cotton wool in hospitals.' Dunsany always hated to be out of things, now he felt rejected, useless and bored as well. They had a butler, a cook and housemaids and asked officers to meals as before but Beatrice – perhaps significantly – recorded in her diary their presence only, not their conversation.

Dunsany was complaining that he was 'lamentably bored' but Beatrice, on a visit to England, still found time to slip away and see her friend Georgie Buller, who was running a hospital with dynamic efficiency in Exeter. They had had a spy dressed as a nurse, but he heard the police were coming and escaped. Newbury racecourse had a sign saying 'Next Meeting ????' On the way back London was impressive, quiet, slow, 'a few darkened lights in the streets beneath the absolute blackness of tall buildings. Bright colours almost made one start. The old glare and fuss would seem vulgar.'

It was not unreasonable for Dunsany to be lamentably bored alone in Derry. Even after Beatrice's return, life remained dismal. On November 10th a subaltern told him an anecdote. His sergeant had once taken off his hat, knelt down in front of the men and said, 'O Lord Almighty, send down one of thy most patient angels to drill this bloody squad for I am damned if I will.' In December Dunsany sent a letter to Sime with a seal on which he had cut a holy man. Sime replied, 'The God on your last seal received due salutations from me. I can guess from the sinister gleam of satisfaction in his left eye that he has just created a world a little bit worse than this one.' There was little else to smile at. After Christmas Dunsany had a few days leave and spent them at Dunsany. He went hunting, but came back depressed, more aware of the war than ever when trying to escape it, and said he would not hunt again. The drains at Brachead refused to work, so Dunsany spent some days in barracks. He gained popularity by acquiring coal, now scarce, for his men. Beatrice had her fortune told, which she does not disclose but was relieved not to believe, and her character read, with great accuracy she thought.

Really my character sounds quite dull when I hear it spoken – shy, fastidious, highly-strung, none of them qualities I admire, ready to give up most things for peace; independence of thought (a useless quality when power of expression is denied one) things grate on me but I don't show it (that is very little) a good friend (true but too easy), good-tempered (cheap), ruled by affections (absurd), and the only qualities worth having that she suggested she was wrong in, for I am not especially artistic and cannot write.

. . . Well, other people's sons are going to the war so it must be a little thing for mine to go to school.

It was not a little thing to her. She had dreaded the day that Randal must go to school when there was peace. Now she decided that he should risk the Irish Channel twice every holidays rather than go to an inferior local school, but she was desperately anxious.

Dunsany's mother died of pneumonia on February 28th 1916. He had not been informed that she was ill and much regretted not having been to see her at the end. Though they had never been able to meet without the risk of an explosive quarrel, he had loved her deeply. He had influenza and the shock made him really ill so that Beatrice went across for the funeral at Charborough by herself. As Uncle Horace said, Lady Dunsany had revolted both by nature and upbringing against all convention, and yet found neither occupation, health nor friends to make the resulting loneliness possible.

Stormy in her lifetime, Lady Dunsany caused further dissension by her will. Reggie inherited Charborough Park, her house and estate near Wareham in Dorset; Dunsany only obtained possession of Dunstall Priory, the small house in Kent where they had been brought up, after bitter negotiations with his brother. Reggie got married on April 15th to Kathleen Chalmers (now Lady Drax) and this time Dunsany was well enough to go. Beatrice wrote, 'I think it will be all right. E. has an intolerant mind but even when I feel impatient at certain things I do recognise that it is a very noble one.' The unprovoked praise betrays her doubts, which were well founded. There had been a row about the pictures at Dunstall, which

Reggie intended to remove. The brothers had never been close,
from then on they were not on terms of any sort.

That spring history repeated itself in reverse. Just as events
in Ireland had distracted the Dunsanys so that they had been unaware that a European war was upon them, so events in Europe
prevented them from thinking about the dangers in Ireland.

At seven in the morning on Easter Tuesday, Beatrice was
wakened in her room at Dunsany by a noise from outside. She
reached the window in time to see a cartload of armed men arrive
to pick up General Hammond, who was munching an apple.
Hammond was the agent and not a general but a colonel who
had been promoted to brigadier at the beginning of the war;
brigadiers were called general until after the war, when there
were too many of them. English himself, he had a romantic
sympathy for the Nationalists, as had Dunsany, but his loyalty
to the army was unquestionable. Beatrice asked Mander, the
butler, if Hammond had left a message and was told he had
not, but had been heard to say, 'Every available man is wanted.'

At breakfast there was no post. Rumours reached them of a
Sinn Fein uprising in Dublin. Lindsay and Dunsany, both on
leave, hesitated lest they might make fools of themselves, but
finally set off for Dublin in the car to see if they were wanted
and what was going on. They said they would be back for tea.
Now that Randal was going to school his Swiss governess was
no longer needed, and she set off to catch her train. Soon she
returned; the line had been blown up. There certainly seemed
to be some sort of revolt. Had it been timed to coincide with a
general massacre or German invasion? Dunsany and Lindsay
did not return that night.

The Home Rule Bill of 1913 had been postponed by the
outbreak of war, and was not to come into effect until after the
cessation of hostilities. It has been noted that effective control
of the more violent section of the Irish Volunteers, now just
called the Volunteers, had been taken over by extremists who
believed in achieving independence by armed revolt. Plots
were hatched. However when Sir Roger Casement, their
German contact, had been arrested on Good Friday, bringing
in any case not guns and ammunitions but advice to postpone
everything, the crisis appeared to be over. Sunday passed
peacefully. On Monday the chief executives and the Army

High Command went to Fairhouse Races to see the Irish
Grand National. But a section of the rebels struck, and by midday the new Irish flag fluttered above the General Post Office
and the Republic was proclaimed. The Easter Rebellion had
begun, though in Dublin only.

For Beatrice there were ten days of mounting anxiety.
Though she tried to cheer herself up by repeating that she
would hear any bad news, she could not believe it. Panic and
chaos had to be held at bay. The noise of the guns from Dublin
frightened the peacocks, so their dreadful squawking filled the
air. Everyone must sleep in the main building; the maids
came into the drawing-room, shouting and sobbing, but, with
Mander, Beatrice managed to calm and transfer them. She
admitted that she did not sleep well herself, thinking every
owl a Sinn Feiner. There were rumours of bands of drunken
looters and the laundry maid was a red-hot rebel, thought to
be in cahoots with them. She heard that Dunsany was not at
Derry, but she had never really thought he was. The post-
master requested a secret meeting, and, when it was granted,
bicycled up with a newspaper, which was on its way to somebody else. 'I thought I'd let you have it for half an hour or so,'
he said, 'before I passed it on.' But it contained only the bad
news that Kut in Iraq had surrendered to the Turks after a
siege of 143 days.

Randal enjoyed himself hugely, marching about the house
proclaiming, 'We are all Free Irish now,' and then busying
himself building a dug-out. Mademoiselle cried out that if
anyone came she would take him and run into the woods;
Beatrice told her that on the contrary she would do nothing so
silly. A neighbour came to borrow petrol to take a nurse to
Dublin and on his return said that there was a lot of sniping
and many casualties. Of Dunsany he discovered only that he
had reported at the nearest depot and been sent on to Amiens
Street, with which contact had been lost. The rebels staged a
successful ambush at Ashbourne, twelve miles away, shooting
three drivers and eight policemen. A specific band of marauders
was rumoured (correctly) to be heading towards Dunsany.
If they chose to loot the castle, there was no one to stop them.
After a particularly nerve-wracking ninety minutes, word came
that they had turned back. In calmer moments Beatrice con-

centrated as best she could on the rock garden. A story that
Lord Dunraven was dead was disquieting, for she guessed
(again correctly) that it referred to Dunsany. On May 2nd
the news that the rebels had surrendered, first heard two days
before, was officially confirmed (that is, a notice was put up in
the Post Office). But there was still no word of Dunsany.
Beatrice's diary had been calm and factual throughout. Now
for the first time she implies how great the strain had been:
'I thought my nerves were fairly tough, but they are not I
find.' The next day she saw an evening paper that said Dunsany had been wounded under the left eye and was in hospital.

Dunsany and Lindsay had in fact reached GHQ at Dublin
without incident and found no-one had anything for them to
do. He was told to go and help a Major Carlin at Amiens Street
and though a route was suggested to him no-one said that if
he went the shortest way he would run into the Nationalists in
strength. He took the shortest way.

In the distance they saw a row of barrels across the street
and twenty men with rifles at their shoulders. They stopped
the car about forty yards away. The line opened fire. Dunsany
jumped out of the car and lay in the road. His chauffeur,
Cudlipp, held up his hands and had a finger shot off. Lindsay
sat tight. Later Dunsany wrote: 'Though Dublin must have
been echoing to those volleys, to us they were firing in complete
silence, for the crash of bullets going through the air drowns
all other sounds when they are close enough. We saw the men's
shoulders jerked back by the recoil of their rifles, but heard no
sound from them except the tinkling of their empty cartridges
as they fell in the road . . . many bullets went by me before I
was hit.' Dunsany could not stay in the open and dashed to a
doorway which attracted their fire long enough for Lindsay to
dive behind the car. The defenders of the barricade made a
splendid charge with bayonets fixed, but Dunsany noticed that
they had forgotten to unsheathe the blades. The first to reach
him looked at the wound below the left eye which was bleeding
profusely and said simply, 'I am sorry'. Lindsay took charge of
the situation, examining the back of Dunsany's head, in order
to see, he explained, whether he had mud in his hair. There was
no exit wound, but he brushed aside Dunsany's remarks that
he was quite all right and by no means dead and removed

painlessly a jagged piece of lead or nickel still in his wound. The
Nationalists had set up a cry for a doctor, saying there was a
man bleeding to death, and Lindsay refused to leave until he
had seen that Dunsany was being properly looked after. The
wounded man was taken to the Jervis Hospital, which was
behind enemy lines, but treated as a free man.

He stayed a week in a private room with four nuns chatting
most of the time, and sometimes taking his temperature. He
could hear fighting going on all around and literally above, for
there were many snipers on the roof, but saw nothing. When
bullets were chipping the window-sill, a nun described them
with disdain as 'Nasty little things'. The artillery came
methodically nearer, first a boom and then the tinkle of
broken glass endlessly repeated. Once a voice called on the
saints and was silent; 'what struck me most about that clear
cry in the night was that there was surprise in it, as though
the man had not thought he would be hit, though the firing
was heavy and close.'

As the week went by there were fewer nurses to chatter for
shorter periods among the hideous cries of the dying. Although
food was short a dainty chop arrived for Dunsany each day
from an anonymous admirer. On Thursday morning he was
woken at 3 a.m. with the disquieting news that there was no
danger. The sky was red and though the fire brigade who refused
to turn out for anything else, turned out for the hospital, it was
said later that if there had been a breath of wind nothing could
have saved it. The prayers of nuns and the drone of bullets
rose to a climax.

During Friday night the Leinsters captured the hospital
while he slept, though sniping continued the next day.

On Sunday morning I heard a triumphant sound and looking out
of my window I saw a triumphant sight. Poets may picture Victory
with her trumpet, walking the field of battle, but who has seen with
his eyes anything quite so like her as I saw then? I saw one corporal
going alone through Dublin, blowing the Cease Fire, every now and
then on his bugle.

Both sides seemed to obey him.

Lindsay appeared again. Fate seemed to have cast him for a
few days as a cross between the romantic hero of a musical

comedy and a fairy prince none can harm. He had been living for a week on sherry, champagne, port, claret and benedictine as in the Four Courts, where he had been kept prisoner, there was no food, but a fine cellar. He persuaded his captors to telephone Beatrice, but they could not get through. When it became clear that the Nationalists were losing, they had naturally become increasingly despondent and eventually asked if he could give them a little advice. He examined their plans, pronounced them hopeless and said 'I advise you to surrender to me'. So he walked out unsteadily with a sword in each hand and four hundred prisoners. In all this he had mislaid the piece of bullet he had pulled from Dunsany. The other half remained in place, as they had had no X-ray equipment. Now Dunsany was transferred to the King George I hospital, but when they were giving him an anaesthetic, they had to press on his wound and the pain kept him from losing consciousness. He explained this, but they took no notice as it is normal for patients to babble when unconscious and no one bothers to listen to what is said. They prepared to operate. 'I can hear everything you are saying,' he said with mounting urgency. No notice. He then thought of repeating the words of the doctors and nurses and this finally attracted their attention. Afterwards, he was given the half bullet to keep in a show-case, and though he always had a scar and one side of his nose and lip was paralysed, he was not disfigured. When she knew it was not true, Beatrice got a telegram from the War Office saying that he had lost an eye. A curious postscript was told to him long afterwards by a doctor who necessarily knew many of the secrets of both sides. Dunsany's Sam Browne belt was taken from him by the Sinn Feiner who delivered him to the hospital. Seven years later when Michael Collins, the Nationalist leader, was murdered, it chanced to be lying around and Collins was laid out and buried with it.

There had been little support and much hostility to the rebellion in Dublin as well as in the country, less than one thousand being involved on the Irish side. Nor had there ever been a chance of success. But British soldiers had died at a nervous moment in the war; the seven who had signed the proclamation of the Republic and all the commanding officers of the Volunteers, some of them hardly more than boys, were shot. They died bravely and the Irish cause gained martyrs. Within two years Redmond and moderation had lost all influence to the Sinn Fein party and violence.

Dunsany naturally was on sick leave, but orders had come through that he was to join the expeditionary force as soon as he was fit. After all the agonising and anti-climax about his going overseas neither of them could muster the energy to look beyond the immediate future and react to this news. For a month at Dunsany they were just tired. He applied for a further month's convalescent leave, but was refused, for which he was later grateful as he thought the return to light duties at Derry had speeded his recovery. They were not sorry to leave. Dublin had been horrible, handsome well-remembered shops reduced to rubble, the sickening smell of smouldering ruins, these were to become familiar, but were not familiar yet. Even round Dunsany where the people had *done* nothing, they felt that they could no longer trust anyone; The atmosphere after even the most abortive civil war is not pleasant. It was said that the country had only been waiting to see how things went in the city; perhaps they would have been willing to join success. Nor was it easy for opponents to avoid one another. An acquaintance called Bobby Dunville, the son of the local Master of Fox Hounds, had been lined up against a wall with two policemen and shot; fortunately one of the police fell in front of him and, though wounded, he was not killed. At lunch at Killeen Lady Fingall introduced him to one of his assailants and commented, 'But you two are old friends. What a small world.'

Beatrice, having for so long dreaded the day that Randal must go to school, was now thankful when he was safely at a prep. school called Forzie Place in England. Two of the executed rebels had been called Plunket, so he made the journey with the side of his case that proclaimed his name turned inward. When she went to take him out in June, he rushed up to the car shouting, 'I like school very much'. Frank Pakenham, his cousin and now Lord Longford, was ten years old and already installed. 'I brushed Randal's hair,' he said with resignation, 'But it is untidy again.' When Randal was inveighing against an enemy, Frank reassured her that the boy was pretty nasty and it was quite all right for Randal not to like him. She left satisfied that her son was in good hands.

At Brachead, their home in Derry, Dunsany suffered from a recurring and unpleasant dream. 'For the rest of the year I used to wake up nearly every night with a feeling, uncomfortable though unjustified, that I was dying. A mouthful of brandy used to banish that impression and I do not know what caused it, but it was quite a realistic delusion.' Whether this came from the wound he had received or the knowledge that he might be sent to fight at any moment, the Dunsanys were living once more a quiet dreary life, both shadowed and enhanced by the threat that any week might be their last together. So many friends had been killed that this was simple knowledge, not melodrama. That summer they heard that John Hawksley was dead. He had been untouched in two years incessant fighting and they had allowed themselves to get used to the idea that he might be spared. He and Georgie Buller had met in Cairo in 1909, when she had gone out to see Beatrice and he had been in the Egyptian Army; they were engaged though it was to be secret until after the war. She never married. Beatrice wrote, 'It is growing so lonely for us who are left, and this place [Dunsany] was almost home for John. I shall miss him terribly for myself and more terribly for Georgie, whom happiness is always passing by.' Of all his friends, Dunsany missed him the most.

As before officers came to meals and Beatrice recorded remarks she found interesting; as before her terseness implies that there were few of these. There was always someone who thought the war would be over in a few months and this time there was a widespread rumour that the Big Push was beginning. Nor was it entirely mistaken; the disastrous battle of the Somme began on July 1st. More moss and more men were required. The date Dunsany was to go before the medical board was moved forward a month. Meanwhile he played pathetic games of tennis in the rain but he could still only manage one set. A trip to Dunsany in the holidays was enjoyed by Randal but only induced melancholy in his parents.

In the autumn that uncertainty and the mood evaporated. Dunsany was finally passed in October as fit for foreign service but not general service, which meant that he could be posted abroad but not to the front. Meanwhile they had some successful outings. One was to the Giant's Causeway in September, 'two lovely days which we enjoyed immensely. What a lot of days I have wasted in the last twelve years – I snatch at minutes now and so I think does E.' Another was to London.

We *did* enjoy our old world again. There were only the Duke and Duchess[1] and Lady Cynthia[2] – the eldest girl is away doing munition work daily from 9 to 6 or from 2 to 10.30 – and we did not know them well – and of course we talked of the same things as here and I am sure many people here, whether Inniskillings or Derryites, are as interesting. But for all that I did appreciate, as seldom before, the charm of one's own people, the ease with which subjects are talked of and never talked dry, the tolerance and good sense and culture (if that word has not lost its meaning by German misuse) and sense of proportion that smaller societies do not possess. The duke told me that during the Rebellion it was thought safer to arm some soldiers at, I think, a convalescent camp. No arms were forthcoming so they borrowed arms from the Ulster volunteers and gave a receipt for them, and they were subsequently handed back at a time when houses were being searched for illegally held rifles. It is a pretty incident.

At a lunch Aubrey Herbert recounted how he, Lord Castlerosse[3] and Lord Robin Innes-Ker[4] had been wounded and taken prisoner in the retreat from Mons. Thinking it might help to be important, they stressed their titles and his position as an MP, and the Germans said in dismay: 'Surely you have not already mobilised both Houses of Parliament.' Then the French returned and the Germans said, 'The other prisoners can remain, but you are too juicy a bunch.' So they went into reverse. 'Mine is a very new creation, I am nobody,' said Castlerosse; 'Mine is only a courtesy title, I don't count at all,' said Lord Robin; 'I have only just been elected and have no influence,' said Herbert himself. So they were set free.

For a week in November Dunsany was like its old pre-war self. There were snipe and woodcock to shoot. The Gogartys came to dinner and Yeats came to tea – he was said to be

1. 3rd Duke of Abercorn 1869–1953.
2. Lady Cynthia was the second daughter and married the 7th Earl Spencer 1919.
3. Valentine Edward Charles, Viscount Castlerosse, son of the 5th Earl of Kenmare.
4. Second son of the Duke of Roxburghe, christened Alastair Robert.

going to marry Maud Gonne's eighteen-year-old daughter and
he did in fact propose. But conversation always tended back
towards the one topic. Soldiers from the front told them of
Ypres where there was not a house standing; of the trenches
named after London streets and even following their topography;
and of a man carrying an arm and a leg for burial who, when
asked what he'd got there, gruesomely replied 'Spare parts';
but above all they talked of war weariness.

The news came that Dunsany was to go to the trenches in
France in the New Year just for a week as he still had not been
fully passed by the medical board and was only to collect
material to lecture to the troops at home. The threat had
become so familiar that Beatrice found the reality less grim
than the false alarms . . .

I have been lucky by comparison – I do know that.

Perhaps the week of the rebellion will have taken off the edge,
and it is no use saying damn everything. But there is nothing else to
say. He should leave England today [January 15 1917]. I had a lot
of his Mss. to straighten and correct but it is hard to settle to
anything – I will go to bed now and I must get used to it. I was glad
of the Mss. . . .

It is snowing and will be awful in the trenches – I believe they
are waist deep in mud – and the long dark wakeful nights in this
cold will be his first experience of them.

In France under fire Dunsany wrote a poem for the first
time since the war had begun. He found that 'simply looking
up at the stars straight over my head during a barrage, when
all the lower parts of the sky were troubled and scarlet, was a
contrast so amazing that it almost made the poem by itself . . .
Silence had gone, gone utterly, never leaving any second in
which there was not a shell bursting.' This is the poem:

> *Songs of An Evil Wood*
> There is no wrath in the stars,
> They do not rage in the sky;
> I look from the evil wood
> And find myself wondering why
>
> Why do they not scream out
> And grapple star against star,
> Seeking for blood in the wood
> As all things round me are?

They do not glare like the sky
Or flash like the deeps of the wood;
But they shine softly on
In their sacred solitude.

To their high happy haunts
Silence from us has flown,
She whom we loved of old
And know it now she is gone.

When will she come again
Though for one second only?
She whom we loved is gone
And the whole world is lonely.

Dunsany returned unhurt; Beatrice had been wrong about
the mud, which had frozen stiff, so that no one could be waist
deep in it. However he blamed a cemetery where the lines had
stuck for two and a half years without drains, for tonsilitis
which from then on used to flare up every now and then till
he had the troublesome organs removed. He probably maligned
the place as Randal also got tonsilitis and Beatrice thought it
was the drains at Brachead, to which they now returned.

Ledwidge popped up and was something of an embarrassment as he had not taken to the discipline you put on with the
uniform of a lance-corporal. He was court-martialled for
spending a night out, so Dunsany informed Major Willock,
who was president of the court-martial, that he would go down
to posterity as an afflictor of poets. Major Willock was quite
distressed. Only two and a half pounds of meat were allowed a
week and for a time conversation hinged on whether rabbits
could really be regarded as meat and if it was immoral to eat
the baby's share. Soldiers were excluded, so Beatrice thought it
was acceptable for Dunsany, but not for her, to eat any wild
birds, snipe or duck in particular, that he shot. The monotony
encouraged her thoughts to range more widely. A few weeks
before Beatrice had written the only comment on religion in
her diary; 'I rather wish suddenly that I did know of a God – I
would rather like to feel that there was someone to be interested
in the world and perhaps guiding it somewhere and that it was
not drifting at the will of its poor bewildered occupants.' Now

she indulged a sudden and almost as rarely recorded burst of nostalgia:

Oh I *love* peace – I love gardens and books and embroidery and games, dancing, hunting, new clothes, sugar, boats, music, travelling – all the careless wasteful things of peace. We were not always happy then, I suppose, and I suppose we shall never, any of us, be rich and idle in the old way again – but surely we shall recapture some of the old joyousness – anyway we shall see the young ones with it. One beautiful thing has grown with war – an almost universal love of poetry – men who might hardly have read it before have written verse, and good verse. As Eddie says it has been squeezed out of them, and it is read too.

America seemed almost as distant and insubstantial as these memories, but it was real and Dunsany was enjoying considerable success there. In 1914 he had published *Five Plays*, first in England and later in America. The British reviewers bestowed more praise than blame, rating *The Gods of the Mountain* his best effort and *The Lost Silk Hat* the odd-play-out and the least interesting. He was still misleadingly grouped with other Irish writers.

A month later the verdict in America was really much the same but stated with more vigour. Where British admiration had been doled out cautiously, each portion seasoned with a few sharp words, the Americans were fulsome. 'It is fairly safe to say that this [*The Glittering Gate*] is the best play that was ever written for two characters and a laugh,' 'Among the many voices that are clamouring to be heard here is a note that soars above the rest, clear and free. These plays are the works of a master, not only formally beautiful but alive with keen and original fancy.' 'A few nights ago I read Lord Dunsany's *The Gods of the Mountain*. Then after an interval of ten minutes for reflection, I read Lord Dunsany's *The Gods of the Mountain* again.'

Among these admirers was Mr Stuart Walker, who was eager to put on his plays in New York. He wrote and Dunsany replied in a rather grand tone.

June 28 1916

Dear Mr Walker,
I am still in Ireland as I am still recovering from my wound. When

ever I may be abroad or dead Lady Dunsany will make all arrangements. *Argimenes* was the first play I ever wrote about my own country. *The Glittering Gate* I had already written chiefly to please Yeats, but that play never interested me. *Argimenes* was the first play ever in the native land of my spirit and or course it has a first plays imperfections. . . . Though the world may be growing more barbarous in Flanders, what you tell me of your aspirations shows that elsewhere it is becoming more civilised. As a matter of fact it is not the ruin of Ypres or a street in Dublin that shows the high water mark of our times barbarity; it is in London in our musical 'comedies', in much of our architecture and in toys made for children.

Yours sincerely

DUNSANY

Walker replied:

Your suggestion that Sarb's first 'Majesty' is spoken in awe shows me that I shall be able to stage your work as you would like it. I have always in reading the play aloud, read the words in awe. The direction, 'in a voice of protest', was frankly, a shock to me. . . . It seems almost wicked to discuss terms about beautiful things, about poetry, but I want you to know that I am eager to help your name to its rightful place in America. . . .'[1]

The note of sycophancy is nauseating now, but sincere unrestrained praise was what Dunsany wanted and here it was. Though the critics had not in fact treated him so badly, it was many years since he had seen criticism as the second of 'The Torments in Another World' and drawn a trim figure in a vast plain menaced by large grinning hyena-like creatures. He was delighted to be helped to any position in America and cabled 'Right'.

On October 27th 1916 The Portmanteau Theatre Players, an amateur group, presented *The Gods of the Mountain* successfully with Stuart Walker as chief beggar. *The Golden Doom* ran in repertory with it and was also well received. In December *Argimenes* joined them, and was thought excellent though not quite up to the standard of its predecessors.

The world premier of *The Queen's Enemies* was reported in shaky grammar by Alexander Woollcott for the *New York*

1. The first performances of his plays officially permitted by Dunsany, had been at the Anarchist Headquarters of New York, where *Argimenes* and another were produced in 1914. They made no mark.

Tribune as 'mightily suspensive for even Dunsany at his second best writes with uncanny theatrical skill.' One paper said of the triple bill: 'Two are by Shaw. The other one is by Lord Dunsany. The two plays by Shaw hardly count.' That was nice; but most agreed with Woollcott that it was Dunsany at his second best. Shaw sent a generous telegram of congratulation which was appreciated.

If Stuart Walker presented the main force of Dunsany's invasion, he had not presented, though he had wished to, the play that won the day. *A Night at an Inn* tells a lurid story of robbers pursued by Indian priests because they have stolen the eye of their idol. The priests are disposed of by their ingenious leader, the Toff, but then the blind idol gropingly appears. There are eight characters, seven of which are human and end up dead. Dunsany was not fond of it – there is no poetry or mystery – but it was one of his two most successful plays and when it opened at a tiny theatre far from Broadway with a cast of amateurs in the Spring of 1916 it became the talk of the town. The *New York Times* reported that, 'the first audience was half-hysterical with excitement for the play is stirring beyond belief,' the *Evening Sun* that, 'the Dunsany play is the sensation of the hour; the little theatre cannot accommodate all those that flock to see it . . .' Only eight performances were possible so his other plays were presented to a public which had heard about but for the most part not seen his work.

Plans were immediately laid for a professional production, preceded by a tour of the provinces (which in fact were a little less impressed and sometimes laughed in the wrong places. 'Are Baltimore audiences more unsophisticated than those of other large cities?' asked a perturbed editorial). No subsequent performance quite equalled the first but there were many of them and after a return to New York, *A Night at an Inn* went to Dublin, Liverpool, the Everyman Hampstead, all over the United States and has never ceased to reappear at schools, prisons, colleges, and other institutions who like it for, among its other merits, its all-male cast. The Toff was given a wife (who survived) for an operatic version named *The Ruby* which Dunsany did not see. Though pleased with the idea, he expected the play to have 'as much resemblance to the opera as a boiled

egg has to an omelette'. Uncle Horace, who was suffering
from cancer and the X-ray burns with which it was treated,
wrote a letter from Chicago, telling him as usual to come down
to earth (Dunsany commented that perhaps Uncle H. was
right and he might have done well to breed pigs – he'd cross
them with lions and then they could defend the yard and there
would be more bacon) but also that there was a demand for
anything he wrote. Encouraged, Dunsany started to write
again and in two days produced a one-act plan, *Fame and the
Poet*, his first in three years. Constant bouts of tonsilitis gave
him spare time to continue and the toolshed at Brachead was
equipped as a study. Beatrice protested when he asked Stuart
Walker to renew his contract on whatever terms Walker
thought suitable, but Dunsany said he remembered the Latin
motto in a picture in the dining-room which advised you to take
warning of the fate of others, and he refused to be grasping
about money. In 1917 Edward Bierstadt produced a book
called *Dunsany the Dramatist* which stated firmly, 'The three
great contemporary dramatic poets of Ireland are Synge,
Dunsany and Yeats,' and extolled his merits. In America he
was established; in Europe the war went on, expunging any
reputation he had won.

Winter refused to end. Snow and intense cold lasted well into
April. Beatrice went over to Kent to take possession of Dunstall
and found evidence for what she knew to be true – that the
house had been much loved but by an unhappy woman. Small
things were cared for, large ones neglected; nothing had ever
been thrown away, but eight fine candelabra were in the cellar,
spoiling with the damp of twenty years, and the Worcester
china was in the gardener's cottage as if she had grown discouraged and left it there in pique. Her savage poodle, a long-
standing cause of dispute with Dunsany, was given to the vet
who thought he could tame it, mistakenly as it turned out.

While Beatrice was in England, Dunsany went to an indifferent play and, after an argument with the manager of the
theatre, walked round the walls of Derry, thinking to himself
that intellectually he was living in a forest of the Congo. From
these depressed thoughts came his only autobiographical play,
The Old King's Tale, and that only reflects his gloom. The
central figure of the play is the king who tells at length of his

struggles to return to his kingdom, how he is sold into slavery, chased by bloodhounds etc, and becomes so convinced that the gods are against him that finally, when a herald from his people asks him to come back, he does not reply but tells a pair of young lovers that they must struggle on, but that he is doomed. Beatrice agreed with Dunsany that it broke every dramatic rule (no action, no conflict) but found it most beautiful. It never achieved success. Beatrice had written the year before, 'I begin to realise that I have grown old – and one shouldn't have to do that at thirty-five.' Dunsany was not yet forty.

Another play, *Cheeso*, was more vigorous if not cheerful. It tells lightly of a young clergyman who cannot believe in eternal damnation until he meets the world of big business. His future father-in-law markets a patent food for humans though it is fatal to mice and for such wickedness everlasting flames seem just the thing. His faith is saved. Full of vehement tirades against advertising and the wickedness of manufacturers, it pleased Uncle Horace by being 'down to earth'. Dunsany too was fond of his first assault on the modern world; Beatrice less so.

In May Dunsany was passed as fit, in June he was back on the sick list. A visit to Dunsany reminded them how the first year they had at least gone through the motions of rolling the cricket pitch. Now it was a hayfield. The stables were used for storage, onions and cauliflowers ruled where once there had been larkspur and antirrhinums. They had not lived there for more than a year, but appreciated the dignity and space when they could spend a few days and forget the unhappy week of the Easter rebellion.

Times were still bad. Though the convoy system had been adopted with considerable success, submarines continued to sink enough ships to make food increasingly scarce. The Pakenham children were read Dickens and Pansy remembered after the war how she had shed tears not of pity but of greed over Oliver Twist, even without a second helping, and how David Copperfield being given a plate of meat scraps for supper as a punishment was almost more than they could bear. The Tsar was overthrown in March, the Russians might declare peace at any moment. In a discussion with Uncle Horace they all agreed that if Germany had waited a few years longer, British decadence would have gone too far for us to

make a stand, as Russian decadence had. The toll of friends
went on. Arthur Villiers was unharmed and had received the
DSO in July for conspicuous gallantry. But Ledwidge was
dead, struck by a shell while with a working party building a
road.

Ledwidge had written that year to say that he could no
longer bear the army and Dunsany always regretted that he
had not tried to find some way to get him out. In a story called
The Road the poet, who had once scorned to let any part of the
world enter his work, used both rank and Christian name as
well as situation. *The Road* tells dispassionately of a working
party who are hit by a shell. Next day more men appear, the
road continues, troops and the farmers and women use it. It
continues: 'And far away the road was growing longer and
longer amidst, as always, desolation and thunder. And one
day far away from X the road grew very fine indeed. It was
going proudly through a mighty city, sweeping in like a river;
you would not think that it ever remembered duck boards. . . .
And before the flags and before the Generals [of the Allies] I
saw marching along on foot the ghosts of the working party that
were killed at X, gazing about them in admiration as they
went at the great city and at the palaces. And one man,
wondering at the Sieges Allee, turned round to the lance-
corporal in charge of the party: "That is a fine road that we
made, Frank", he said.'

Dunsany had selected and introduced a collection of poems
Songs of Peace the year before and in October wrote an introduction for *Last Songs*. The young poet had held a special place
in his affections and no one was to replace him.

In October Dunsany was passed as fit for general service and
this time there was no delay. The preliminary scenes were repeated – an old man insisted that he take a telescope, which had
once belonged to his father, to France and to his great annoyance it was stolen there; the second chauffeur suddenly said,
'I may never see your Lordship again,' and almost broke down
– and were no less affecting for being part of a now familiar
pattern. Beatrice found paradoxically that she was less nervous
now that there was no question of a swift return. In London
they experienced their first raid, more irritating than alarming,
though as a result he made her promise to leave a day earlier

than she had planned. Beatrice had not meant to accompany
him to Victoria, she had certainly not intended to go on to the
platform, which was covered with weary privates, but she did
have the resolution to leave two minutes before the train.
Randal had to be taken to school the same day and she then
proceeded with reasonable calm to stay with her sister Mary
and discover that she, who was knowledgeable about wild
flowers and birds' eggs, had much to learn about digging
potatoes. A new phase had opened.

They began writing letters to one another immediately.
Dunsany wrote from Folkstone.

You won't have the worry of explaining to people years hence that
I was brought up at home and so of course I stayed at home and
trying to make it sound plausible and natural. Don't stay in London
another night. I am very sorry you are staying Tuesday night. . . .
Don't worry I think my work is not done yet.

and three days later in good spirits from France:

. . . You would be surprised if you knew who was here in this camp.
You naturally think I mean Lord Kitchener, but I don't, I mean
Ethel Stourton [a neighbour]. I have not yet seen her but I am told
she is here. . . I have just had a good story – a soldier couldn't get
his change from a Frenchman due to him from a five franc note.
Can you speak French said he to a pal. Yes the pal could speak
French and would undertake to get the change from him. So the
pal goes up to the Frenchman and they talk like this: –
PAL: *Parlez-vous Francais?*
Frenchman: *Mais Oui!*
PAL: O, you can, can you, you blighter? Then what about this
    bloody change?
So he got the change all right and brought it back to his friend.
You may send all letters here, as I have been promised that they
will be forwarded.

                    Ever your loving
                    PONY

He wrote almost every day, sometimes about forty words just
saying he was all right. He asked her to pay Captain Armstrong
the £1 he had bet that the war would end in 1916, 'however I
shall continue to prophesy and I'll fix November 5th now'. At
first he says nothing of his life or surroundings as he did not

know what the camp censor allowed. In his second week he sent a poem for Beatrice to send to *The Times*, the first of many, mostly descriptive verses like this one:

> *The Monument*
> I saw a pear tree on a garden wall
> Stretching its arms quite twenty feet each way
> There was no garden near, nor house at all:
> Flower and wife and child were passed away.
> Many memorials can the Kaiser boast
> Yet this may stand for him as well as most.

But Dunsany revealed only that he had enjoyed a Charlie Chaplin film or had been for a walk and met an Irishman who had heard of him, 'but he had recently been to America; I told him that a man must travel far from England to have heard of an English poet'. However he found this admirer to be 'one of those persuasive world-travelling Irishmen, who can talk persuasively and emphatically without really knowing what they are talking of, a real type, a swashbuckler, something of a Mephistopheles, an ideal Toff for *A Night at an Inn*, an equally good President of the Patagonian Protected, a mine in which there was never any gold, but then the President is such a sound man. He knew nothing of me or my work.'

Later he wrote:

When we were out of the line we lived at a place that had been Ervillers, four miles back, where the bombing planes used to call on us every morning, but never hit us. That was in the desert of the Somme. We never saw any animals there except mice, and an army horse or two; and when the rooks flew over at evening they passed out of sight before they could find trees. There was something melancholy about watching this flight over land that had been fertile for centuries.

Beatrice could not enjoy sitting in a warm room surrounded by pretty things, while she wondered what the British Expeditionary Force were up to that evening. So she went to help at the hospital that Georgie Buller ran in Exeter, where she was as useful and uncomfortable as she had hoped. Her job was to arrange for soldiers to be transferred from one hospital to another as they got better or relatives clamoured for them. At first she found it difficult to telephone when surrounded by people, who were all jammed into small echoing rooms, and the welter of forms looked confusing; but soon she decided that if she could correct the faults of thirty-seven years in four days, she could do it very well.

Through all their letters, like those between a schoolboy and his mother, there runs a scattering of references as to what she should send him, whether it arrived, and if it was nice. Brazil nuts were obtainable; was Mexican chocolate an acceptable substitute for Cadbury's? Did he like preserved ginger? He was probably given sardines by the authorities, but she sent some anyway; and Devonshire cream seemed worth a try.

Dunsany was still quite cheerful and healthy though he thought he was 'more sensitive than most to concussion'. When there was a possibility of a safe job, though he did not try for it, he would have been happy to accept it in spite of the lack of glory. On the 18th he acknowledged the ginger, which he found very good and asked for dental wax, indelible pencils, in which the letter was written, and socks, as his servant had burnt a hole in his.

He also sensibly told her to show a letter from the Baronne de Sauvergrente to the police. The letter asked for £5 which the Baronne said she had lent to Lord Dunsany at a dance, as he had appealed to her with the words, 'I, like you, am of gentle birth' and explained that he had no money. At first the Dunsanys thought it was some form of blackmail, easily dealt with as Dunsany had been in France on the suggested date. The police, however, insisted that the Baronne was very respectable, and the police were right. It was a confidence trickster who had given his name as Dunsany who was at fault.

Generally their tone is light. The letters were designed to inform and to please, with his emphasis on the former and hers on the latter; neither wished to depress. Beatrice passed on from the papers an Egyptian official excusing himself with the words, 'It is impossible for me to come as expected because someone has removed my wife. My God I am annoyed'; and, 'My God I am annoyed', became a catch phrase between them. He noted that the safe job he had hoped for had been abolished. Occasionally she betrayed anxiety or he would write in his literary as well as his private voice. They had stayed at Amiens before the war (while showing them the Cathedral, the guide had caught a pigeon with his hands and as he continued to discourse they gradually realised that he was going to keep and eat it). Now Dunsany wrote:

Once more the Hotel de l'Univers shelters me at Amiens. What a changed town! Or rather how changed the personal view-point. Then as a tourist, an alien, something beneath the notice of the soldiers, now an equal participator in their dream. I come as it were as the connecting link between the battalion and the lights of London, as a missionary between the 20th century and the ancient abomination of desolation. I have descended upon the shops. For half my way the journey lay through the abomination of desolation, for the other half France smiled; and I noticed that we have no way of knowing where we are, that it was autumn. Verily such a journey as I made this morning was never until recently made by man. Imagine Waterloo, Sebastapol, Ladysmith, Pompeii, Troy, Timgad, Tel el Kebir, Sodom and Gomorrah endlessly stretching one into the other; and twisted, bare, ghoulish trees leering downward at graves; and scenes very like Doré's crucifixion and realities like the blackest dreams of Sime; tanks lying with their noses pointing upwards still sniffing towards an enemy long since stiff or blown away in fragments like wounded rhinoceros' dying. Imagine the wasted ruin of a famous hill that once dominated all this, now no more than a white mound with a few crosses on it, standing against the sky to show that Golgotha was once more with us. And over all this dreadful triumph of iron over man, and the spirit of man over iron, one feels that Nature is smiling softly to herself as she comes back with all her flowering children over villages that are no more than famous names and farms and roads and bridges that none can trace but those who remember them. At Albert in the Cathedral the desolation culminated, as though the Kaiser had knelt there before Satan to hear the Lord's Prayer said backwards and receive the blessings of Hell, and we passed thence into happier fields like one who wakes from dark dreams on a summer morning.

I go back again immediately after dinner, which shall be eaten at l'hotel de l'Univers. I bought you a little golden dragon who has caught a small diamond and gave as a convenient address 18 Montagu Square [Lady Jersey's house].

Je Mangerais

Ever yr loving
PONY

New London Hotel
Exeter
Oct. 24, 17

My Darling Pony,
I have had many wonderful letters from you in my life but I really think the one from Amiens the best. I wonder if you would let me copy it for Mr Gogarty on condition that he lets nobody take it from him or have a copy, so that no press has it – but he would love it and might read it to A.E. or some appreciative ones.

Dunsany bought a piano at Amiens for the Battalion and got it to the front in a motor-lorry provided by the Royal Flying Corps. They had a concert and it turned out to be a good buy. At the end he was thanked and asked to make a speech. According to his version he thought he would not 'come the orator', but they started to push him up and when he put an arm round each of his neighbours to anchor himself to his chair, they promptly stood up, so he finally spoke, as of old, though briefly. Randal commented to his father: 'When there is an advance the piano would get rather in the way.'

Beatrice was delighted with her dragon and asked that it should be given a name. She had met a Colonel Young, who had stayed at Dunsany and recalled shooting bottles in the river and the notorious sugar incident (Dunsany had been expounding on the hardness of glass during tea at Killeen. He claimed that however hard you threw a lump of sugar at a window, it would be the sugar-lump that would shatter. He turned out to be wrong and Lady Fingall had been extremely angry).

7th Royal Inns: Fus:
Officers Club
November 4 1917

My Darling Mink,
I got two letters from you yesterday. Shall I tell how I came to this club the night before last with three other officers of D. Co. and how I thought that perhaps I was the only one who was feeling a great strain. Then we dined and some day there shall be told the great retreat from ——, how I led it, how we met others upon the way whom we would have fought with, how I made alliances so that there was no fighting but increased thereby the weight upon my arm, how I sang to them, ordered them, lifted them and beguiled

L.D.   K

them so that the motor-lorries killed not one, how seven men would have fallen if I had stumbled. And after two miles the others being safely home, I found myself alone with my company commander and his senior subaltern with only a few more hundred yards to go. I stumbled then nearly exhausted and stood looking remorsefully at what I had done, while thoughts like these probably passed through their minds:

'Dunsany has been very hard on us, but he has let us rest at last. It is a nice place too.'

And the others thought 'Dunsany knows what he is doing. He has put us here, we're not going to argue about it, he has got his reasons. It was nice of him to choose this good soft mud.'

And I got hold of them as Odysseus got hold of his lotus-eaters and I shouted two words in their ears they had often heard before when lying in mud all sick for sleep, and shouted them grimly, 'Stand to'.

'Why yes,' they thought, 'the war and misery,' and made 5 per cent of an effort and with 95 per cent I got them up and so brought them home. That is one of the ways whereby men try to escape from the strain of the greatest war, I try other more philosophic ways. Pity those that have no way.

Ever your loving
PONY

The next night was rather similar:

7th Royal Inns: Fus:
B.E.F.
Nov. 5 1917

My Darling Mink,

The officers of D. Company gave me a dinner last night at the Club. We walked back arm in arm with me in the middle, either to show that that was their natural and usual way of going home, not a necessity, or else to show that if ever I wanted help to get home after dinner, I should have it.

I'm sorry that I cannot give you any information about the raid that you tell me was undertaken by Inniskillings on Oct. 29.

Ever your loving
PONY

Dunsany was rather impressed by a piece of arrogance on another occasion when he was walking back from dinner arm-in-arm. He saw a lorry coming and said, 'a bit more this way. We're in front of the lorry.' His companion moved a little towards the side of the road. 'We're not clear of it yet,' Dunsany continued. 'It's not entitled to another inch,' said his friend and had to be pulled out of the way.

> 7th B.E.F.
> Nov. 7

My Darling Mink,
We are well out of the way of shells and will still be when you get this letter. I hope you may some day meet all the officers of D. Co. with whom I have soldiered. They are all my friends, even Lacey, a typical ranker: they probably all started with a prejudice against my inexperience, which I think changed in every case under shell-fire ... and another is Williams. The latter is a journalist on the *Manchester Guardian* with a good appreciation for poetry. One night I was rummaging among philosophy to find comfort and he said did I know Wordsworth's *Ode to Duty*. I asked him to repeat it, which he could not do, but he said what he could remember of it as we went along the line and I certainly found it inspiring. I don't think I told you that I was hit one night but not hurt. It was that night, but it was later on that we were talking about Wordsworth, towards dawn.

> *Ever your loving*
> PONY

Beatrice copied out and sent the whole 'Ode to Duty'. She also passed on the comment of her neighbour at a charity performance of *A Night at an Inn*. 'What a creepy-crawly thing.'

> 7th R. Inns: Fus:
> B.E.F.
> Nov. 12th 1917

My Darling Mink,
You've been a most dear Mink to me always. Words cannot express my gratitude. Perhaps I too seldom tried to express it, but you knew it was there however much concealed. God bless you.

> *Your loving*
> PONY

> Nov. 13

Fit and Well
My Darling Mink
It is your bad luck only to get flattering expressions of devotion from me when I see something bad ahead as I thought I did last night. However, nothing bad came, though I am sick of this square peg in a round hole business, which is good for neither. I am excused

all duty for forty-eight hours at least and I write this far enough from the Boche. I did not go sick but I started talking to an officer of the R.A.M.C.[1] and before I knew where I was one of his orderlies had innoculated me in the chest with anti-tetanus serum which I enjoyed so much last time. I don't know why unless that while crawling about I had stepped with my left hand into a coil of old barbed wire (British).

Ever your loving
PONY

'Crawling about' was going into No Man's Land to put up wire, which he said afterwards he disliked doing intensely.

Before Christmas Dunsany had some leave. The day after he arrived a man accosted him in the street, having seen by his badge that he was in the 16th, and asked for news of his own division. So Dunsany took him to lunch with Beatrice at the Savoy, where they were staying. They exchanged horror stories —the man had himself been blinded by a wounded German he had spared, though now his sight was returning – and suddenly said together, 'It's a great life.' Eager to see *Chu Chin Chow*, because all his comrades went to see it on their leave, Dunsany went to sleep in the second act.

After he had returned to France, Beatrice went to Dunstall. As she walked up from the station she counted twenty-one separate searchlights stabbing the clear frosty night. War could throw up such moments of beauty, accentuate them by contrast or uncover qualities that might have remained unknown. In her diary she wrote

... Contrasts are trite things – still one can't help being struck when the cowman's wife here cried almost ceaselessly for some months after her boy (she had seven fighting) was killed – and only a month after old Mrs Cheesman lost her two sons I met her serene and smiling and she told me that they were 'always with her'.

A windless sunny day and the loneliness of these Kentish valleys is perfect, just one gravely buzzing aeroplane overhead and then the silent chalky slopes and old black yews, – I do understand the air men who thank God for 'the sweet seclusion of the sky'.

At the end of January 1918, Dunsany was offered a job in

1. Royal Army Medical Corps.

the War Office. He was pleased to accept it, though, however
unsuited he might have been to a military life, he remained
emotionally attached to the army and always spoke of it with
the greatest respect. Now he worked in an office for the first
time and was quite content with a room to himself on the
Embankment in a building taken over by the War Office which
had inefficient blinds and so broke, with impunity, the black-
out restrictions. Before he arrived someone went to the London
Library to find out what sort of books this fellow wrote. He
was given a work by Lord Dunsany, *Teuton or Gaul* which
asked 'should we not therefore rather ally ourselves with the
sober and solid Teuton than with the sprightly and frivolous
Gaul?' It had been written by his grandfather over fifty years
before.

Overcoming any suspicion this aroused, he joined MI7B,
which meant that he wrote short pieces for newspapers all over
the world, to show how just was our cause, how fine our troops.
His speed and eloquence were well suited to this, and he was
drawing directly on his own experience for the first time. He
wrote mainly of the front – the different sounds of shells, the
loneliness of sentry duty, the destruction, being shown the
Chaplin film. Sometimes he told a simple story, often he wrote
of the personal guilt of the Kaiser, while other Germans are
seen as pleasant ordinary people who wished the war had
never begun. His total sincerity and the fact that he describes,
without mentioning politics, the destruction of war and
incidents of British courage stop him sounding like a professional persuader. The published collection of these pieces,[1]
identifiable by subject and tone, do not stand apart from his
other work.

Dunsany, happy to be home and at Dunstall, easily put up
with commuting and the minor irritations of bureaucracy –
such as not being allowed to refer to a paper he had himself
written, because it was too secret for him to see. He remained in
the job till the end of the war and realised he had been very
lucky. He would have felt ashamed, left out, even disappointed
if he had not fought at all. Yet with the best will in the world,
he had been kept at home during three years of mud and
slaughter, survived unhurt for four months at the front and

1. *Tales of War* 1918. *Unhappy Far-off Things* 1919.

finally found a job that was both worthwhile and congenial. The climax of his war was over, though the climax for his country was yet to come.

In the spring they were quietly happy. It was good to be in a home of their own again after other people's ugly villas and hotels. It was better not to keep making new friends, only to lose them. It was best to remain in England, together, and not worried about personal safety. They were exhausted. If it seemed selfish, they were prepared to leave the moment they were needed; but, for the moment, to them, fate was being kind.

Inevitably public events shattered their mood. On March 21st the Germans attacked successfully on the Somme. During the next week the British were in retreat. Beatrice wrote:

March 24
It is awful. You could feel the tension all through the church this morning – it has nothing to do with the strained faces, the throat clearings and special prayers – you can *see* it too; a thick unnatural hot haze hangs over the valley. They don't seem to be talking in the village even, the only signs are of men working on the line, Sunday though it be. Perhaps there were 100,000 casualties yesterday – we believe we hold them because we believe we are invincible, but everyone is madly anxious in secret, and we know what the price is likely to be even at best – the word best is a mockery. And one can't do anything about it. Eddie said that at the W.O. conference that his department have on Saturdays, Capt. Dawson opened it by saying that he knew they all felt they were on the wrong side of the channel.

The next day she worked in the garden as she had during the Easter Rebellion.

March 28   Dunstall
The battle still goes on and the Germans seem to have advanced some twenty miles [in fact forty] – but we still have faith. For four still moonlight nights they have not raided us which looks as though they were staking all they have on this. Raids! How trivial they seem! At Eddie's department at the W.O. they wanted three important articles in a hurry and selected nine of the sixteen writers there to do them. Then three judges read them all and were each to choose one – and each chose Eddie's. That was on the 26th.

The glorious weather has broken and we are thankful. I have made bandages till I cannot see to do more.

The Allies were in unco-ordinated retreat. Lloyd George took over direction of the War Office, delivered the reserve to Haig in France in a week, and appealed to President Wilson for American troops to fight immediately. Wilson overruled his own commander, Pershing, to comply.

The second German attack, once more against the British, began on April 9th. Once more the British retreated, but the line did not break. Haig made his appeal, 'With our backs to the wall and believing in the justice of our cause, each one of us must fight to the end.' On April 12th Randal and Beatrice hay-making at Dunstall could hear the guns in France. They made her feel that she could not stop; at last she became so tired, she lay back on a damp haycock to rest – and suffered from rheumatism for weeks and intermittently for years.

Through the summer months the Allies received more men, many of them British, and gradually the initiative passed to them.

In August Dunsany had two weeks' leave and they went to Ireland, first of all to stay with the Gogartys in County Galway. They had been away long enough to find it like a curious pre-war dream. Healthy young men were selling race-cards at the stations, there was as much bread, butter, meat and sugar as you could eat, coal fires were normal, cars and the petrol to run them abounded. Beatrice ate, but resented. She was fond of her host, but found it hard to accept the luke-warm support he gave to the Allies. The boys fished all day and nobody seemed to care if they went to bed or not.

At Dunsany they found a batch of Eton boys gathering the harvest, for seven hours a day, and later nine; that was more like her idea of war-time behaviour. Dunsany went back early and wrote a letter from the club to which he had just been elected:

The Athenaeum,
Pall Mall
Sept. 7 1918

My Darling Mink,
I have been instructing my mind with the Library catalogue here.

They've heard of Tennyson, Meredith, Yeats and Wilde but not Shaw, Galsworthy, Masefield, J. E. Flecker, William Watson or me. I am glad to say they have not got Marie Corelli or Garvice, but they have one book of Conan Doyle's. This selection baffles me.

I suppose its sound, but *deadly*.

Here old volumes rot in tropical profusion, and it is hoped that any young man disturbing their silent vistas may breathe their decay and die.

At the beginning of October, Dunsany went briefly to France again to collect fresh material. He was reminded by a rather grisly incident of Tennyson who wrote of '. . . a ghastly dew from the nations' airy navies grappling in the central blue'. Dunsany noticed a piece of brown paper on the wind-screen of a staff car and was told that it was to preserve a splash of German blood that had dropped from an aeroplane – a ghastly dew indeed. He was cheered, as always, by meeting someone who had read and liked his work, in this case a Canadian officer with a pocket edition of *A Dreamer's Tales* and a Captain Moncrieff, translator of Proust, who came up and said: 'I am glad to meet you here. *The Sword of Welleran* greatly increased my martial ardour in 1914.'

He came back full of new material, notes of such things as an old refugee pointing to a heap of rubbish and saying *Voilà ma maison,*' and taking no further interest in anything but revenge, or a potato that had fallen from some grocer's shop and was sprouting large and strong in the broken pavement, though the shop was gone.

When Beatrice went over to England with Randal she travelled with her sister Mary whose four daughters were following later. Mary Longford tackled the captain as to whether it was safer to travel by day or night and he replied, though they were about to set out on a night crossing, that it was now quite safe by day but at night they had to travel at full speed with no lights and he still did not like it. So Mary Longford took the trouble to change her daughters' tickets. Next week the ship was sunk in the daytime with all hands lost but no Pakenhams aboard. Beatrice had made twenty-three crossings and said she did think there had been a better chance of being saved. The old Leinster was a painful loss, it had been so familiar and friendly.

By October they were almost ready to admit the feeling that had been growing for weeks; that the war was going to be won, and won soon. When Dunsany had written to Ireland, he had written not of the war, but of books, and of being 'a young writer'. Beatrice too was for the first time looking beyond the end of the war not as a speculative dream, but with interest, though she was unsure whether she felt enthusiasm or dread. In Ireland she wrote: 'The world is a grander, realler and more terrible place than it seemed – but I am no heroine. Sometimes I want to remain awakened after the war, and sometimes I am poor-spirited and want to care only about the old trivialities. Revolution may settle it the first way and time the second. I don't know.' At lunch with her mother and sisters on November 1, Lady Jersey declared that as there would be no more raids, they should uncover the street lamps. Her three daughters disagreed, saying that, 'people would think it was over and eat all the bread'. Mary was planning to send her son Edward to Oxford and not into the army and Beatrice thought Markie looked ten years younger with the relief that her son Charlie, who was at Sandhurst, would probably not have to go. (In fact he volunteered for Russia, but returned unhurt.) Beatrice's version of 'a land fit for heroes' was, 'Of course all worlds are great worlds for the next generation, but surely that notion is less trite than usual, and Randal and his generation will be muffs if they can't make something of it.' But when the reality came her mood changed:

8th November 1918   Dunstall
Eddie came home last night with War Office news that the war is over. I would give so much to feel joyous and elated, but instead I feel like crying when I think of it. Eddie said he had been depressed all day too. If we had been able to prophesy such a complete victory a year ago we should have been happy. But it is no use. It was too terrible; and they are all dead, Tom, John, Channy, Ledwidge and all the rest, and it is over, and we can look back on the four and a half greatest years in history and feel that nothing can atone for them. And it is not that I am a pessimist, I haven't seen anyone since the beginning of the end who was able to feel otherwise. ... There is Peace coming and I *will* try to be glad – I am glad of course, but I will try and understand the gladness of it.

Eddie woke in the middle of the night, Nov. 7/8, and wrote part of his dirge of Victory and finished it at the W.O. next day.

Lift not thy trumpet, Victory, to the sky,
Nor through battalions nor by batteries blow,
But over hollows full of old wire go,
Where among dregs of war the long-dead lie
With wasted iron that the guns passed by
When they went eastwards like a tide at flow;
There blow thy trumpet that the dead may know,
Who waited for thy coming, Victory.
It is not we that have deserved thy wreath,
They waited there among the towering weeds;
The deep mud burned under the termites breath,
And winter cracked the bones that no man heeds:
Hundreds of nights flamed by; the seasons passed,
And thou hast come to them at last, at last!

Evening
Bells ringing, in Shoreham and farther away – and I looked in the
map at all the countries where bells are ringing tonight. No more
raids, we have left the shutters open tonight.

I travelled by train to the Eynsford Work Depot (news not then
official) and there was a private soldier in the carriage wild with
excitement, and telling us all what he'd do when the news came.
'I have a bottle of 3-star at home – I shan't stop to draw the cork,
I'll knock the neck off, I'll have a week's leave and if they don't
give it to me I'll take it.' Then, with a sudden jerk, 'there'll be
aching hearts today – my old Mother for one – I am only one left
out of five.' Somehow his jumbled confidences were so like what
everyone felt.

It is over, it really is. The bells have not been allowed to peal for
four years at night.

There were three days of joyful rioting in London and a bonfire burned in Trafalgar Square when news of the armistice
broke. But the mood soon changed. All attention had been
fixed for years on the day of victory in the future. When it
arrived, and then receded, it was not easy to look to the present
and future again. The country began to count the cost.

MI7B(1) was disbanded within a week and Dunsany
joined the 3rd Battalion of Inniskillings at Tregantle Fort in
Cornwall, and later at Devonport. There was nothing to do.
Eventually he was free to go home.

Dunsany Castle
Well we are here again and Ireland never changes. The Sinn Feiners talk big but they are only the Fenians of former days for all that.

9th December   Dunsany Castle
A soft grey Irish day with a mild wind blowing, and I borrowed a horse from General H. and went for a ride, and am teaching myself to read without knitting and Eddie is writing, Act II of the *Old Folk of the Centuries*.

But the past is dead for all that and I can't bury it.

PART THREE

Post War 1919 – 1929

At Dunsany it was impossible not to remember their life before the war and make comparisons. This was a melancholy pastime. The war was a great division for everyone, but the contrast was particularly painful for the Dunsanys; before the war they had been young, now they were not. Dunsany's greatest friends were dead and he did not replace them. A photograph album of army friends has the dates when they were wounded, missing or killed underneath in red ink and the entries are terribly frequent. Everyone was poorer but they still had no need to think about money; Dunsany was not working much. He cut out a phrase quoted in a paper, 'It is a great responsibility to have survived the war,' and pasted it into a blank book in which he intended to write. The pages remained blank.

Dunsany was still in the army and returned to England. Beatrice went abroad with her mother. It became clear that the troubles of Ireland had by no means been settled by the war as they had hoped. Before the Sinn Fein made hunting impossible, Randal went out for the first time and liked it. Though a letter addressed to 'Lord Dunsany, try British Isles, please find him,' reached Dunsany, he was still almost unknown and his letters show his increasing bitterness and feeling that it is the London theatre and not his plays that is at fault. Sometimes the implication is light as, 'I went to see Doris Keane, just before she went to bed, which as modern drama demands, she does on stage'; sometimes direct as in a letter he wrote to the *Sunday Express* which he describes to Beatrice: 'It is pretty violent, but never mind I don't mind sticking to it. It's about fat men with beady eyes and the drama in England.'

His relationship with the Irish Renaissance group, if it had

1. The Post Office seems to have been accommodating and flexible. In 1910 a letter of his to Beatrice had been successfully addressed 'The Lady Dunsany 1st Class Passenger to London from Downes, Friday morning probably by 11.23 a.m. c/o Station Master Crediton'.

ever existed, was now dying. In 1917 Ernest Boyd could write, 'His work is as much a part of the movement which has given us the fantasies of Synge as is that of James Stephens', and find evidence in his faults as well as his virtues, saying of *The Golden Doom*: 'The fable is a pretty one, but quite Yeatsian in its lack of dramatic quality.' A nationalist pamphlet in 1918 called *The Glittering Fake* used his *The Glittering Gate* very closely, to ridicule not Dunsany but the hopes and promises of a settlement, and this seems to imply wide knowledge of his work and, less reasonably, an essential Irishness in it. In fact he had almost lost contact with Yeats, always the dominating force, and was not to see a great deal of him in the future.

From a literary point of view the post-war decade was a period of frustration for Dunsany. He was over forty, an Edwardian survival out of tune with the times. He believed as a matter of course that the task of an artist was to produce Beauty, but in the 1920s there was little demand for what was small and exquisite. Theatre managers no longer wanted curtain-raisers, publishers scorned exotic tales, and Dunsany's problem was how to remain true to his talent and yet hold the attention of the public.

Managers expressed themselves delighted and made wonderful promises, but their plans repeatedly collapsed and the constant oscillation between hope and disappointment made him irritable. He also exerted himself to stretch his tales to book length, and between the wars he wrote nine novels, but the short story always remained his natural form of expression. When demobilised at last at the end of April, he went to Dunstall and wrote in a room over the stables.

Peace was not all anticlimax. Merely the presence of civilian clothes and young men in shops and on the tennis-court was cheering. It was still impossible to go abroad just because you wanted to, but Beatrice's rheumatism was sufficiently painful for her doctor to sign a certificate and she went to Cannes in a surrendered German train with her mother. The flowers and the sunshine were glorious, the company interesting. In Paris the *Daily Telegraph* correspondent told her, not quite accurately as it turned out, that Lloyd George would have everything his own way at the Peace Conference, which had been reduced from ten to four. Of the others remaining, Orlando did not speak a word of English, in which they invariably talked; Wilson had influenza; and Clemenceau had never got over his wound and slept much of the time. Talks between King Faisal and the French also seemed set fair for the British. Faisal asked his friend Colonel Lawrence if anyone else present spoke Arabic. No one did. 'In that case,' said Faisal, 'when it comes to my turn to speak, I shall recite a chapter of the Koran and you can translate it how you will.' And, according to the *Daily Telegraph* correspondent, Lawrence did. However neither stories nor sunshine cured her and when she returned Beatrice went to a spa at Droitwich.

In June Dunsany was attached to the American 3rd Army on the Rhine for a few weeks. As he drove past a cemetery in Burgundy he observed that the difficulty in building one's life after the experience of the Great War was that the war was a brick greater than the building. His mood of uncertainty persisted, though he liked the Americans, and appreciated baseball. He was relieved when, after many smiling friendly Germans who stood aside to let him pass, a boy scowled horribly at him. The right attitude, he felt.

When he got back he had his tonsils out and with them lost his depression. In eight days he wrote a full length play, *If.* Beatrice had a week's season and felt like a mole that had shed its skin. Music was there for the asking. She greeted old friends rapturously and found they had nothing to say to one another, ran across others and could not make time for all that needed expressing. The 'Hooligans' of her dancing days, just after the turn of the century and the Boer War seemed to have no memories as they shook their matronly heads over the wild ways of the young girls. The upper classes were behaving admirably, some selling silver, some deer, some land, to adapt to the post-war world. However the restlessness and the threat of Bolshevism had not finally passed. In Ireland there were agricultural strikes and the Dunsanys hurried across for ten days. They decided that the majority were loyal, led astray or intimidated by half-a-dozen trouble-makers. These were not allowed to return and the house was shut down.

So they spent the rest of the summer at Dunstall, having dinner under the trees by the tennis-court, watching the glow-worms and smelling the tobacco plants round the house.

People came from London and asked if they could come again. Americans were charming but warned them that other Americans were not. One, who managed two London theatres, Mr Miller, motored down. He heard *If* and took it away with a satisfied air; but he did not produce it. Miss McWilliam, the sister of Dunsany's army friend, and Henry Ponsonby, a cousin, were sitting outside, when they saw a column of smoke and then a blaze from a neighbour's house. Dunsany and Randal rushed over. Miss McWilliam and Beatrice walked more sedately, for it was a hot day. Henry Ponsonby, who had always been neat, went into the house, changed into old clothes and, when the women arrived, was sitting on the roof, directing operations. Below Dunsany managed the buckets with the men from the village who had instinctively divided into a dozen who helped and about thirty, who watched. They had it under control before the fire-engine arrived.

Dunsany had planned to give a series of propaganda lectures in America as part of his job but when the war ended, the plan naturally collapsed. However a Mr Pond appeared and revived the idea, with Dunsany to speak of anything he chose, preferably himself. Asked later how he knew that Dunsany was even a competent orator he admitted that he had not. 'However,' he added, 'it didn't much matter as the Americans come to see you, not to hear you.' Dunsany was well paid and did indeed find that if tired he could simply read his stories aloud. Uncle Horace, about to have a serious operation, offered his advice:

'. . . I gather you are going on a lecturing tour in America, about which don't forget to have a talk with me as I may be able to save you lots of trouble. I have always been pestered with reporters in America, and this time on account of the part the Irish question is playing in their domestic and foreign policies, I suffered almost as much publicity as a football hero or Music Hall artiste. I could have made quite a fortune by selling myself to lecture agencies, and I had independent offers for speeches, the best being £100 for a single speech of half an hour upon any subject I liked to choose. You will be lionised and if you are not careful those who are running you will give you a War record that would make Foch blush, in order to increase the revenues from your audiences.

'I missed Stuart Walker in New York but saw one of your plays, not I think by any means one of the best. It was at a small theatre called The Punch & Judy a more silly name even than the Portmanteau. I don't know why Stuart Walker jokes so heavily in these things . . .'

Mrs Cornwallis West (Mrs Patrick Campbell) came down heard *The Queen's Enemies* and promptly decided to take it, though nothing came of this. Dunsany said that he would never contribute to any theatre, lest his aunt say that he paid to have his plays put on.

'I never heard such a paltry reason,' said Mrs West firmly. 'Your aunt! I should like to meet her to see if she is worth it.'

'She is not,' said Dunsany.

'Let us despise your aunt – now, at once. There it is done; and you need consider her no more.'

Dunsany enjoyed the conversation, but did not put money in the theatre.

Mrs West was keen to go to America and when she heard that Dunsany might be going to lecture she boomed that she would go as Beatrice's maid – 'I cut ribbons beautifully'. She also insisted, 'You must take a large net hat, for when you go to restaurants. If you don't take those kind of garments, they will all PITY you.' Beatrice took the hat, but did not wear it, or notice their scorn.

They duly set off in a French boat from Havre because there was a strike in England and Beatrice had to share a cabin with a woman who squirted scent over everything. It was very rough, but there were no other hardships. Dunsany thought one day that you should be able to see the sun shining through the water on the horizon at sunset; he looked and found he could. It was green. A few fans and a handful of addresses, but almost no personal friends, were their only guarantee of a welcome and, in spite of Uncle Horace, they were unprepared for the swarm of interviewers that greeted their arrival in New York; not that Dunsany objected. He was interviewed day after day for a week, by among others, a rather amateur young C. Vanderbilt who was seeking experience; but he never ran out of comments. Only once was he unco-operative. Two reporters started asking questions and he gradually realised that they had no idea who he was, so, in the friendliest way, he refused to tell them. The uncritical warm-hearted praise of which there seemed to be an unlimited supply was just what he had been missing and he revelled in it. With Ireland troubled, England licking her wounds, and both full of sad reminders of the recent past, America was an escape, a dream and an adventure, if a little fatiguing. They loved him and he loved them, even when they misrepresented his leather waistcoat as fur underclothes. He, who never ate sweets, swallowed a box of fudge. The lectures were always successful, though those that asked about Ireland got answers they did not like. When asked what he thought of de Valera, he dropped the hand of his interrogator and fired back, 'What do you think of Crippen?' His first lecture was delivered on October 16th in New York and he was allowed to stay there a few days – long enough to look around and have his portrait painted by Orlando Rowland, 'in very good likeness' Dunsany thought.

He saw *A Night at An Inn* and *The Queen's Enemies* and was impressed, turning to Beatrice to say almost with surprise of the former, 'Why, this is a good play'. Afterwards he stood in the street signing books and was delighted when a woman told him that at one performance the man behind her had leaned forward, seized her shoulders and, at the climax, 'he dug his nails in'. A light play, *Fame and the Poet*, which might seem to be directly inspired by the hurly-burly of this trip, had in fact been written in the war and was being performed in the autumn at Harvard and in St Louis. A poet longs for fame, one day she appears, a vulgar and impertinent strumpet, and will not go away. A more ambitious play in his usual dramatic vein, *The Laughter of the Gods*, had been a moderate success at the Portmanteau Theatre, in New York in January, and was now in Baltimore. It has a slightly more complicated plot than usual but the familiar theme of the Gods striking down arrogant man. The Babylonian King has moved his palace to Thek. The ladies of the court, finding it dull, persuade a prophet to foretell doom if they remain. He does but is ignored, indeed he is to have his head removed if doom fails to materialise, and wanders about miserable at having made the Gods lie; but the Gods have not lied and with hideous laughter Thek is duly destroyed. Dunsany thought it 'superior to *Gods of the Mountain*, just as I thought *A Night at An Inn* inferior'; but it was not played professionally in Britain.

Yale had put on a little thriller called *The Murderers* in the spring and were to present a new minor work *The Compromise of the King of the Golden Isles* in a few months. Also revivals of earlier plays continually popped up, so that there was enough Dunsaniana about to sustain public interest.

Soon they were off on a gruelling tour accompanied by a solid ex-army Englishman named Williams. Blasco Ibanez, the author of *The Four Horsemen of the Apocalypse*, was also on Mr Pond's circuit and Williams compared notes with his manager. Dunsany, though he denied it, was accused of pouring water over his own head as a protest against an over-heated room; Ibanez took off his hat and jumped on it when irritated. Williams decided he had the easier artist. He had commanded the necessary tact and force to hold Church Services in a remote and unenthusiastic lumber camp when he was twenty, and managed Dunsany remarkably smoothly.

In New Hampshire 'the maples at that time of year were scarcely a subject for prose. Each tree was like the flame of an explosion. There are such colours in the sky at sunset and dawn, but I do not know what other leaves can equal the glory of the maple in the fall. And there were apples there as red as any that I have seen in our islands and larger than any that grow here.' Then he was off, one night at Portsmouth Naval Prison to see *Fame and the Poet* acted by inmates and one old boy who had come back to help, the next at Boston, the next in Brooklyn, the next in Yama Farms in the Adirondack Mountains. This pace kept up and he could often snatch only a few hours sleep between trains or even on them. Fortunately he spoke almost without preparation, needing only ten minutes to himself before he began and sometimes a note or two. In Washington he found a house named after, or the same as, one of his stories, so, as no one was at home, he wrote his name on the wall.

Beatrice had accompanied him on this first assault on the continent but now went to stay with a new friend, Mrs Coomley Ward at Hillside, Wyoming while Dunsany had a brief pause – but scarcely a rest – in New York before setting off again. Mrs Ward was a generous democratic puritan, who called her under-gardener Mr So and So, asked strangers to stay until sometimes there were sixty people in her house and the sur-rounding cottages, but would throw out any girl caught smoking. At seventy-six, she announced over breakfast, 'I feel full of mischief today,' and though Beatrice escaped a good deal by being slightly ill, she still received the impression that, 'The American idea of a rest is to motor all day and call upon everyone they have ever known.' At meals she read aloud, sometimes Stevenson, which was not so bad, but once a long German-inspired magazine article, which was trying. A little deaf, she merely raised her voice over rebellious murmurs and at the end said placidly, 'Well I call that beautiful.' Beatrice was popular and after a week Mrs Ward said cheerfully, 'I wanted Lord Dunsany more than you, but now I don't think I want him at all.' She accounts for this success, 'I suppose I am exotic here and that's why.'

Meanwhile Dunsany was being catapulted up and down the country. 'At Minneapolis I got out of the train, which kept its own atmosphere, still remembering the palms and huge flowers and butterflies of New Orleans, till the cold gripped me like a mighty hand.'[1] In Chicago he saw a performance of his *Tents of the Arabs* given by puppets and regretted in a speech afterwards that no puppet had been knighted. This remark was wrongly taken as a sneer at Sir Johnston Forbes-Robertson, who was in the neighbourhood, though not by the actor himself. Dining in a crypt in St Louis with the Artists Guild, Dunsany was asked if he could not write a play about monks as it could be acted so effectively there. He delivered a lecture, 'at more length than necessary', as he admitted to Beatrice in a letter, about the forces that go into the act of creation and the impossibility of whistling up inspiration to fit mundane, practical wishes. However, he continued to think about it and on the train to Chicago next day wrote *A Good Bargain*, which was duly acted in the crypt the following January. He had another great success that evening, particularly impressing one member of his audience by reading the new play from the untidy scraps on which he had written it. Beatrice met him there and took him back to Mrs Ward for a rest after nineteen scattered lectures.

At Mrs Ward's house there was a girl who deemed it an honour to be allowed to type anything for him and a boy of sixteen who loved stories about Lords, Ladies and the Royal

1. Letter from Dunsany to Beatrice.

Family. He bombarded Beatrice with questions as to whether it was necessary to be a lord's daughter to marry a lord, and if it would be all right for the Queen to snub a duke. He approached Dunsany on the same topic with confidence. 'Everything goes by precedent in England,' he stated. 'The king could no more go about without his monocle than he could go without his crown.' Dunsany replied seriously, 'As a matter of fact if he had his crown he couldn't be without his monocle.'

'Why so?'

'Because, as you say, everything goes by precedent. One of our kings had to wear a monocle hundreds of years ago, so our succeeding kings had to have it too, but as their sight was good and they did not need it, it was let into the front of the crown, and is there to this day.'

'I believe you are making game of me.'

But not all Americans were taken with the charm of the eccentric British peerage. A guest of Mrs Ward's said that he would allow Beatrice to be a Lady, because of her quality, but he couldn't bring himself to call Dunsany anything but Mr. After an extra day because he had hurt his back defending a snow fort, the unworthy peer returned to his circuit. In a small town in Connecticut, Dunsany almost got into a fight. Very tired, he lay down on a sofa in a hotel and put his feet up. The manager said he could not do that. He asked why not. 'Because,' came the reply, 'if you do that, we can't know if you're drunk.' Dunsany, a near teetotaller, curiously and surely mistakenly, decided that the way to prove his sobriety was to fight the manager and, preferably beat him. He offered to do so. However Mr Williams intervened and prevented a blow being struck, though he muttered afterwards, 'It's a long time since I've seen a good fight.' In the Portland Naval Prison Dunsany watched a performance of *Fame and the Poet* and then made a three-minute speech giving no good advice but simply saying: 'My philosophy is that life is made up of sunlight and shadow, just as it takes nights as well as days to mellow the orchard, and therefore one should never regret any experience.' The Governor had his words taken down, printed and a copy given to each prisoner. When he wrote his autobiography he called it *Patches of Sunlight* and omitted, without denying, the shadow.

Dunsany was in New York for December 9th, which was Beatrice's last day – she was going home for Randal's holidays. At eleven in the morning he gave a lecture to the League for Political Education and then they went to a huge lunch, which was followed by speech after speech. An Indian felt that Dunsany had, as a god-maker, an affinity with India, where there are more millions of gods than of people; a Chinese woman considered that of Western countries, England was most like China because the fundamental wish of each was to do right however clumsily (a doubtful compliment that would be more likely now to go to the Americans); a war correspondent asserted that a decline at the mines did not matter as the future of England was founded on the manhood of England and not on coal; a Mrs Kelly told strange stories of American Indians, among whom she had lived; Edna Ferber, then known for short stories rather than novels, thought herself inappropriate to speak of Dunsany, together they were like cabbage and lilies, sauerkraut and pomegranates; Mrs Robinson spoke of her brother Theodore Roosevelt, who had been President from 1901–1909. The Dunsanys thought it all most interesting, and after a reception in their honour at Barnard College – 'such nice, happy, keen girls' – went back to a pleasant dinner with Mrs Robinson. They liked her and found her relaxing, partly because she understood that they could enjoy and admire America without wishing to live there.

In the morning Dunsany was off to Boston and Mr Williams saw Beatrice off. 'You might have been so different,' he said gratefully. She had been in America two months; Dunsany stayed on over the New Year, meeting H. L. Mencken, then Editor of *The Smart Set* at Harvard, and Maeterlinck, whom he admired. He discovered Mrs Maeterlinck on a swing in her drawing-room which he thought rum; otherwise his impressions are not recorded. Maeterlinck found him an odd man, 'with a smile like the brass plate on a coffin'. Mr Pond was eager to exhibit him in Texas, but he decided, prudently, that he should go home and do some work. On the boat he bid a formal good-bye to the hemisphere in which he was recognised and fêted, saying to American friends: 'I shall talk no more about the drama tomorrow for we shall be half-way across, and on that side I do not count as being a writer of plays, and so it

would be silly to talk about them.' He reports the Americans
as puzzled but coming up the next day to admit that he was
right.

At Dunsany the old pattern struggled to re-emerge. House-
parties and cricket matches and hunting could be arranged,
some of the old verve regained, but the political situation, which
was bad and growing worse, intruded, and the carelessness of
pre-war gaiety would not return. '

February 10th 1920   Dunsany Castle
I hunted today on Randal's Jack, the first time for seven years. I
enjoyed the old feeling but I don't mean to really take to it, only,
the meet being here, it seemed giving way to old age not to go.
Winifred Leigh is here and taking it up again, and Eddie came out
on a borrowed horse of General Hammond's.

It took twelve men in masks to raid Mrs Chaytor at Smithstown
and take three useless old guns – they did not discover the butler's
good one hidden away.

At a performance of *The Lily of Killarney* in Dublin they
heard of a mail van being robbed and of a particularly deliberate murder, but Beatrice found that the list of horrors had
been growing so insidiously that she no longer reacted as
strongly as she felt she should. In the interval a man in the
gallery sang a rebel song in a plaintive Irish voice and though
there was scattered applause the majority went on talking and
munching their chocolates, which she did not think indicated
a sense of oppression.

Gradually much that they had thought ended with the war
was being restored, not least a gap between themselves and the
people round them. Home Rule, and how to get it, dominated
conversation once more. Magee, the vet came 'and ranted
S.F. – he called himself a moderate because he didn't advocate
murder – he excused it though – he had no arguments but
two or three stock epigrammatic sayings of somebody else.'
The next day the doctor, Murnane, said that the police
murders were turning the farming class back against the Sinn
Fein. The real pleasure was when Captain Fowler arrived for
tea and talked about hunting; but even he was political enough
to keep the guns in his house loaded.

While disapproving utterly of their actions, the Dunsanys

stayed on friendly terms with those whom they expected to be nationalists. Upper-class sympathisers they found more difficult to forgive. Toomey, their keeper, was an ardent Sinn Feiner though he wore his medals from the British Army. He was valuable to them as he could dissuade anyone who thought of bothering the Castle. Attacks were more personal than ideological so your fate depended on local popularity more than on religion or politics. Fortunately Dunsany had been an amiable landlord. Nevertheless they did not dare to dismiss any servants and when Beatrice was asked to give a girl who had worked for her a character she waited until her questioner came to tea before telling her that the girl had forged General Hammond's name on a cheque. She would not have put such a thing in writing.

The village shop was closed. Sometimes the papers and letters did not come. Race meetings were cancelled, trains arrived with their windows broken. The Sinn Fein held trials and carried out their own death penalties. When the Dunsanys had tickets for a matinée in Dublin, they did not go as the motor would probably have been smashed or stolen. It was a relief to be leaving for England.

If circumstances were grim, Dunsany himself was buoyed up by his success in America and hopes for his plays, in particular *If*. He wrote a new one, *The Flight of the Queen*, whose characters were human but their behaviour and the plot came from bees. Even distantly-reflected glory was not rejected. When Oliver Plunkett, a cousin, who had been the Roman Catholic primate of Ireland before he was hanged, drawn and quartered in London in 1681, was pronounced 'Blessed' by the Pope in May, Dunsany said he would take a halo above his signature. In July he was asked to go to Prague with a party of journalists and four or five writers as guests of the new state of Czechoslovakia. He went, and enjoyed himself enormously. A brass band played at the station. Men with eagles' feathers in their hats met them in the waiting room. There were speeches, the first of many, for one speech was expected for each course of a banquet and, 'though the people here are said to be starving, I have never had as many or such long banquets.' Dunsany was happy to speak whenever required.

He went to the Sokols, athletic schools whose sort of displays later gathered Nazi overtones but impressed him at the time.

'I had never before seen twelve thousand men on parade being drilled by one instructor, nor had I ever seen smarter drill. As one man could not drill twelve thousand, the instructor was the band and their words of command were the different notes of music. I had never seen sound travelling before but I saw it travelling then over the heads of twelve thousand young men; for though they all moved instantly with perfect precision as they heard the note of music, they could only move as it reached them, and one saw their movement going like a wave over them at exactly the pace of sound.'

He also saw a successful performance of *Smich Boha – The Laughter of the Gods* in Czech.

When they were leaving, Dunsany went into H. G. Wells's room and found him 'on his knees on the floor over a portmanteau; and then he explained something of our social system as he saw it . . .

His views I gathered were upon these lines: there was a class of highly educated men, trained in the best universities for the better kind of activities; such men could not be required to do menial tasks like packing, nor even be expected to know how to do it, men of a humbler caste and less highly trained should do this for them. That, if I got it right, was part of his social philosophy; and having given his son a very fine education, he was now packing his clothes for him.'

Back in England, Dunsany got a telegram from Lindsay, who had been with him at the Easter Rebellion in 1916, saying that he was ill and would like a visit. He seemed cheerful and they talked happily for some time, but when Dunsany asked a question of a nurse she 'said something beginning with the words: "Well everyone here . . ." And I understood I was among dying men.' He met McWilliam in London and told him the doctors only gave Lindsay a few weeks. 'Then they don't know Lindsay,' said McWilliam, but though he lasted longer than they had allowed him, Lindsay died of consumption within the year.

Though friends told them it was foolish and they did not look forward to it, the Dunsanys crossed to Ireland at the end of July. At Holyhead their luggage was thoroughly searched for arms. On board they heard tales of murder, where no witnesses dared come forward and passers-by openly jeered in a town street, but at Dunsany all seemed deeply peaceful. This ambiguous calm continued. The keeper Toomey personified it. He was a staunch republican and a loyal friend. The doctor, always well-informed in such matters, advised: 'Useful now. Sack him later.' Dunsany scorned such behaviour and Toomey stayed at the Castle till he died forty years later. His relationship with Dunsany was of the feudal sort that can seem like one between equals; as long as neither stepped out of his role, they could say almost anything to each other and it never occurred to either of them to do such a thing. Failing to find a bird, Dunsany once said angrily: 'Toomey, you're a fool.'

'Yes, my Lord.'

'Toomey, I'm a fool.'

'Yes, my Lord.'

Few could agree so simply with a distraught Dunsany. Toomey's command of English led Dunsany to say, 'The best education in the world is to go to Oxford or Cambridge; and the second best is not to learn to read;' which rated Toomey above Dunsany. The keeper returned the compliment when Dunsany, straying on to politics, asked what the Government were going to do and was asked in reply, 'If you do not know with your Oxford and Cambridge education, who would?' It was hard to believe that he could be ambushing policemen on his afternoon off or even that he knew people that were; but the latter at least might be true.

The first cricket match for six years was held at Dunsany against the Worcestershire Regiment. They had the team to stay and played Moucat after dinner, in their pre-war manner. But some friends could not stay because they were expecting the police barracks opposite their house to be burnt down any day and it would startle the children, if they were not at home. Bryan Ponsonby, a cousin, was on the court-martial of a man who cried all the time and said that he had been trying to miss the policeman, who had done him a kindness. They decided that he must be speaking the truth, as the pistol could only have reached if he had fired it into the air; but the policeman was dead. The Sinn Fein raided the whole countryside to get arms. The Married Men had played the Bachelors at Dunsany and, with Randal the Captain of the Bachelors, it had been a tie. They were having the replay when they were warned. Dunsany played on, while Beatrice went to tell Toomey to hide the only two guns they kept, as everyone knew that both Randal and Dunsany shot. They were not bothered; this was a sign of remarkable popularity as Dunsany never thought to change his narrow Unionist views, nor to make a secret of them. General Hammond lost his puttees, belt and field-glasses. The Dunsanys could not repress a 'faint feeling of vulgar triumph' when they heard that the Fingalls, who had been much more cautious in what they said to whom, had been raided at Killeen. They heard of only one farmer who threatened to fire back and he was left alone.

Ten days later the other side raided for guns in its turn. The soldiers were most accommodating and allowed Dunsany to keep his rook rifle and it seemed such bad luck on Randal that Dunsany told him to hide his 16-bore, which he did successfully. In fact there was not even a search. What the Dunsanys heard – that week a girl's hair was cut and acid rubbed into the roots because she went out with a soldier, a man of eighty shot dead – was shocking; what they suffered was merely inconvenient. When Terence MacSwiney, the Lord Mayor of Cork, was on a hunger strike, fifteen policemen were murdered during the first three weeks. The Dunsanys watched his health, anxious lest his death should cause an uproar that would prevent Beatrice getting Randal back to school. It was not heartlessness; they felt strongly for the policemen. But from slightly different angles they did not recognise the Sinn Fein as worthy foes. Dunsany thought they were rebels and so traitors and should be put down with whatever force was necessary. Beatrice did not object to their cause so much, but could not allow their right to fight for it in such a manner. The boasting, the cowardice and the comedy put her off, the disloyalty and the cruelty sickened her.

Randal got to school without difficulty though MacSwiney eventually died. Beatrice did not relent. When a sister, who had encouraged him, destroyed herself, she wrote, admittedly in the context of having been moved by the courage and dignity of the widow of another the rebels had murdered, 'I can bear less than ever the mawkish nonsense talked in the papers about Miss MacSwiney – what should a woman who has killed her brother do but commit suicide and why should anyone stop her?'

In London Beatrice had a minor operation. While she was convalescing at Dunstall she heard that there had been reprisals by the police at Trim. While seven of eight police were at Mass, the barracks were attacked and burnt, and the eighth policeman wounded. In return the Black and Tans burnt the Court House, which actually belonged to Dunsany. Beatrice thought it regrettable but inevitable. As in the war there were theories and rumours that it must all end in a few months, but she could see no reason to believe them. Mrs Robert Gregory came and told how the Sinn Fein had recovered some fleeces for her. First they took two suspects to a lonely house and gave them no food for twenty-four hours. Then they flogged them and told them separately that the other had confessed. One did confess, but the other would not, so they blindfolded him, told him he was to be executed and fired shots all round him. Still he would not, but they did not kill him, they banished him. He turned out to be innocent.

On November 10th an anonymous body was brought from France as 'The Unknown Warrior' and Beatrice stayed awake to hear the train going by. A week later she walked past the Cenotaph in London and there was still a queue almost the length of Whitehall of people waiting to put flowers. Men kept their hats off as they passed. Dunsany felt that he had indirectly named this symbol of those lost in the war with the title, *King Argimenes and the Unknown Warrior*, remarking that 'to call a man a warrior is not a normal English custom.'

In Meath the penalty for being caught with a gun in your hand could be death; for mere possession you could be imprisoned. That no one had wanted to confiscate it would be no excuse. Dunsany shot on. 'The state of the country certainly made snipe-shooting more exciting than it normally is, and, being the only person shooting, I made good bags [327 that year].' He had narrow escapes. Once he was stopped by a platoon of soldiers looking for firearms. Though he had a game-keeper and a labrador with him and his gun was under a rug on the front seat, such was his confident air that they let him through. Another time he simply hid his gun behind his back. He hopefully tried to justify this behaviour to a disapproving Beatrice by claiming that he was keeping his normal life going and that this was valuable in the circumstances. Though it seems probable that he continued to shoot basically because he liked shooting, this was mixed with a pride that would not allow them to be chivvied. A similar feeling that it would be shirking to leave kept the Dunsanys often in Ireland, when the easiest course would have been simply to abandon it until the troubles were settled one way or another.

Relations of men he had never seen appealed to Dunsany to help get them released: 'Sure your Lordship has only to give the boy a good character.' He considered that to agree to such a request would be a betrayal of principle. Only once, when a local protestant asked him to sign a petition to save a rebel from execution, did he feel that he should help. He wrote a private letter to the Governor-General, which had no effect. He did aid his gardener, Brudell, who had bought a ticket to go to America. Then Brudell was kidnapped by the Sinn Fein, who let him go unharmed (he was supposed to have been concerned in a robbery) but told him he must be out of the country by a certain date, simultaneously and illogically removing his ticket and passport, as well as his Mons star, military papers and gold locket and chain. Dunsany lent him £10 to reach a brother in Canada, from where he sent a postcard. There was thirty years' silence. Then after a lecture in Chicago a letter and ten pound notes were thrust into his hand by a prosperous Brudell. Perhaps it is pedantic to think that the money could have been posted. Certainly Dunsany was delighted to have found 'such an honest man'.

At the end of the year a footman was dismissed for stealing, after being twice forgiven. Apparently he told the police that Dunsany had a roomful of automatic pistols. In any case early in January, 1921, the Black and Tans came from Navan and removed the remaining guns and even the useless old pistols hanging on the walls, which were presumably the inspiration for the roomful of automatics. The Dunsanys were not at home and the butler, Mander, showing the rough intruders out, asked impeccably, 'Whom shall I say called?' Though they took and did not return a brass cannon, the Dunsanys resented the informer but not the confiscation.

Three days later thirty-five soldiers arrived in two lorries to enquire into a story that Dunsany had a special Sinn Fein permit to shoot. He wrote a strong denial and they went away, but a nervous week followed. Then another lorry load of soldiers and a Ford car arrived at 9 o'clock in the morning. Everyone was polite and friendly, but he was taken to Dunshaughlin to make a statement and in the afternoon the butcher and the grocer bailed him out. Though Dunsany made jokes about the charge being reduced from 'feloniously shooting a snipe with intent to kill' to 'shooting a snipe while trying to escape', they were seriously worried. Later it would appear ridiculous that Dunsany, who held his extreme Unionist views at the top of his voice and had been wounded by rebels in the Easter Rebellion, should be in trouble with the Government. For the moment it was real enough. No one who knew him would believe it, but there were those who did not know him, and his lawyer talked of a prison sentence of a year or two. Rumours of his Sinn Fein sympathies circulated, based on his shooting unmolested for so long. Beatrice rang up friends from the Commander-in-Chief to an Assistant Under-Secretary, she wrote to her mother, who wired next evening that she had 'enlisted powerful advocates', and Georgie Buller expressed a letter to Lord French, the Lord-Lieutenant, at Cannes. The head constable at Dunshaughlin came to assure her that he had nothing to do with it and was very sorry.

There was a pause and Beatrice went to London, talked to the Irish Office and was told that the case was definitely being dropped and 'they were only, as would have been reasonable, confiscating the guns and stuff', that is, keeping the ones that they had taken before Dunsany's arrest. She had influenza and had planned a trip with her mother to Cannes and, at Dunsany's urging, she went. In fact he had been warned that day that there would be a trial, but unselfishly delayed telling her so that she would go and then sent an emphatic telegram to Lady Jersey saying that on no account was Beatrice to be allowed to undertake the idiotic journey back. On February 4th he sent a telegram, 'Lost twenty-five pounds – coming soon', and the threat was over. Soon she was able to write: 'One ought not to blame them when one knows all that officials are suffering now and what their nerves must be, and of course they see now what fools they have made of themselves, for the American papers for one thing mock them delightfully, but one wonders with a gasp how many more mistakes and some that are not put right they have made It was long before I could hear a lorry at Cannes without jumping.' Dunsany was stimulated by the excitement and worked well on his first novel in France, where they remained for two months.

When they returned to Dunsany in April there was still a curfew and fairs and meetings were forbidden in Meath, but oddly race-meetings were allowed. Beatrice, Randal, Winifred Leigh and another friend went to Navan races and, apart from a bridge which the Sinn Fein had made the local people destroy at gun-point, there was no difficulty; the weather was fine and a good time was being had by all. Then a shot rang out. Immediately there was a stampede, not particularly in any direction, but everyone took a step or two from the feeling that to move was better than to stay still, except for those who threw themselves to the ground. Randal, who to his mother's gratification, had lost the first bets he had ever made, took cover behind the fattest bookie he could see. That was in the enclosure; outside there was panic. Some cried 'Don't run', others 'It's a mistake', and a wounded policeman was carried off; but no one knew what had happened.

Later it emerged that it had been a deliberate attack, but not a successful one and, as all the doctors in the neighbourhood had naturally been present, the victim had been well cared for. When Beatrice said, 'Well no more races,' on the way home, Randal protested, 'Oh Mummy, really, there was only one shot.'

The custom house with its beautiful copper dome was blown up. A pretty girl of twenty-three came to tea at Dunsany. Later they heard she had been killed. On good terms with the Sinn Fein, she had thought they would not shoot her fiancé, if she was in the car. They did not mean to harm her and went to her funeral. Mrs Robert Gregory was driving home from tennis with another girl and two soldiers, who were not then targets, but also a policeman, who was. The gates of the drive were shut and when one of the men got out to open them, ambushers opened fire. Though someone shouted to her to take cover behind the car, she stayed where she was, which saved her life. As she crouched on the floor among the bleeding bodies of her friends a boy came up and asked, 'in the gentlest voice I have ever heard, "Are you all right?" '[1] She was the only survivor. Beatrice adds, 'Yet they [the Irish] have this quality of inspiring affection – why can't they have the other one of deserving it? Sometimes one feels sick with wrath and helplessness and yet I would hate to live elsewhere.' Her comments on the troubles remain resolutely one-sided, but for the first time she admits affection, however qualified, for more of Ireland than just her home.

They clung to London as something stable in a reeling world, but when they went over they were forced to realise that it was no longer the city they had known. Talk was all of big houses for sale and no one to buy, collections and pictures scattered, dowdy clothes, no coal, no parties, no servants and everyone living on capital – 'till I fled, steadying myself with trite consolations about moth and rust and lilies of the field and the blessed sun.' *If* was really being produced, and while they would have him, Dunsany attended rehearsals. The similarity of their taste was shown when Beatrice decided there was just one picture at the Academy, *The Witches' Fire*, which she would really like to own, and Dunsany bought it independently the same afternoon.

On May 30 she wrote in her diary only '*If* – a success'. It was her briefest entry and Dunsany's greatest triumph in the theatre. His first full-length play to reach the post-war stage, begins, amazingly to those familiar with the exotic nature of his work, with a prosaic scene in which a happily-married man misses his train. Even when, years later in his suburban home, he is presented with a crystal that will take him back in time, he wishes only to catch that train; but on it is a pretty girl who owns a mountain-pass in Persia and the second act is more typically full of Eastern adventure. He returns penniless, wishing he had never gone, but, by giving away the crystal, breaks the spell and is reunited with his wife.

The heroine of *If* combines two types which always intrigued Dunsany – the beautiful lady who is utterly ruthless and the

1. Mrs Robert Gregory quoted in Beatrice's diary.

beautiful lady who talks with a common accent. He was delighted with Gladys Cooper's acting and used to say that he only had to tell her one thing, which was to say, 'I should kill *Hussein*', and not, 'I should *kill* Hussein'. The scenery was by the young designer, C. Lovat Fraser.[1] Dunsany liked the daring of Henry Ainley's scarlet against Gladys Cooper's pink; but he objected to the idols being made comical.

Beatrice judged by the reaction of the audience at the Ambassadors' Theatre – a few boos, when the girl on the train failed to get the hero, which were swiftly drowned by cheers. The morning's reviews were mixed. The contrast of East and West and the acting of Henry Ainley and Gladys Cooper (whose oriental clothes were a sensation) were praised and the complaints were inconsistent, it was facile yet clumsy, too drab but too exotic and, incredibly, too obscure. Rebecca West in *Time and Tide* wrote in a long review:

'There can be no doubt that Lord Dunsany was sent into the world to aid in the great task of cheering us all up . . . *If* is full of his special quality . . . It is not a very original nor a very profound parable but it gives a magnificent opportunity to this pictorial gift . . .

'I have not the slightest ground, except my low view of human nature, for alleging that Lord Dunsany himself is responsible for the portentously reverent pace of the production, that he himself has insisted on the dialogue being regarded as as precious as a string of pearls, but I feel sure that it is so . . . this particular error is just the one into which an intellectually unrobust artist like Lord Dunsany would be likely to fall. For what it means is that he cannot bear to think that he has written a play that is intellectually negligible. To admit that he thinks would be the same as admitting he has written a bad play . . . but he has not.'

Miss West's low view of human nature led her astray. Dunsany had attended rehearsals, and used to offer advice from the dress circle, but he found this led to argument rather than alteration, and made him miserable. So he stayed away. A similar charge had been made by Frank Harris two years before:[2]

1. C. Lovat Fraser had made his name with his sets for *The Beggar's Opera*. He died during the run of *If*, on 18th June 1921.
2. *Great Contemporaries* 1919.

'The stories and tales of Dunsany fall into a lower class than his plays; though studded here and there with very beautiful passages they are usually almost meaningless. The truth is the lack of thought becomes painful to me on a prolonged reading; his originality is of imagination or rather of Celtic fancy and rarely of insight. If we go to his beliefs we shall hardly find an original word in it, much less an original idea.'

Dunsany disliked all criticism, but to this he could be indifferent, as he did not regard lack of ideas as a fault and was content to be intellectually negligible. Indeed he found it hard that his early work was sometimes found obscure and highbrow when he admired clarity and simplicity and thought he had achieved them. He complained constantly of those who worried 'meanings' out of tales that were simply themselves.

The success of *If* was said to owe much to the fashion set by *Chu Chin Chow* and the Russian Ballet, but such causes are not convincing; in the same manner if it had failed, a heatwave it survived would have been blamed. Miss Gladys Cooper had contributed much, but when she left the cast in September Miss Madge Titheradge replaced her effectively. It figured in lists of the best plays in London, it was published (with a dedication to Randal), Desmond McCarthy was friendly in the *New Statesman*, above all it ran. If it has not been revived, as its success would seem to warrant, that is largely because it is expensive and demanding to stage. Dunsany went often, sitting on the floor if necessary. The attitude of his wife's relations to Dunsany changed. Instead of being a relation who wrote, he became a writer who was related. He and old Lady Jersey still sparred gently; he appeared at one of her dinner-parties in dark glasses as a protest against the glare of her chandeliers – she gave no sign of having noticed. When he asked innocuously, 'I believe you knew a relation of mine, Richard Burton?' she ended the topic, 'Yes, he drank'. But they had learned mutual respect and even liking. As the first president of the Victoria League, a society for fostering friendship within the Empire, she gave Overseas tea-parties, and two or three times he read from his works. Also he enjoyed meeting the new generation and was a prominent figure at family weddings or other clan gatherings.

At Dunstall Dunsany examined the weekly takings of *If* and

his share of them (about £50 a week if it was full) and worked
on his novel in the hut in the garden, which he had named
Thule. Some neighbours used to ring a bell before each meal,
including tea, and this invariably annoyed and interrupted
him. Sometimes he would try the house with Beatrice playing
the same pieces by Schuman and Grieg over and over – a
change disconcerted him. At the end of October *If* completed
its five-month run and the Dunsanys gave a successful supper-
party for the cast. His total earnings from it were £1500 and in
the wake of this success, the Everyman Theatre at Hampstead
did four of his short plays for two weeks – *The Tents of the
Arabs, The Lost Silk Hat, A Night at an Inn* and, for the first time,
Cheeso. They went well without causing a sensation.

What would have been a tranquil summer, resting on a
present success and working for future ones, was invaded by
Irish politics. Uncle Horace came for a day, downhearted and
something of an outcast both from politics and his family. He
thought that it was because Dunsany was a nephew of his that
he had been arrested and another nephew, meeting him in the
street, had told him that he was doing the family no good. All
his relations disapproved of Lady Fingall and his actually quite
mild politics; only the Dunsanys remained friendly. A truce
was declared in July and Michael Collins and Arthur Griffith
came to London to try to negotiate a settlement. Uncle Horace
said there would be no more burning whatever the outcome
and Beatrice thought him wise, plausible and convincing, but
she had seen him be wrong again and again and when they
went to Dunsany she brought back two Chinese ginger jars as
a small form of insurance. Normal insurance was now unobtain-
able and it seemed both humiliating and asking for trouble to
move larger things.

On the boat going over Dunsany was asked about his guns
being confiscated and he commented, 'I am snaring eels now,
like a reformed drunk drinking soda-water,' Life there was for
the moment uncertain, almost furtive, and they did not enjoy
it. In September Lady Jersey sent a telegram asking, 'When
will Eton reassemble?' This was code for 'the negotiations are
breaking down, danger', for she was a friend of the wife of the
Lord Lieutenant and had privileged information. So Beatrice
and Randal put forward a plan to go to swim and shoot rabbits

(now a treat) in Wales. Dunsany remained to keep up the cricket team and appearances. Mary Longford received a similar telegram but decided to ignore it, which she did with impunity. The settlement was finally achieved in December but the Dunsanys hardly felt relief, let alone enthusiasm. The Irish Free State was recognised as a Dominion, the fact of a separate unit of six northern counties was accepted. Though the delegation had returned to consult him, de Valera, who was Prime Minister of the Sinn Fein Cabinet as well as President of the organisation, rejected the final draft of the treaty; he was overruled by the Cabinet and Arthur Griffith replaced him as leader. The party was split, and the only issue that mattered became whether or not you supported the Treaty. This isolated the Dunsanys as they disagreed with those who did only fractionally less than with those who did not.

In the New Year, 1922, Dunsany was planning a safari. In London he had his hair cut, made three visits to his dentist and wrote that he was 'a bit tired after buying the chocolate etc.'[1] His journey went smoothly though he got a headache 'and arrived in Algiers full of misery, I chewed a steak as desperate men sometimes do for the sustenance that is said to be in it and tho' there was none I had some tangerines and champagne and some of the misery lifted.'[2] He decided against joining up with an acquaintance in Biskra: 'after all why cling to relics of civilisation when one has left it for the desert? To bring another white face with me would be like taking a tall hat, and I think the desert would be huffed at either and would hide his mysteries behind yet one farther ridge.' In the same vein he wrote later, 'I think that the desert is to the mind what the bath is to the body: of all the little specks of dust that stick to one's skin there may be no actual harm in any one of them, and yet one is the better for a bath; in the same way the trivial pieces of information and empty phrases that daily fall on our minds are swept clean away by the desert, and the mind is fresher and clearer for them. All athletes wash; all prophets come from the desert.'

Dunsany liked the colour and atmosphere of the desert and he liked shooting. He wrote of each but as he got nothing for the first ten days he concentrated on the landscape and sent

1. Letters to Beatrice.   2. *Ibid.*

pages of description daily. The setting of the sun is recorded in detail each evening. Before he set out he also noted a conversation with the *valet de chambre* at his hotel.

D: *Vous avez de moustiques ici.*
V de C: *Oh oui.*
D: *Beaucoup?*
V de C: *Neuf.*

Dunsany was about to add that he had killed one, when he realised that the *valet de chambre* thought he had said *domestiques*.

In the desert with Smail who had been his guide nine years before, seven men, four camels, two mules and nothing to shoot, Dunsany was not always happy and his spirits were not improved when he received a cutting from an English paper which referred to him as 'among less-known titled people connected with the stage' – the familiar taunt to which he was peculiarly sensitive. Astride a mule, he wrote some verses to a Dublin critic, the spirit of which is in the lines:

> 'And lesser journalists have said,
> That cannot see such things themselves
> The man is clearly off his head
> To write of things like Gods and elves.'

He also argued religion with the Mohammedans. They can eat meat only if it is properly killed by a Mohammedan with a knife. Dunsany claimed that there were many causes of the death of a beast he shot – the captain of the ship that brought him to Africa, the maker of the guns and indeed himself; there was, however, only one life to be had. So if an orthodox Mohammedan knife could be thrust into a breathing carcase, it was the sole immediate cause of death, though his bullet happened to be lodged in the heart. His men conferred and then asked the advice of Si Amar, 'a sort of combination of Master of Hounds and Archbishop.' He said no. Dunsany did badly by claiming that the earth went round the sun, but regained some ground by announcing his kinship to Sir Richard Burton, the traveller.

After a poor start the shooting was successful and he began mentally rearranging the positions for his trophies at Dunsany, '... I have planned for him [a mouflon] one of the places of honour, where the biggest pig is now, he is going up one and displacing the lesser pig. . . .' His return was as efficient as the journey out had been, untroubled even by headaches, and in Biskra he received the pleasant news that he had been elected to the Beefsteak Club.

Beatrice had three pleasant months, visiting Winifred Leigh and Georgie Buller, enjoying the Russian Ballet in *The Sleeping Beauty* in spite of a neighbour who explained it to her, and finding *The Gondoliers* 'the gayest and merriest thing'. Then she waited at Brown's hotel.

On the day after his return Dunsany signed five hundred copies of his first novel. He was pleased and a little surprised that he could sustain a novel and was proud of the *Chronicles of Rodrigues*. The form is not perfect – the hero simply goes from adventure to adventure until the book is long enough – but once labelled 'picaresque' and compared to *Don Quixote* it suffices. The comparison is natural as it is set in the Golden Age of Spain as Dunsany felt it should have been; there is a curious moment when robbers clad in green attack the hero with bows and arrows as he wanders through the forest – Robin Hood seems to have got into the wrong book – but the tone pleasantly reasserts its combination of adventure and comedy. The reviewers were friendly if a little patronising. 'It is a pretty plaything and no more,'[1] is an annoying comment, because it was, like almost all Dunsany's work, designed only to please, even if there are gruesome touches like a bell-rope that elicits an effective scream because it is attached to a hook in some unfortunate's stomach. Of writing novels he commented: 'The labour of writing seventy thousand words is not easy and that is how long a novel should be. It may be longer but God forbid that I should take longer than that to tell a story.'

They were apprehensive about returning to Dunsany. Beatrice felt that after more than seven centuries they could not grumble about four or five bad years but also that she would like those that came after to realise that it had not been easy, even if they then thought the effort pointless. In fact it was depressing, but not frightening. People were closing their houses, or writing from abroad of their intention of doing so.

1. *Times Literary Supplement* 30 March 1922.

The future of the Treaty remained uncertain. They were glad
to leave after a month. In May Beatrice wrote at Dunstall,
'These first hot, lazy days – one can sit with one's odd jobs on
the verandah looking over the valley all the morning and evening
and at the wood all the afternoon, and believing, at the moment
anyway, that one may do this every May until one dies and
that by that time one will have drunk in beauty enough. I'd
like to *die* in England.'

Irish politics pursued them. Field-Marshal Sir Henry Wilson,
who had been involved in the creation of armed forces in
Northern Ireland, was murdered on the steps of his London
house by two members of the IRA which had formed itself
from the anti-treaty Volunteers.

20th May 1922   Dunstall
E. and I went up to London and stood in Hobart Place to watch the
funeral procession pass. As E. said one thinks one can imagine that
sort of thing but one can't. The vast silent crowd in the rain, the
Guards with reversed arms, the grey generals, even old Lord Grenfell
at eight-two, walking grimly past, the Ulster Constabulary following
last of all – and then Chopin's funeral march played softly yet every
note heard in the silence – a little boy near us began crying under
his breath – and there was the moment when the gun-carriage
passed and hats came off. And never a word even when it was all
over. Are the English roused at last?

In Kent Dunsany wrote *Mr Faithful* which is based on the
contrived situation that a penniless suitor has to hold down a
job for six months to show his worth and a friendly but simple
MP (Dunsany's politicians are never shrewd *and* nice) is
persuaded to let him do the duties of a dog. He sits in the
corner, sleeps in a barrel, chases rabbits off the lawn and eventually gets the girl. It was performed without great success
at the Lyric Hammersmith but adapted successfully to the
wireless; Beatrice in cutting it had to omit one of Dunsany's
favourite lines when the butler, regretting that he never carried
out the dreams of his youth, mutters ominously 'Never mind
now. And perhaps it's as well the way it was. It saved a lot of
bloodshed.' (Dunsany is particularly good at these startling
asides. A fanciful narrator once says in passing, 'A couple wore
a look on their faces such as you see on the faces of rabbits down
in a burrow when a ferret is loose outside. No I forgot; you've

not had the opportunity of being there; but you know what I mean.')

On June 16th there was an election in Ireland and the supporters of the Treaty won fifty-eight seats while its opponents received only thirty-four with thirty-five new members uncommitted. A large section of the IRA refused to accept this verdict and civil war, more destructive and vicious than anything yet, broke out.

Free State troops shelled the Four Courts, where antitreaty supporters of de Valera held out for two days, after which the second great green dome of Dublin was destroyed. Mander, the butler, had a notice pinned to his door advising him to leave Ireland in fourteen days. It was thought that it was probable that this was only local spite, but it seemed too dangerous to risk his staying. As well as no butler, a summer in Ireland promised no cricket, no rifle, almost no neighbours, sometimes no papers and not many bridges, so effectively, no motor. So Beatrice and Randal went to a hotel in Minehead and hunted stags across Exmoor, and when Dunsany, who was putting on a bit of weight, joined them, he did so too.

On August 20 Michael Collins dined with Uncle Horace, who wrote in his diary: '. . . an interesting personality. Too fat, but virile, thirty-two years old. Forcible, direct, simple and yet cunning. A bit crude (perhaps due to shyness) in the expression of his views. Collins said one thing which was significant: "After we get over the present trouble we shall have to fight Bolshevism." He took a risk coming here without an escort. I fear he is too careless of his life. His car was bombed only yesterday, when luckily he was not in it.' Three days later Michael Collins was killed in an ambush at a place aptly named Kilmichael; it was four hundred yards from the site of an ambush he had himself arranged two years before, in which sixteen had died.

Uncle Horace went to his funeral, but Dunsany, whose Sam Browne belt was being buried also, though he was not aware of that, did not disagree with the verdict that, 'It was the judgment of God'. Arthur Griffith had died naturally ten days before and now W. T. Cosgrave led the pro-treaty majority party in the Dail. The Government decided on harsh measures and made possession of arms a capital offence once more.

There were sixty-six executions and four prisoners were shot when a deputy was murdered.

They went to Dunsany just the same, but with some apprehension. All was well. Mander returned, slept in the castle instead of his house and was not bothered. The men on the place told General Hammond that they would watch the castle, but he thought it best not to attract attention by taking precautions. After a wet summer, the wind and the rain departed to allow a glorious September.

Dunsany went to shoot grouse, rabbits and partridges staying at Arden with the Mexboroughs as usual and at Helperby in Yorkshire with Sir Clive and Lady Celia Coates. She was a tolerant hostess, but Dunsany sometimes approached the limits of her tolerance ... 'all their family were then young, and I was fortunate enough to be able to amuse them. This I did by building a factory chimney of toy bricks about six feet high in the drawing-room and, as all children love realism, I lit a fire inside and the smoke came out of the top as in real factories. I shall always remember Lady Celia's sympathy with her children's delight, which, though she did not express it in words, for on account of the density of the atmosphere she could not speak, or even easily breathe, was yet unmistakable.'

On October 5th he started for the Sahara once more. However a strike of the Marseilles dockers delayed him for ten days which he spent miserably in Paris. 'I knew one man in Paris, but he had changed his address and I could not find him.' The tedium was momentarily a little interrupted by a stranger walking into his sitting-room at the Crillon and announcing 'I am the *Sun*'. An American journalist, he wanted to know what Dunsany would shoot in a few months' time, which Dunsany was unable to tell him.

Then he saw an item in an English newspaper about the Voronoff treatment for injecting monkey glands to restore youth. Immediately he started a play whose plot depended on such treatment, though in his daily letters to Beatrice he does not mention his mundane source of inspiration. He has almost the whole plot in one burst, and it is a complicated business, hinging on an old duke who has the injections in order to have a son who comes to spend much of his time in the tops of the trees in the park, hangs about the zoo, particularly by the apes, and finally has to be destroyed by the faithful keeper. He reported progress daily, though suddenly he wrote a letter on other things:

> Hotel de Crillon
> Place de la Concorde
> Paris.

My Darling Mink,
The strike continues at present. Lalique's[1] man read a rumour that it would end in a few days. I have been buying a few absolute necessities for 66 [66 Cadogan Square, the house in London which the Dunsanys had just bought]; a tray for cards, without which the hall would be a mere faux-pas; a bowl for electric lights without which guests of different Christian sects would be murdering each other in the dark; an ink pot so that I can write; a paper-weight so that my writing-table may be as tidy as it ought; two little bowls for flowers; a photograph frame, only one for the whole house; and a tiny little scent bottle as a stray present. And I got the whole lot for 130 odd pounds. Of course I got them at Lalique's and amongst them I think are one or two pieces of Lalique's best work. You'll pay about that for three carpets. I exercised restraint and bargained. You needn't show any restraint at Eastwood's sales: all that you get will be a joy . . .

His tone is rather defensive because he had been told not to be too extravagant.

Though he wrote again that day about the work, which was to be called *Lord Adrian*, it was not finished when the strike ended and he was able to continue to Africa. There, after a few dull days, he shot some mouflons and commented, 'of course, compared with this, East African shooting is more like making a good shot with a bun at the zoo.' He got a head which Si Amar said was the biggest ever shot; anyway it was his record.

Beatrice had gone: 'To 18 Montagu Square to see about getting into and furnishing 66 Cadogan Square. Frequent panic lest it be a white elephant or an unjustifiable extravagance, but it does seem desirable for both D. and R. while we can afford it, though it is a warning to see six to let in the same block.'

The new house in Cadogan Square was really both an

1. 1860–1945. A French designer of glass, jewellery and furniture in the Deco Art style fashionable at this time.

unjustified extravagance and a white elephant, but the Dunsanys never regretted it. They bought it partly because the future, indeed the present, in Ireland seemed so uncertain and partly because there was an idea then that Randal might go into the Foreign Office and it would be nice for him to have a London base. The troubles passed, Randal went into the army, and the supply of money, which was still no problem at this stage, became, if not short, finite. The house remained and was used and appreciated; they had after all taken one each year before. When they were not there it was sometimes let, like its six neighbours, which 'we did not mind doing because we had no relics there'.

The inside was basically conventional but as time passed acquired some characteristic touches. The spacious drawing-room had the green walls that were then fashionable, soft carpets, big armchairs and heavily shaded lights; only the idiosyncratic choice of pictures and bric-à-brac suggested that the owner might be an unusual man. Not everyone would notice, say, a cabinet made by Ernest Gimson[1] which Dunsany picked out from the Wembley Exhibition two years later and installed.

The Cadogan Square district was extremely respectable but it was not far from the traditional haunt of Bohemians. The extent to which he was not of them is shown in a letter he later wrote to Randal from safety:

> 66 Cadogan Square, London.
> I penetrated as far into Chelsea last night as any traveller has been. The great river that I spoke of in a former letter was as a matter of fact not Moet or Chandon but Krug and it flowed with a superb grandeur. Tho' I thought I was to reply for the guests, after I had sat down they nearly all replied for themselves, but I was what they call the 'principal guest' and my speech was luckily an enormous hit . . . If ever you are lost in Chelsea mention my name and they might help you on account of that speech.

He makes the district sound like a partly-subdued colony where the natives are, if hospitable, restless. 'At one o'clock Sir Roger Keyes and I found ourselves in a Chelsea studio in

1. Ernest Gimson 1864–1919. Furniture designer, Leader of the Cotswold School.

which ladies seemed to be about to have afternoon tea, tho'
the drinks we actually did have were brandies and sodas. About
1.30 I suggested that we might be keeping them up, but our
hostess said, "Oh no, we never go to bed early".'

Beatrice felt she had no particular gift for furnishing, but that
her surroundings had given her standards. She bought a
buddha and a llama that Dunsany had admired. At her mother's
birthday tea-party, general opinion was that the Conservatives
would creep in with a small majority, Asquith be safely out of
it, though some gave Lloyd George a chance. Beatrice addressed
envelopes for Sir Samuel Hoare, who was returned and made
Secretary for Air. For general opinion had been too cautious;
the Conservatives with 345 seats had a majority over all the rest
combined, the coalition was ended and Bonar Law became
Prime Minister. The Labour Party dropped their plan for a
capital levy half-way through the election and won 142 seats
compared with 117 for the Liberals which divided roughly
evenly for Lloyd George and Asquith. The great dynamic
force, Lloyd George, never held office again and Britain returned to normal, orderly times. Ireland did not.

Uncle Horace was a supporter of the Treaty and deeply
grieved that there should be civil war. Beatrice visited him in a
nursing home where he was looked after by a Mrs Percival, a
political sympathiser, with whom she talked.

'Of course there is no pessimist like your reformed Nationalist –
perhaps they feel responsible – and then she was reacting from the
strain of cheering him up and said so. I said something about his
heart being broken and she said "Quite broken, and all I hope is
that he'll be safely in Algeciras before they burn Kilteragh"."But???"
I said. "It will make an impression in America, and they are too
crazy to care that it is the wrong impression," she said.

She had seen some of the leaders, of both kinds, at Kilteragh
recently and felt utterly hopeless and said that there was nothing for
it but to save what one could and clear out. Well of course we have
been incredibly fortunate so far at Dunsany and therefore until they
throw us out we owe it to them to stay even if our sentiment did not
point the way. And then one little thing experience has taught one
is that one is always afraid of the wrong thing – one can only meet
things as they come. We talked of how a little recognition might
have soothed him in the failure of his life's work and I said that
Eddie wrote to him when he was President of the Convention and

how he answered that E. was the only one of the family to write. 'I wrote to him' she said 'and sent it to my cousin [Mr Heard] and told him not to give it to him if he were inundated with congratulations, and he answered that there were not a dozen letters.'

Dublin looked hectic and squalid. Untidy green soldiers held up the motor and stared in, but said nothing. A porter making conversation, instead of commenting on the weather or the crops, asked pleasantly: 'Your house has not been burnt yet, has it?' Dunsany itself still retained its atmopshere of calm. Dunsany was again able to shoot snipe unmolested, Randal's harriers were welcomed; but the threatening noises were growing closer and more insistent.

Kilteragh was burnt. Uncle Horace, luckily in London, had been made a Senator. If his family considered this an extreme position, the supporters of de Valera did not and he suffered as moderate reformers of goodwill generally suffer. Dunsany commented later, 'He was like a dog on a tennis-court. Both sides stopped play in order to get him off.' His secretary, Gerald Heard, was at Kilteragh, and though the two mines which the attackers exploded removed several doors and windows and brought down ceilings, when they had gone he managed to put out the fires and the house was still standing. Exhausted, he took a sleeping draught the next night, for which he was given a guard. But the rebels were watching and when the guard returned to barracks at 2.15 they lit the house once more, and Heard was lucky to be saved. This time Kilteragh was utterly destroyed and with it a great number of A.E.'s pictures and a fine library with many Irish first editions. Uncle Horace never lived in Ireland again. It was also a financial blow for, as he had written to Dunsany in 1921, 'I tried to insure Kilteragh and Lloyds wouldn't look at it. I don't wonder.' That night Beatrice could only lie awake thinking of 'that happy hospitable house with the wind blowing all cold through it'.

Comic incidents continued, but became harder to laugh at. While Lady Susan Dawney was away there was a battle in her house and garden, with quantities of firing but no blood spilt. 'Both sides,' wrote the gardener, 'admired the antirrhinums.' However as they were stealing her car they overturned it and two men were killed. So the gardener sent a large wreath of the admired antirrhinums to the funeral with the inscription: 'With Lady Susan Dawney's deepest sympathy'. A boy of nineteen told how he had been offered a stolen car as a present, but warned: 'Be careful how you move it, as there is a bomb under each wheel.' The Republican was hurt that his gift was refused. Two British soldiers laughed at the marching of the Free State Army, were put in prison, escaped, became Republicans, were caught and executed.

When Beatrice found Randal sleeping with his house colour scarf on his bed, she asked if he wanted another blanket. He admitted later that he liked to have it by him, 'to save things'. In Ulster they took prisoner an armed Free State man just as they were starting a game of football; not knowing what to do with him, they made him referee.

Randal was simply being practical; the danger was real. A marauding band from Louth burnt Kilmessan station, hid in the woods at Dunsany for two days, burnt a train and passed on. Yet in a discussion about going or staying, the Dunsanys felt that if the Castle was burnt, they would still cling to the land that was left and hope that Randal could some day return. Cromwell and the rebels of '98 had entered but spared it; it was not right to be the link that broke. They were heartened by an incident with Riley, the old vanman, which seemed to prove that 'it was not all terror and cowardice'. Aged well over sixty, he was coming back from the bank at Trim with £145 for farm wages and was stopped while walking the horses up Swainston Hill by a masked man with a revolver. The man put one hand on the reins, a foot on the step and pointed the revolver. Old Riley simply whacked the hand on the reins with the butt end of the whip. The man dropped the reins, fired wildly and Riley got off. 'I suppose the shot luckily made the horses gallop,' said Beatrice. But Riley would not allow that even his horse was frightened by it. 'It did not,' he said, 'I skelped him with the whip and made him gallop.' At first he refused the £2 Dunsany offered him, thinking such an obvious piece of duty needed no reward.

April was the cruellest month. They received a promise that 'we will leave your house in ashes before New Year'. Threats were many, Dunsany's ridiculous arrest as a Republican helped, they could do little but wait and hope; but it was not reassuring. At the end of the month (she did not risk a diary in Ireland) Beatrice wrote:

'On April 1st we heard a motor in the night at Dunsany but could see nothing and were thankful. In the morning it turned out seven armed men came for General H's Ford car, which he keeps in our stables and took it off to blow up Clonmellon Railway Bridge to stop Fairyhouse Races, de V. having ordered a time of "National Mourning" and no races. The car was left derelict but unhurt near Crosskeys and we felt happier to hear that the raiders told Mick Flynn, his chauffeur, that they "heard his Lordship was a good man and they didn't wish to disturb him or his family". We went to the races; and so did everyone else by road. A few days later some men drove to the Dunsany stores, took petrol in a trap (stolen from Knockmark) and burnt Lismullen; giving the old Dillons twelve minutes in which they saved their Gainsborough, King William's relics and a few more things. Old Sir John is eighty and spent the night in a barn. They drove back by Baronstown and set fire to it but after they left the Wilkinsons managed to get it out as they had run out of petrol. They returned two days later and set it alight again, but again only burnt furniture and a floor or so.

'F.S. (Free State) soldiers searched our woods but of course found nobody.'

April 12 1923   Dunsany
Toomey was arrested and we can't get him out – they can't catch the perpetrators so take sympathisers – or those said to be such. Also a gardener of ours. . . . On April 16th they burnt Ferroms – Major N.B. [North-Bumford] escaped in pyjamas – she dressed, but they poured petrol on her bed before she was dressed – little David was so busy saving his new puppy that he did not feel the shock. They had sent away two vanloads of their best stuff before; luckily as they saved nothing but the horses. And then Kilmesson station was burnt for the 2nd or 3rd time (the temporary buildings) and Dunshaughlin police barracks, and many ricks at Kiltale and a big train wreck near Knockmark – why go on? Just one month's record and other districts are worse? And though the country people don't openly approve still all sense of right and wrong is shaken and they do really feel that Mr Wilkinson's not employing enough men, or Mrs N.B.'s unpopularity (she was an indiscreet talker) or old Sir John's quarrels with his herd, are quite good reasons for the outrages. But it is little bits of personal cruelty that throw such a nasty light on the Irish character. When for instance they burnt the stationmaster's house at Kilmessan (Mrs Preston

L.D.   N

and we had to refit them entirely with clothes and furniture last
March) they would not let him run upstairs to save his dead wife's
pictures and his money. Sometimes one feels sick with impotent
rage, sometimes utterly indifferent . . .

And yet if one could just speak one's mind and shake off responsibility and go, one would not be happy – one would miss the gentle
friendly helpless country people, whom one loves, though without
trust or respect, even as one would miss one's home or memories.
We talk of it very little – there is so little to say – but we are weary
of barbarian ways and of incapable tyranny, and though one laughs
at it more often than not it takes the heart out of things for me.

Lady Fingall, according to Beatrice, went round saying that
Dunsany and Toomey had a Republican ammunition dump in
the woods. This made Toomey's release no quicker. When he
did come out of prison after several months he was full of new
learning and sophistication. He no longer believed in Will-o'-
the-Wisps, and said 'By God' instead of 'Begob'. He retained
enough of his old way to reassure Dunsany who asked several
years later if there was still witchcraft in Ireland. 'Sure and isn't
the whole country rotten with it,' said Toomey – but then he
knew that that was what Dunsany wished to hear.

On May 1st the Dunsanys returned to England and could
hear noises in the night without worrying about being burnt
in their beds. Gogarty came to tea, a high Tory now and
begging them to save what they could from Dunsany, where a
year before he had assured them that with such a good landlord, the castle was 'asbestos'. They had not brought much:
the best of the plate was at Barclays, some of his manuscripts,
some jewellery, china and a few pictures, among them, because
it seemed only fair, the Opie with the Latin inscription that had
prevented any danger of Dunsany becoming mean about
money, 'Take warning by the misfortunes of other men.'
Beatrice was careful with Gogarty and agreed with him, or
rather helped him to agree with her that his wife would find
English ways strange and difficult and was right and reasonable
to be reluctant to uproot herself; but in her heart, she thought
her a fool. 'She has married a charming flibbertigibbet and a
sacrifice is required if she is to keep him.'

In London Mr Bourchier, a distinguished actor, came to
breakfast and was wild with excitement when Dunsany read

him *Lord Adrian*. He cried, 'You have H. G. Wells beat to a frazzle', and took it away to read to his wife.

Uncle Horace came to Dunstall and, for once, there was no need to divert him from politics. All were grateful not to think of them for a while, which was easier there. They had a triumph; Dunsany asked the neighbour if he would stop ringing his bell before each meal – he had suffered in comparative silence for two summers – and he said that he would. The year before he had raced through *Mr Faithful* in order to finish it before the bell-ringers arrived, but now he was working, sometimes before breakfast, on a novel *The King of Elfland's Daughter*. He had thought about it years before and Beatrice had made sure it was never entirely forgotten. She was said to have 'a tired heart' and had to stay in bed much of the time.

In their absence the tension in Ireland relaxed. The republicans gradually laid down their arms. In an election, they were again defeated. De Valera was not returned to power until 1932. In August there was a dance and Randal, aged seventeen, went as a grown-up for the first time; his mother recognised that boys were asked at that age since the war. There was cricket, a village match, where a batsman who was unable to believe that his leg had been in front of the wicket, pleased them by coming out muttering, 'Begob, that's too Irish'. Perhaps nationality was something to joke over, perhaps they had weathered the storm?

They returned once more to England before the answer was certain and drove pleasantly through a crisp afternoon to Lincoln where they admired the cathedral. Then on to Hull and the purpose of their journey, which was to see Arthur Bourchier, who was now rehearsing *Lord Adrian*. Immediately there was a row, similar to the one about *Alexander* and for a time as serious. The end was unacceptable. Dunsany talked of Greek tragedy and fate, Bourchier said that he understood that interesting point but the public would not and Beatrice was sure they would lose. Next day Dunsany thought of returning to his first draft which was a compromise and all were happy. However the play was presented during the election, the quarrels returned and somehow *Lord Adrian* never got to London. It was published in 1933 and ran for a fortnight at the Gate Theatre in Dublin in 1937, when it was praised by all for its dexterity and by James Agate for its charm and fantasy; it reads well. Bourchier died of a heart attack in South Africa and Dunsany used to claim that he was responsible and that Bourchier, inspired by the play, had been experimenting with rejuvenation. Yeats underwent the treatment and was referred to, behind his back, as 'The Gland Old Man'.

In London Dunsany had become an enthusiastic clubman and enjoyed such office as President of the Poets' Society. In particular, he went often to the Beefsteak, where he made friends with Elgar. Dunsany admired 'the natural simplicity with which he regarded his genius; he never boasted of it and never doubted it; his attitude was somewhat that of a child who has got a bird of paradise in the poultry yard at home: it is strange that it should have got there, but there it is'. Perhaps he envied Elgar his calm certainty. He would listen attentively to a creative artist and when Elgar said something like, 'Man has only added two arts to the world, music and architecture; all others he imitated', he remembered and repeated them. Naturally Beatrice was excluded from such club-bound friendships, but Sir Edward once came to tea at Dunstall to meet the Otto Kahns, who owned the New York Opera House and had been kind to the Dunsanys there. They talked easily of music. Arthur Villiers was present and remarked afterwards that Dunsany could no longer laugh at his, Arthur's, Jewish friends in the City, for he had capped them all.

In the spring Ireland was mercifully uneventful. The troubles really were ended. A reunion went off successfully:

23rd April 1924   Dunsany
Mr and Mrs Yeats staying. I wish I could remember Yeats' conversation accurately – not that it is lost as I believe he puts it all in lectures and essays, but because it is such a delight. The clearness and beauty of his phrases, and never without an interesting idea. He was developing the theory that shock is necessary to achievement – he cited Wordsworth, whose young revolutionary ideals had such a shock when he saw the French revolution in practice, that it made a great poet of him for 10 years and then drove him out of active life altogether after which he inevitably deteriorated. Perhaps unconsciously he was explaining his own new absorption in politics as necessary to his literary life. It is often pathetic to find great minds finding the most ingenious excuses for murders; it

makes for tolerance no doubt, but also for insincerity. I had not met Mrs Yeats before, but they seem a happy well-assorted couple; she is practical, appreciative, not a shadow, and has a sense of humour (being English it has not been lost in the late mess) and we thought him improved in little ways.

Yeats had married Miss Hyde-Lees seven years before, with Ezra Pound as best man. Mrs Yeats had family customs which Yeats tried for a time to adopt. 'I have given up twoing and fouring [going to sleep in the afternoon]' he said, 'but still read detective novels.'

If Ireland was no longer frightening, it was still depressing. The Dunsanys were glad to be back enjoying the evening in Kent:

'Rain; but it was fine after dinner so we walked along the terraces by the Mildmays' woods and up the hill at the south end and waited over the crest, and from 10.30 p.m. to 11 were surrounded by nightingales – I counted five quite close. It was quite dark going back through the wood and down the hill – and though Maude[1] and I had agreed earlier that we did feel much older and had reached a dull age, I am afraid we giggled like schoolgirls when I asked, "Is the path slimy?" and Mr R. saying sadly, "You will soon know", put a foot down and crashed to the ground. But the nightingales had gone to our heads.'

Dunsany was fond of nightingales and sitting on a summer evening to listen to them at Terling he was goaded by another giggling girl into saying 'What a bore these nightingales are, we can hardly hear Lady Betsy[2] laugh'.

The King of Elfland's Daughter, finished in March, was published and received favourable but rather automatic reviews, which tended to concentrate on the story and at the end include a phrase about the beautiful writing. Dedicated to Beatrice and the Dunsanys' own favourite, 'nearer to verse than most I have written' and 'seventy thousand words of very hard work', it was also nearer to being a fairy story and less a romantic adventure than *Rodrigues*. There are trolls and a magic sword and a beautiful princess whose hand needs winning and finally, as often in his early novels, not so much a

1. Maude Roundell had known Beatrice before either was married and her husband had been in the Coldstream with Dunsany.
2. Lady Betsy Gore.

climax as a descent into a foreseen happy ending. Sime contributed an effective frontispiece of the climax of a Unicorn
hunt. (After the war the publishers said they could not afford
more than one Sime per book and at the end of the 'twenties
ceased using even that.) However over another drawing Sime
and Dunsany disagreed – a rare event. For a collection of plays
Sime's conception included a squat monster and Dunsany
wrote to Beatrice 'part is beautiful, part is complicated, part
is unhealthy and the whole thing is unwholesome and intricate.
I've told Huntingdon *NO* and if he wants further talk to
telephone you.' So Sime substituted a charming and inoffensive
Pegasus.

Sime had a successful exhibition and was particularly charming when he stayed at Dunstall for a couple of nights. He quoted:
'last year I think summer was on a Wednesday', for its lack of
application to the summer they were enjoying, while Dunsany
and Beatrice picked enough wild strawberries for three pots of
jam. Some chess players emerged in the village, and though
Dunsany won, the blacksmith in particular could give him a
game. Slowly, six years late, peace was descending on both
their homes.

Not that Ireland was yet entirely free of hazards. The Taillteann Games, called after an ancient Queen and planned for
every four years, were really an all-embracing festival. The
Dunsanys did not think they would go and listen to the 'fatuous
self-glorification' that was sure to be talked, but they did grace
the Governor-General's Garden-Party: 'I didn't think Dublin
could produce such a dowdy collection – it was the forlornest
party I ever saw. I have only once been to a garden-party at the
Vice-regal Lodge before, when the King came after his coronation; now not only the beauty and interest, the very life of the
place seemed gone. However I curtsied to Tim, who was doing
his part well.'

Tim Healy, the Governor-General, had defended Parnell
and was sufficiently popular and moderate to be acceptable to
a large section of the Irish. Realising that many would make a
point of not bowing to the representative of the King, he shook
hands with his guests immediately at the top of a flight of steps
so that their position could not help being ambiguous. Beatrice
was determined to curtsy properly and found it dangerous. She

was mistaken at this party for someone who looked quite unlike her and Dunsany commented: 'Well, of course, you were the only two who had washed your necks.' Altogether it was an occasion to live through rather than one to enjoy. Later Beatrice sat next to de Valera himself at a dinner at Government House and, with so many likely topics and personalities to be avoided, got through by talking of her nephew, Frank Pakenham.

In spite of the garden-party being as bad as they expected, the Dunsanys softened towards the Taillteann Games. They were happy to put up two 'Distinguished Visitors'. One was the head of Sheffield University, Sir Henry Hadow. He was called Sir William Hadow officially and one of his labels read Sir James Hadow but his actual name was Sir Henry Hadow, so they called him Sir William Henry James to each other and introductions became a blur. The other was Augustus John. Gogarty, a mutual friend, told Dunsany that it would be unwise to give John too much whiskey. Dunsany was indignant and replied that a guest in his house should have as much as he wished. But Gogarty also told John that Dunsany was teetotal and that he would fly into a rage if his guests accepted alcohol. The result was that the poor painter refused everything, but went for a five-mile hike on Sunday to escape such a household and simultaneously qualify as a traveller and so be allowed a drink. The incident was much repeated and embroidered; Beatrice has no recollection of Dunsany teaching him to play the Irish harp as Compton Mackenzie alleges. As distinguished visitors they went to a banquet with 270 guests and, perhaps because they could drink what they liked, enjoyed it. Sir Henry was put out at not drinking the King's health, which pleased the Dunsanys as that was why they had not gone themselves, and the evening was threatened by a speech which was planning to run through all Irish History, but was mercifully stopped by force after half an hour at the battle of Clontarf, AD 1014.

They became still more involved in the Games when Dunsany entered the Chess Competition. He claimed later that he had been goaded into it by Yeats. Gogarty had entered a book of his for one of the competitions, assuring him that it would win. Yeats heard of this and was thought to have used his undoubted influence to stop it being so much as mentioned. So Dunsany decided to enter for something that Yeats could not control.

He went to Dublin each day with increasing hopes. Not wanting chess to loom too large in his life, Dunsany had played little over the last few years, though that May Uncle Horace had thought it worthwhile to write a detailed list of his defects from his failure to seize the initiative to his throwing away of winning positions. For once he was glad of his title. He felt that it led people to brush him aside as an aristocratic idler, which he usually resented; but for a chess player, especially one who could not remember the openings and badly needed practice, it was useful to be underestimated. His first opponent was from the North and returned there in defeat after lunch though he had more matches to play. At the end of another victory there was spontaneous applause. After a fortnight he had drawn once and won the rest. He was given a silver-gilt medal of the eponymous Queen of the Games, 'who has been dead', as he remarked, 'too many thousand years for one to know if it is like her'. When he returned to Dunsany, everyone leaned from the windows and cheered.

While he was busy winning, Randal ran the house-party, whisking the guests off to the races before a ball at Headfort, after which those who still had energy played tennis in their evening clothes until 7.30 in the morning. Dunsany liked cheerful young people and they thought 'The Lord' great fun and egged him on to tell stories and to sing songs in his tremendous voice which made nonsensical words sound doubly ludicrous. Sometimes the songs were personal or topical; often they served the purpose of channelling off his annoyance. Irritated by a pompous announcement that the Irish Free State had no war with Turkey, he bellowed a parody on 'Yes, we have no bananas', and fury gave way to laughter.

Visitors flowed through the house once more: Randal's friends, cricketers, Padraic Colum and his wife for one night. They had an anti-Yeats story, which seems to have been almost obligatory equipment for the Irish intelligentsia:

YEATS: My wife can read Plotinus in the original Latin.
GOGARTY: Arabic, Yeats.
YEATS: Er, Arabic.

Mrs Ford, a literary American, was a trial. She stayed for a month and claimed to have read every book of the Irish Renaissance. So Beatrice took her to Tara, of which she gave no sign of having heard and she did not care to get out of the car. However when they passed the ruins of a house burnt the year before, she was all eagerness and only a locked gate thwarted a minute inspection. Beatrice was disgusted. Mrs Ford was a keen supporter of agitators the world over as Dunsany was not. She was also deaf and became deafer when she sensed hostility. Towards the end of her stay at Dunsany it seems unlikely that she heard anything at all.

They crossed to England in October on the anniversary of the torpedoing of the Leinster and the ship slowed to drop a wreath over the place where she had gone down in 1918. Beatrice was exhausted, but Dunsany went to shoot in Yorkshire with the Mexboroughs, a family who knew what they were taking on by having him without Beatrice and could, more or less, cope. A letter reveals him in high spirits:

Arden Hall, Helmsley, Yorks.

D. to B.D.

. . . We started capping verses at dinner last night till we came to V. Mrs [Guy] Baring said she could only think of veal, vine and violets; so I suggested 'Veal, vine and violets have layed waste my days' BYRON. And when that didn't pass I tried

Veal that first led me
To these paths of sin.

Same Author.

Then Agnes[1] said 'But *how* could veal etc. etc.'

And tho' Marjorie now and then interpolated, 'Don't be too literal-minded', an argument ensued between Agnes and me in which I pointed out that if Byron had mentioned veal (and if he didn't he was of no use to us) that is the morbid introspective way in which he would have blamed it for his errors. And above Agnes reiterating, 'but how *could* veal . . .' and her mother's appeals to her not to be literal-minded I argued that in my own dislike of it I could suspect veal of anything . . .

Politics were at last taking an acceptable course. The first Labour Government lasted less than a year and the Conserva-

1. Lady Agnes Savile, the Mexboroughs' eldest daughter, then about sixteen.

tives swept back into office, where they were to remain under Stanley Baldwin until 1929. Armistice Day was declared in Dublin with much singing of *God Save the King*, a woman in a red white and blue scarf, who could boast, 'A ruffian tried to take this scarf from me but I used my hatpin till I spoilt it', and no counter-demonstrations till nightfall. At a dinner-party Beatrice sat next to Neville Chamberlain, whom she admired for turning down the Chancellorship for the unpopular Ministry of Health. She asked why Americans minded *Main Street*, a detailed and depressing account of life in the mid-West, more than the British had minded Dickens fifty years before, and he said that nobody could take Dickens for anything but a satirist, but that there was an uncertain feeling that Sinclair Lewis might be writing truth.

In January 1925 Dunsany went up the Nile which he had not seen for over fifteen years. After some sight-seeing in Cairo he travelled in a comfortable steamer 'though one of the staff said to me, deprecatingly, of dinner 'Cook, he is no great business'.[1] From Wadi Halfa he was in a train looking out on the desert and longing for it. At Khartoum he was introduced by Sir George and Lady Schuster to Beethoven's Symphonies, which he had not known, 'a deficiency as deplorable as for a mountaineer never to have seen the Himalayas'.[2] He set off; once more by river, with a gramophone and the whole of the Seventh Symphony but the needles he ordered did not arrive in time. However, 'Africa grows such things more abundantly than Europe grows grass, and I found that mimosa thorns did very well.'[3] It makes a curious picture, the enormous bearded peer winding his gramophone and changing his mimosa on the most deserted stretches of the Nile; he knew and loved every note by the time he returned.

On February 8th he could write to Beatrice: 'Last night there was a full moon and we heard the hippos roaring: Bag so far 1 Mrs Grey, 1 Python, 4 White-eared Cob, 2 Reed-buck, 1 Tiang, 4 Waterbuck. 5 p.m. We are going through papyrus swamps again, probably the least explored part of the earth.' Mrs Grey is a waterbuck, not a tragic error. The first hint of the python was when his guide put his slippers on. 'I interpreted this as a precaution against a snake, and so it was, but such a

1-3. Letter to Beatrice.

snake as could have eaten him as well with his slippers on or off, a nineteen foot python with his head rested on one of his hugest folds looking at us with big yellow eyes.' He could not bring himself to shoot hippo or giraffe.

On the way back he saw more sights, the spot where Gordon fell at Khartoum, the temple at Karnak, and the Valley of the Kings, where he had a special pass so that,

'the sweating crowd was parted on my left and on my right, and I walked through dry.

'And four or five of us were led into the tomb down the slope and given about three minutes there, and we saw Tut-Ankh-Amen lying in his coffin, not a corpse without illusion, but the body as he desired it to appear, a form entirely of gold, lying calmly there gazing upwards.'

Though he revels in writing about them, the Egyptian Gods and temples do not seem to have had any greater effect on him than they do on most tourists. They seem so much in his style, but his response was respectably enthusiastic rather than overwhelming. It is true that he was no longer writing in his early strain with which they particularly accord.

The Dunsanys recorded an instance of telepathy (or a remarkable coincidence if that is preferred) in the letters exchanged while he was on this trip. Beatrice wrote saying she felt 'so uneasy. Are you all right?' which was an uncharacteristically illogical gesture as there could be no answer for weeks. Dunsany replied that he was fine but told her to look up his letter written on the day she had worried (but naturally received after she had written hers) and she found that he had said, 'Tomorrow is a dangerous prospect. We are going after buffalo.' In fact the engine of the boat went wrong, they could not land and so the danger was never real, though Dunsany's apprehension had been.

Beatrice spent the time he was away in Italy with her mother. On their way home they saw John Barrymore play *Hamlet* in London and thought him magnificent. He came to tea to hear *Lord Adrian* and took it away in delight. 'Didn't you like him very much?' asked Beatrice, excited herself. 'I always like them at first,' replied Dunsany, thinking of past disappointments. He was right not to have hopes of Barrymore.

Dunsany was having a fine time, but he was not working. He had written two pages of a sequel to *Rodrigues* almost a year before, but let it lapse. Beatrice felt her conscience prick, knew she had followed the path of least resistance for too long and successfully roused him. He re-started *The Charwoman's Shadow* and though he stayed and shot with, among others, the Mexboroughs at Arden, and the Talbot-Cliftons at Kildalton, he finished it by the end of October. It is a distinct technical improvement on its predecessor; the plot progressing to a foreseen end instead of just stumbling forward. The hero, Ramon Alonzo, is sent to study alchemy to restore the family fortunes and has a horrid time with a magician who tricks him out of his shadow. There is an effective scene when he has made himself a new one and spends a pleasant day in the ordinary world but as evening is drawing on, the girl he is with suddenly screams; all the other shadows have lengthened but his is still the short neat one he had designed for the morning. However all turns out well in the end.

Meanwhile everything seemed to be turning out well for the Dunsanys. Peace was real and, if *Lord Adrian* was not going to follow up the success of *If*, which it still might, surely other plays would; meanwhile he was enjoying the novels. Trouble came as before from an unforeseen quarter. This time it was money. In the second week of May 1925, Dunsany winkled an answer about tax out of his lawyers. It was worse than the worst he had feared, roughly that he must pay in both England and Ireland. Beatrice had been sad that the only member of her family who understood what she felt about Ireland, her sister Mary, was leaving now that her son Edward was married. Now she wrote that her melancholy had been mistaken, for:

'It is our turn. Dunsany, which we kept going all through the bad days, where at last we were feeling we had come through and the future was easy, where we had managed to keep on all those dependent on it, will have to be closed down. I doubt if we could face it if we were there, but it is the only thing to do. As usual one never fears the right thing – I left it more light-heartedly than usual, full of summer plans, and the garden full of tulips and hyacinths and the grass of daffodils. And Randal's beloved harriers must go – we'll keep some hunters and picnic there at Xmas. What a stupid book this has become.'

Things were not as bad as they seemed. She was able to add, 'Lawyers go by law only, but the Treasury does mitigate the law with a little common sense.' The extra tax could be reclaimed. Unfortunately there was another half to the crisis, the almost traditional failure of a trustee.

Since the war relations with Uncle Horace had been friendly. If he wrote of Dunsany's chess, 'my criticisms of his mistakes will I expect greatly improve his game', the patronising note was forgiven. When he told Dunsany in 1922 that he must decide whether he was British or Free State Irish, which might be a nice point for him, but was running close to treason in his nephew's view, it was accepted as part of his known political instability. Two years before he had written from Oxford, 'I have had a little set-back and realise, *Non sum qualis eram,*' and gone on to quote the Poet Laureate, Robert Bridges, saying of Dunsany, 'He writes well – he writes well', which according to Uncle Horace was the highest praise he bestowed. Kind opinions were always popular at Dunsany and his courage in illness and adversity was recognised. But he had claimed, and been granted, not only affection but respect. His self-proclaimed status as a sophisticated business figure and man-of-the-world had been accepted at face value. He had written impressive letters full of figures and efficient-sounding language about the future of the coal mines – now it appeared that the coal was running out, nothing had been put aside and so a large slice of income was to be cut off without warning. Uncle Horace was relegated irrevocably to a lower category, whose members should be ashamed of themselves. That he had lost a great deal of his own money was no excuse. It appeared that he was perilously close to being 'not quite straight', guilty of at least culpable negligence, if not of dishonesty.

Time softened censure a little but their old relationship was never even faintly restored. A letter from the Beefsteak to Beatrice in 1928 shows the difference and that it remained.

'I saw Uncle Horace. I was there a long time. He said "20 years ago you had 100,000 where you now have 200,000. Even if you lost 50,000 you'd be 50,000 richer than you were twenty years ago. I utterly fail to understand how you can think it matters. You have menservants and keep up three houses." When I said Irish land is worth half what it was twenty years ago, he said "that doesn't affect you. You don't have to sell it." Tell the General these points. He may see them. I'm sorry I can't.'

So Dunsany could be kept going but economies were needed. Beatrice made plans:

'We can cut all cricket, schooltreats, dances at Dunsany, try and let 66 [Cadogan Place], but these are drops in the ocean. We met a man at the Ainleys yesterday who will probably take *If* for U.S.A. [He did not.] And we have *Alexander* coming out this autumn [it did not] and Ramon Alonzo – *The Charwoman's Shadow* – should be ready for the Spring for it is slipping along easily [it was]; but there is a lot to make up, and the leaf-sweeping industry seems to absorb endless Clynches and McTaggarts who can't all be thrown out. My only feeling is begin somewhere at once and other economies will follow more easily. But I don't see how we can keep the harriers.

Neither E. nor I are really extravagant so that personal economies won't amount to much; nearly all, except perhaps letting 66, must be things that will affect other people and that is so hard to do.'

Mrs Ainley had been named 'The Opium Dream' by Dunsany and lived up to the name with a promise to put on *Mr Faithful* at the Lyric, Hammersmith, which came to nothing, apparently because Arnold Bennett wanted changes but did not say what they were. The hope of earning a significant amount from Dunsany's writing was never fulfilled. Five men were sacked from the garden, nine from the farm. They chose those that would be least hard hit, but knew that they would not find other jobs in Ireland. Things had not changed so much that they did not get a letter threatening to burn the castle if they did not take the ex-soldiers back; but the sting had gone out of such words. Dunsany surprisingly disapproved of Randal steeple-chasing for reasons of safety not morality, though Randal was good at it. However the terriers were permissible and he had one last season. Standing on a bank at a meet a farmer was heard to say to a priest, 'The young Lord is a terror to go,' and the priest replied, 'Nothing stops him.' Next year he was to go into the 16th Lancers. The house in Cadogan Place was let for a few months, as they had in fact planned before the worry about money. *The Charwoman's Shadow* appeared and was greeted with the same pleasant reviews as *Rodrigues* except for an increase in the still small minority who found them sickly or artificial. It sold better than any of his books so far, but novels, then as now, were not likely to earn huge sums.

Dunsany does not seem to have been downcast. A man came to the door with a battery wireless, which Randal and Beatrice bought. He was strongly against the purchase, and almost instantaneously became an ardent listener. He resisted television in its turn and there he did not recant, though he appeared on it. His snipe bag for the year was an impressive 570, beaten the year after with 600. He sent four birds to Lady Celia Coates and only the labels arrived. So he sent four more and labelled them all over the box, 'Four Poisoned Rats'. They arrived intact.

When first the Coal and then the General Strike began in May, Dunsany's reaction was consistent with his other views, naïve but not vicious. 'We all had jobs in those days; it was a queer time . . . There appeared to be no malice upon either side; it was only a test.' He admired other strike-breakers such as Lord Montagu who drove a train and had grime in the cracks of his nails, 'deeper than soap would go,' and told Beatrice to be sure to tip the lift man at Victoria as he was Captain Fane, a friend of his. He heard the story of a woman who shouted at a lorry-load of strike-breakers: 'You bloody bastards', and thought the retort, 'Hullo, mother. Are you here?' neat.

This was conventional for his class and generation. He was not heartless but could fail to imagine other people's difficulties. In this case Beatrice agreed with him. She in her turn admired a friend, Lady Lloyd Martin, who had been on canteen shift for milk distribution since 6.30 in the morning and was planning to work all night. Though uninterested in politics she was serious about such crises, and where Dunsany's attitude seems to have been tinged with the feeling that it was all an enormous lark, she wrote that nobody could ever forgive the Government if it backed down. They both consented wholeheartedly when a friend said: 'I have seen too much history made; my father died in 1905 aged seventy-two and had seen nothing but the Crimean War and the opening of the Great Exhibition.' Moscow was thought to be making a big effort, the threat was real enough but Beatrice, recognising it, still could not feel excited or frightened – only bored. Dunsany wanted to be a special constable but was too old, and when he got a job, he started on Monday only to find that it was officially all over on Wednesday.

In the summer he went through some old notes and ideas and turned them into four short plays. These and three more were published in 1928 as *Seven Modern Comedies*. They are more conventional than his earlier plays. The writing is simple and as they are set in contemporary England with more humans than Gods or fairies, they reveal something of their author's views. There is Dunsany on the Modern Girl: 'you smoke when they smoke, you drive their cars, you play all their games, you talk their talk, you . . . there's nothing apparently different between you and them. Of course they know you're a girl when they stop to think' – but he likes her for all that. This one, *Atalanta in Wimbledon*, as a result of reading Tennyson, offers her hand and income to anyone who can beat her at ping-pong, unsuccessful contenders to be put to the sword by her faithful retainer.

Personal experience and politics appear. The author of a short play keeps interrupting rehearsals and resisting changes in his work – to no avail. Russian peasants planning revolution have a vision of the future, full of starvation and misery. With *The Jest of Hahalaba* we are back with magic; on New Year's Eve Sir Arthur Strangways summons a spirit who gives him a file of next year's *Times*. Browsing through share prices which will make his fortune, he works his way back to tomorrow's paper and sees his obituary – which gives him a fatal shock.

Dunsany had re-met Kipling, whom he greatly admired as a writer and a man. He found him 'full of mirth, so lightly repressed and so near the surface, that it was ready to break out at any moment, and a zest that one can only call boyish and a deep sympathy which made him probably the kindest man I ever knew.'

The Kiplings asked them to lunch at Batemans, their house in Sussex, and Lady Jersey's brother, Rowland Leigh, was there with his wife Mabel. 'I haven't married a genius, as both of you have,' she said to the other two wives, 'but I assure you he can be quite as temperamental and tiresome.' The Dunsanys saw a mill that had paid tax ever since the Domesday Book, and admired the house, which they found as charming as their host. 'His eyes dilate,' Beatrice wrote, 'in a way I never saw quite equalled. He told me Tim Heely turned atheist for a brief time but was quickly brought to heel by the priests and that during an argument he told Kipling that he believed everything they said. "You believe they can shorten your grandmother's years in purgatory?" said K. "Certainly." "Then I won't argue with you," said K. "Bring me the man who pulls the strings." '

A lunch at Dunstall led Beatrice to the conclusion that 'Actresses can be a bit catty'. Nancy Price had married a member of the cast of *The Gods of the Mountain* and the friend-ship that had resulted with the Dunsanys outlived the run of the play and the marriage. She brought down Ivor Novello and another actress, Miss Doble. When Miss Doble refused wine, Nancy Price said, 'She lives on cocktails,' but all the other had to do to win the round was look dreamily beautiful and murmur, 'Now who invented that?' Novello sat on a cushion on the floor, presumably looking dreamily beautiful too, listened attentively to *Lord Adrian* and was charming and polite, but nothing came of it.

Things were coming to nothing a little too often but this was the year of 600 snipe, and his new novel, *The Blessing of Pan*, a greater achievement and the forerunner and equal of his best novels. The plot is more than a string of incidents, the language is vital but controlled and he is writing of something more immediate than the Gods and fairies that enchanted him. His hero is a vicar; all clergymen are good in Dunsany's work, though in this one his superiors are foolish and his predecessor is wicked (and so turns out to be a false clergyman). This is a particularly nice vicar and the book concerns his struggle with Paganism in Kent. The lure of the wild is in conflict with respect for civilised order and decency. As a gentleman who came of age before Victoria died yet sought to express emotions he did not understand, educated at Eton, Sandhurst, and on the bogs of Ireland, an admirer of fairy stories and the British Empire, Dunsany's own nature was deeply involved in the struggle. In the book, Pan is the victor and, though never an orthodox Christian, Dunsany cannot but disapprove.

His passion for the countryside round Dunstall floods through the book which is lent further interest by the suspicion that the

hero and heroine may be an unconscious portrait of himself and
Beatrice. In superficial ways Elderick Anwrel, the vicar, is
similar to Dunsany in that he knows about orchids, flints and
chess, preaches without notes and makes speeches to the village
cricket team. His wife Augusta (a name with the same 'feel'
to it as 'Beatrice'?) is a woman of strong principle, a pillar of
sense and understanding in his reeling magical world; and
naturally he knew no other marriage so well. This is scarcely
evidence, let alone proof; but the passages between them strike
a familiar note of mutual understanding.

When the villagers are following a strange, threatening music
that comes from the hill in the evening, we see how Elderick
relies on his wife in difficult times.

He entered the house and there was Augusta reading, a welcome
sight, a new world to him. There at last was someone who would
never go over that hill, never find any lure in that nonsensical music.
    She looked up at him coming in so late.
    'They have all gone over the hill with Tommy Duffin,' he said.
    'Have they?' she said quickly.
    'Yes. It is very foolish of them,' he said.
    But she did not answer at once. 'Yes. Yes, of course,' she said
then, looking straight in front of her.
    And he knew it was no use saying to her things that he did not
feel.
    She too must have heard that music but she did not speak of it.
    Then he broke the silence by asking about their maid.
    'Is Marion here?' he said.
    'No,' she replied.
    And he knew that Marion had gone away after the other.
    Whether or not Mrs Tweedy were gone he did not ask. They had
cold supper in any case, so she might be still in the kitchen.
    And the meal passed almost in silence. Augusta could not make
light of it all now as he had so much hoped she would; for he felt
the need of being woken out of a dream that was too dark and much
too long.

Elderick needs assistance still more in small things as when
he writes to his bishop of his doubts.

    'I shouldn't sent this letter, dear,' she said.
    'What?' said the vicar, 'Not send it?'
    'Not quite as it is,' she replied.

'But, it's a thing he must know,' he said.

'Then, whatever it is, I should tell him,' she said. 'Go and see him, you know. But not write.'

'But why not write it,' he asked. He relied so much on her sense that he did not question her next remark although it much surprised him.

'I don't think he wants a letter quite like that,' she said.

'He doesn't want it?' was all he said.

'I don't think so,' she said, 'but of course you could tell him verbally.'

'But I can't put it clearer than that in conversation; I couldn't put it as clear.'

'But you could see how he was taking it,' she said.

'Go over to Snichester?' he said.

'I think that's best,' she answered.

'Oh dear me,' said the vicar, he was thinking of all his friendly familiar surroundings and how he must take farewell of his knick-knacks again almost as soon as they had been restored to him.

'You need only go for one night,' she said, 'You could take the 2.45 and put up at the Crozier.'

'If I went in the morning,' he said hopefully. 'I could get back the same day.'

'The afternoon would be the time to see him,' she said.

She seemed to know, and he said no more.

And without knowing the news or the bishop, the reader is sure she is right. That seems a convincing example of how small decisions might be taken by the Dunsanys except that he may perhaps have been somewhat less tractable at times and used a stronger protest than, 'Oh dear me'.

The reviews were less favourable than usual finding it uneven and deploring the final triumph of Pan.

Dunsany took up painting in oils and comments honestly: 'I do not think I had any aptitude for painting, because I found it very difficult and I only got there by hard work ... I soon selected trees to paint: they are full of interest and character and I think I had the feeling that I could paint a tree and perhaps get a branch a yard out of place and it would not be much criticised whereas ... if I got a nose an inch out of place, the picture would be absurd ...' A.E. gave him advice and encouragement. About his writing A.E. said in a letter, 'I think that more people read your books in Ireland than you imagine

and I doubt whether Yeats, Lady Gregory or myself fare better
with our own countrymen than you seem to think you do.'

A.E. later sat for his portrait. Dunsany reckoned that he had
a style of his own and an ability to catch a likeness, soon learned
to place noses, and continued to enjoy his new hobby.

In August 1927 Randal came of age and there were celebra-
tions at Dunsany Castle. The Irish Free State was now running
so smoothly that it was possible to light a big bonfire on a hill,
and Randal's sardonic remarks about blazes in the past evoked
appreciative chuckles from the crowd. The following year he
joined the Indian Cavalry and set sail on February 22nd for
three years abroad.

Dunsany asked, 'Have you any feeling against it?'

Beatrice began to say the obvious things she minded, such
as not being prepared for the idea of losing him altogether,
and the drawbacks of India.

'That's logic,' said Dunsany. 'I meant feeling.'

And she said no, for as a matter of fact, though hardly daring
to admit it, her instinct was that it would be all to the good.
'Neither have I,' said Dunsany.

Yet he missed Randal so much that he, who never smoked,
smoked every day for a week; and Beatrice was ashamed to
miss him as she did.

The pattern of their life was settled and remained so. It
was agreeable and productive if a little repetitive. Even the
expeditions which broke into it were to places he had visited
before. In March Dunsany left for America to lecture at the
University of Philadelphia.

He felt about American hospitality that, 'if anyone deserved
such kindness on account of his work, he ought to get on with
his work'. But this was not a lecture tour, it was to teach students
and he felt justified. On arrival he wrote: 'interviewers much
the same as ever, photographers worse.'

Major George Putnam, his publisher, put him up and
explained the Battle of Gettysburg in which he, the Major,
had fought. Mr Pond popped up and persuaded Dunsany,
without much difficulty to give a few lectures after all, but he
turned down a rival's offer for a series next year.

New York was 'the same mad rush. Very stimulating.' At a
party where Dunsany was getting more attention than James

Stephens, the short poet generously said, pointing, 'He is so much larger than I; he *needs* more recognition.' Perhaps he did; in any case there was enough to go round.

He wrote cheerfully on April 6th:

300 Park Avenue.
No radio folk pay, damn them. But I suppose it is something to talk to 16 million people.

. . . I went through Putnam's offices today and stung them. I did not go like the hurricane, but tactfully like the mosquito, stinging the right people in exactly the right places . . . This really is a marvellous city; there is a vast building at the end of this avenue with a curving road running through it and Mrs Rockefeller tells me that trains run through this building in the basement where other people have rats. And the shops are like Paris and the hospitality is like that of romantic fiction.

Mrs Avery Rockefeller asked him to stay at Greenwich which was 'like an English country house, of course with beautiful things in it, well worth seeing for the £5 that I gave the butler and the £5 that someone stole.' The marvellous city was changing: 'They are pulling down New York. One no longer sees along Fifth Avenue a chalet from Switzerland and a castle from Normandy, side by side with a pyramid from Egypt, but great American structures going up, as they should, expressing America and the age.'

He completed his lectures and classes in Philadelphia pleasantly enough, though there was a slight stirring from the uncritical acclaim that had washed around his last visit. His audiences were told that the only test of a good play was whether or not it could quicken the pulse beats of an audience. A bad play was one of which people said the dialogue was very good, which was like a house that was praised for being made of excellent bricks. They were emphatically not told anything of technique. He gave other lectures. At Cornell after a lecture someone said what a good name Sime was for Sime and he offered Rhibelungzanedroom and Rhibelungzaha as improvements.

Back in New York he fought with unfamiliar central heating. 'I asked a housemaid if there was any way to open my window. She seemed amused at so simple a question. She came and said there was a way to open it but that she was not strong enough.

Nor was I, nor was a log of wood, but the handle of the tongs did it for evermore.' A clash with Irish Nationalism was inevitable in America, but he remained unruffledly patronising:

I don't think Americans can ever mean to be rude; they would go far out of their way to show the field of Waterloo to a Frenchman because they believe it to be interesting. Lunching with as good a family as there is in America I went on with one of their guests to a lecture-hall where she was to introduce me. Dialogue in the car.

She: Do the Free State recognise your title?
I: I don't care whether they do or not.
She: It is a title that was given by the Crown is it not?
I: Yes.
She: Then I don't think I quite know the status of the Free State.
I: Canada.
She: But there are no peers in Canada.
I: No.

And when she introduced me, she did deliberately so as Mr. Dunsany, twice.

She apologised afterwards. Dunsany was still lecturing a bit, but social engagements were thrust on him so he simply booked a passage home and stuck to it. Meanwhile he heard Paul Robeson in *Show Boat* with Mrs Percy Rockefeller, and *Tristan and Isolde* with Mrs Harriman; he was photographed by a woman whose 'line is the Higher Smile for Bigger and Better Celebrities', received a letter from 'an *admirador* in Cuba who collects the *autografas* of the most important *personalidades* of the *Mundo*' who thought him 'one of the most genial literary figures of all the epochs', decided 'the movies are perfectly worthless' and calculated he had earned £1,000–£3,000 less expenses.

Back for springtime in Kent he wrote a lot of verse and 'the *Saturday Evening Post* took all my best poems and, with a very accurate judgment, refused all my inferior ones'. Some were printed in England too and in 1929 he published *50 Poems*, which reviewers found pleasant, though in one case 'pleasantly platitudinous', the acceptable offering of a minor poet. His verse never rose above this level. Four lines from *Ode to a Dublin Critic*, a rare reply to a public attack, show how he still felt he was abused for being a peer:

From little fountain-pens they wring
The last wee drop of inky spite:
'We do not like the kind of thing
That lords', they say, 'most likely, write.'

That spring he played Capablanca, chess champion of the world. Selfridges arranged for each of seven counties to play three men simultaneously against him and Dunsany was eager to prove that he was not representing Kent only because he was president of their chess association. He muddled his opening, thought that he was to be humiliated by a swift disaster but regained his position at the cost of a pawn. Uncle Horace had always said that it was his middle game that was fine and he excelled himself by winning back the pawn and eventually extracting a draw from the champion. The game was recorded in *The Times*. Another Kentish player drew and Capablanca lost one game to another county so Kent scored two half-points to tie first place. It was the zenith of Dunsany's chess career and he was given a cocktail-shaker as a prize. This he found 'as useful as reindeer-harness' and exchanged it for 'the most useful Thermos flask I ever had'. Capablanca became a friend and played at Arthur Villiers' boys' clubs.

Though he wasn't working on any major project the pattern of life was filled in with poems, stories and sport. Toomey managed after years of effort to cajole a flight of ducks to a pond at Dunsany; later, during the war, a neighbour, who had been trying to lure him away in his master's absence, asked Toomey how to attract ducks, and was told to cut up car tyres and to spread them around. Whether he followed this curious advice is unknown; certainly Toomey was completely loyal. Dunsany bicycled about from time to time putting his long legs down to stand steady while he shot a rabbit. In the house he would occasionally break off a conversation and ask a nephew or friend to open the window through which he would then dispatch another.

His hamper of food for a day's shooting was complicated and must not be skimped though he rarely ate any of it; it included whiskey, which he never touched, but Toomey enjoyed. This ritual went on for thirty years.

Dunsany stayed with Gogarty on an island in Galway Lake and then went to Arden for grouse and Kildalton for stags.

Lady Dunsany recorded someone earnestly asking Lord Balfour for his view of eternity, and his reply, 'Julia Maguire, when she comes to luncheon and stays to tea.' Also Sir Ronald Storrs stayed and told of a man sailing back to England during the war who drank a bottle of champagne each day. 'You seem surprised,' he said, 'but I drink this because I have never been able to afford it.'

'That is why I don't drink it,' said Storrs.

'I am quite sure,' said the other, 'that this ship will be torpedoed and all the wine bills lost.'

Next day it was torpedoed and the man finished his glass and said, 'You see', before taking to the boats.

In the autumn Dunsany left gaps in some stories of the East to be filled with local colour later, for he planned to go to India for the first time that winter. Though it was successful he disapproved of this technique and did not use it again. He sailed with Beatrice in December and 'as usually happens in ships on long voyages we had a chess-tournament, and I won a small silver cup.' His reaction to Bombay was akin to his feeling for the purity of the desert – a positive pleasure in the absence of civilisation. Seeing the mud houses on the outskirts he thought not of the horrors of poverty but of their unity with nature, the lack of artificial encumbrance in their lives.

They had several letters of introduction and blended sight-seeing with visits to friends and friends of friends. The Taj Mahal by moonlight, far from looking like a biscuit-box, inspired two romantic poems. A visit to the Nawab of Rampur was so successful that they stayed almost a month and then returned twice. The first evening was perhaps the stickiest, with the Nawab cross-examining Dunsany.

'Why does so-and-so not marry?' he asked. 'Why does his father not command him to do so? I command my sons and they marry. Do I not?'

Receiving no contradiction on this point, he turned to Dunsany.

'Does he not like women?'

'Oh yes.'

A happy smile came over the Highness's face. 'Ah,' he said. 'Tell me something about that.'

'Well,' Dunsany struggled on, 'he does to a certain extent.

And then on the other hand ... What I really mean is, he doesn't like them too much nor on the other hand, too little. But just right.'

The whole large house-party sat round in silence, but the smile of anticipation had faded out of His Highness's face and he said: 'You are very discreet.'

But if Dunsany was a disappointment as a gossip, he was an appreciative guest. On a wide lawn surrounded by plantations of peaches and mangoes he watched flocks of pigeons being drilled by men who could make them wheel to left or right by flapping a white cloth. Far away to the north-east over the elephant stables shone the white peaks of the Himalayas. Having drawn a game of chess with the champion of the world, Dunsany here found 'the Master of the Universe', who, moved 'rapidly but with absolute composure; adopted too rash an opening and lost.' Dunsany decently kept silent. Their host admired Britain greatly and had sent his cook to Edinburgh to learn how to make porridge.

Randal got some leave and came to Rampur. On Christmas Eve, he, Dunsany and Prince Dillon, a younger son, went on a shooting expedition. About twenty miles from home the car broke down and simultaneously the sun set and a storm began. The Nawab sent out five motors, his second son in one (which eventually found them) his eldest son with the Cavalry, and started himself in a Rolls-Royce which soon stuck. The only thing that cheered him was that he consulted the Koran and opened at the sentence: 'They shall return but with difficulties.'

When they returned in a bullock cart, Dunsany got out saying, 'Happy Christmas, Your Highness.' They had to stay up an hour and a half saying how little it was Prince Dillon's fault and how well he had managed the bullocks in spite of his painful toothache, for it was not a small thing to have mislaid two honoured guests and he was likely to be beaten. At last Dunsany said that he had not asked the Nawab for anything, for his every wish was granted before it was half-formed, but now he had a request. The Nawab was delighted. Pause. 'Forgive Prince Dillon.' He pondered a moment and then he said yes. Beatrice saw that the episode needed rounding off and leaning forward suddenly, took the Nawab's hand and shook it.

For a Christmas present the Nawab gave Dunsany a huge walking-stick with a great gold knob at the end engraved with the Crown of Rampur. He was dared to carry it in London, but surprisingly refused. Dunsany wrote of this time:

'A gun fired at sunset and dawn throughout Ramadan so that Mohammedans should not make the mistake of eating at the wrong time. And every now and then throughout the night a watchman at the edge of the fruit trees would cry out loudly that he had seen a thief, so that if there happened to be one he should consider himself detected. In the palace a band such as one hears in large London hotels [not surprisingly as it had been brought intact from a large London hotel] played for us every evening, and it was some while before the Nawab realised how greatly I should have preferred to hear Indian music.'

When he was to leave to visit the Maharajah of Benares, who was a Hindu whereas Rampur was a Mohammedan, Rampur protested that he should take a cook as 'he will feed you like a dog'. Indeed there was no porridge but as compensation the Maharajah's palace rose sheer from the Ganges with the exotic beauty that most appealed to Dunsany.

On his return to Rampur, the Nawab mounted a much more elaborate shooting expedition than any they had yet undertaken. Police guarded the road for twenty miles 'to protect me from either imaginary dangers or real ones of which I knew nothing'; the camp included rows of shops and a triumphal arch (which was unfortunately blown over). Mounted on an elephant, he shot pigs, swamp deer, peacock, crocodiles, panther and partridges. The last allowed him to make less travelled countrymen guess what animal that is not a dog had retrieved his birds. The answer was an elephant, who passed them up to the mahout with his trunk. When he left Rampur, with many thanks and a promise to return, the Nawab promised that next time his camp should have a thousand men, and that he would come to Dunsany. He could wash only in running water for religious reasons (on trains servants had to stand on the roof and pour) but Beatrice, confident that she would not be tested, said that was the easiest thing in the world to arrange.

A trip North to Mardan where Randal was stationed and

then they stayed with the Viceroy, Lord Irwin, later Lord
Halifax, in the building designed by Lutyens in New Delhi.

'One of my impressions of the Viceroy's house is of a long passage
leading to the drawing-room, and as one walked along it in the
evening, one would pass the sweep of a large archway through
which the sunset was shining and then another and another, so that
sunset after sunset would flash into view like great pictures. And
another thing I remember was walking about at night, while the
ball was going on, looking at various rooms, and suddenly seeing
stars over one's head: the bold fancy of that open space amongst the
stone was very imposing at that time of year, whatever it may have
been in the monsoon.'

They continued their tour and stayed with the Maharajah
of Gwalior. There was a large party at the palace their first
night and 'the finest chandelier I have ever seen.' The next
morning Beatrice received 'ten silver bowls of milk which had
been put out in the dew all night and beaten up into froth at
sunrise, for my breakfast.' There had been one thing missing
from the pleasure of Dunsany's shooting – a large omission.
He had not had a shot at a tiger though several attempts had
been made to give him one. So that morning he was whisked
to the top storey of a little stone tower past which the many
beaters were to drive a tiger. He had listened to much talk of
the correct technique and kept quiet. Now he simply walked
downstairs without explaining himself, asked someone to un-
block the door and took up a position outside. His only response to agitation from the tower was to ask for a second gun.
He did not have long to wait.

'One thing astonished me as I saw my first tiger, and that was that
he was like a tiger. I remember my surprise clearly still. I had been
accustomed to see Zebras, fairly close in bright sunlight, look as
though their hides were of unstriped chocolate, and Barbary sheep
as though they were mere sunlight shining on bare rock, and rabbits
like patches of mud, and spotted panthers looking jet black; in
fact everything in nature appears to a hunter delusive and yet here
was a tiger looking just like a tiger as a public man of whom one
has seen many cartoons may surprise one by looking exactly like
himself . . . And here the story ends. For when you press the trigger,
and are lucky, it is all over; if you are unlucky there is a lot more to
think about and to say. But this tiger was dead.'

After a pleasant stay they went to Bombay, accepted some ripening mangoes from an agent of the Nawab of Rampur as a parting gift and set sail for London. Dunsany started to write on the train to Bombay (*The Electric King*, 'my best story') and had much material stored up in his brain.

PART FOUR

The Thirties

IT was 1930 when Dunsany returned from India. In the past decade a repetition of the success of *If* had seemed at first inevitable, then likely, always possible. Now fashion that had been friendly was turning decisively away from all that he admired of poetry and imagination to realism and social conscience. He thought of himself as a dramatist but had almost given up hope of recapturing the London stage, and in fact he did not do so. This was part of his reason for turning to novels, which, with collections of stories, were to prove his most lasting works. Dunsany had left half a book of stories to go to India and to these he eagerly returned. As long ago as 1925 he had created Jorkens, a senior member of the Billiards Club, which had no billiard table but a deal of conversation. Jorkens has travelled much and tells tales that enable Dunsany to use his own experiences in Egypt, India and, particularly, Africa, without being confined by mere accuracy. Typically he will recount fantastic events in exotic but real surroundings, as for instance when Jorkens marries a mermaid in Aden. Dunsany considered even this a step down from the realms of pure imagination towards drab reporting but over thirty years he wrote five volumes of these stories and left more unpublished at his death. He regretted only the name as too similar to Jorkins, a lawyer in *David Copperfield*.

Jorkens was a satisfactory device that Dunsany used effectively without ever working out. The narrator joins the club and reports Jorkens' tales, protesting that he believes them, but protesting too much. Whatever he is asked to swallow, the reader is left feeling that Jorkens is a liar, and the new member, in spite of his occasional doubts, excessively gullible, but he has no criticism of Dunsany himself. Some of the more extreme events, such as a flight to Mars on fifteen gallons of petrol, are even distanced a further degree as they purport to happen not to Jorkens himself but to friends of his. This looks like technique, but may be described as instinct. An effect Dunsany is fully aware of is the contrast between the gloomy clubroom, dark on foggy winter afternoons, and the steaming jungles or sandy plains most frequently evoked, the brilliant tethered to the mundane.

But Jorkens is more than a device, he is the only lively, varied character Dunsany ever created. He talks of his exploits, not his character, and he is not truthful about either, but with evidence drawn from over a hundred stories a portrait cannot but emerge. At first glance he might seem to be like Dunsany himself – a loquacious traveller who spends much time at his club – but this is not so. After all his strongest wish is for a glass of whiskey. Equally his characteristics may seem to derive from what is convenient for his creator – boastful and talkative if he is to tell so many stories about himself, naturally adventurous and in constant need of money to make him more so, that he should get himself into strange situations, ingenious, that he should get himself out again. This is true and applies to his physique as well; he turns out to be surprisingly small, less than nine stone when he was twenty-five and capable of losing two more, and it is hard not to feel that this hitherto unhinted lack of stature fits too neatly with the fact that, in order to escape from an otherwise impassable valley in which he is trapped by a jealous Mediterranean, he captures and harnesses some wild ducks who are just able to fly him out. Snippets of his past are sometimes vouchsafed or hinted. On the first day of the Eton–Harrow match in 1938 he 'was wearing a button-hole of a rather uncertain blue'; but wherever he was at school he learnt to speak ancient Greek well enough to converse with Pan when he ran into him once in Greece. Indeed he says modestly: 'I am no linguist but I have smatterings of about 20 languages one picks up as one goes along.' He has been 'in with a firm in the city' from time to time and is often doing deals but, as always in Dunsany stories, unsuccessfully. He has had a house in Surrey, lived in Pimlico and there was a boarding-house he thought of as home but by the time we meet him he is a little pathetic, with few, if any, friends and the centre of his existence the club where his standing is shaky. At first a story from Jorkens is a treat to be coaxed from him with tactfully offered whiskey (or whisky, he drinks Irish or Scotch equally happily). Later we find members desperate to avoid giving him an opening, certainly keeping away from any mention of Africa. On one occasion he is heard in the doorway, so a member says, 'Icicles in his hair, is that really possible?' solely with this in mind.

'Quite possible, if I may interrupt,' said Jorkens. 'I have seen that very thing.' Seeing that we were in for a story from Jorkens, another member muttered: 'Oh well, I don't mind as long as he is not thrusting Africa down our throats.'

But Jorkens heard the mutter.

'What's the matter with Africa?' he asked.

'It's too dry,' said the other.

'You are perfectly right,' said Jorkens, 'but we can correct that. And then I'll tell you about those icicles. They are perfectly possible. I saw them thick in his hair.'

The other fellow was really neatly caught and there was nothing for it but to order two whiskeys and sodas. There passed a few moments with which my readers will probably be familiar, moments that in a club are merely routine, and Jorkens continued.

'Yes,' he said, 'there were icicles in this fellow's hair.'

'What fellow?' said Terbut.

'A man I met in the Sahara,' said Jorkens. 'I'll tell you how I happened to be there.'

'Oh? The Sahara?' was all that Terbut could find to say.

Hostility to Jorkens is most open in Terbut, a pedantic lawyer. The reason offered for his perpetual and suspicious badgering of Jorkens is that he has aspirations to story-telling himself or 'some unaccountable jealousy, Terbut never having travelled much beyond Paris'; but this seems inadequate. Like Iago, Terbut has a motiveless malignity, an overwhelming desire to destroy and humiliate a character built on a grander scale than his own; unlike Iago, he fails. He is continually asking exactly where events took place; it frequently happens that Jorkens cannot remember or assures him that he will not find the name on any map. Mostly his sceptical questions are tersely answered but even in the first volume, *The Travel Tales of Mr Joseph Jorkens*, our hero, and with all his failings he is certainly that, trembles on the brink of open insult: '[scientists wish]' he says, 'to prove that there is a definite unbridged gap between us and the apes. That must always be our first interest, so far as biology goes. 'Some,' he said, looking at Terbut with his dark hair and rather low brow, 'are naturally rather more interested in that than others.' As Terbut's doubts are so often reasonable, the reader may occasionally feel he is harshly treated, for he rarely scores, is often snubbed, and sometimes even loses money, as when he bets £5 that the distance from Blackfriars Bridge to Westminster Bridge is the same as the distance from Westminster Bridge to Blackfriars Bridge (They agree to measure it by taking a taxi and, as the road bends with the river, the first journey on the outside track is the longer. Bertrand Russell writes in the second volume of his auto-biography how he and Littlewood, the mathematician, 'used to debate whether the distance from us to the post-office was or was not the same as the distance from the post-office to us, though on this matter we never reached a conclusion.' Which seems to leave Jorkens one up.) But it is difficult not to enjoy Terbut's downfall in the Neapolitan Ice when Jorkens tells how once his soul was liberated and soaring northward from the green of England until it reached the Arctic where,

'I knew that my lips were freezing. After the pain came numbness, the first symptom of frostbite.'

'How could your lips be frostbitten,' said Terbut, 'if they were still indoors in London?'

'Well they may not have been quite,' said Jorkens, 'but I went to a doctor next day, and he said that another three minutes would have been sure to have done it.'

Jorkens continues his dramatic and vivid account of the Arctic ending, 'cold snow like a world-wide jewel, and a scent of strawberries.'

Terbut complains predictably about strawberries in the frozen wastes and it emerges that Jorkens has fallen asleep with his head in the Neapolitan ice-cream, leaving little doubt that the whole tale was an elaborate exercise in Terbut-baiting. After that their exchanges are more straightforwardly rude, for example:

'I was on a holiday in Greece,' said Jorkens.

'On a holiday from what?' said Terbut.

Support for the Jorkens stories came from one of the men Dunsany most admired and whose praise he most valued. He had re-met Rudyard Kipling and saw him occasionally at lunch at the Beefsteak, his favourite club. On Jorkens' re-appearance in 1931 Kipling wrote:

Batemans,

[This is not erse but my own typing. (R.K.)] Burwash

Sussex.

Dear Dunsany,

At first I resented the introduction, as camouflage, of your *Mister Jorkens*. Now I begin to see why your imagination *in vacuo* (and you've got more of it than anyone I know) had to have that peg and the background of the Billiard Club's atmosphere.

From my point of view it *is* real proper imagination, which is a very scarce article indeed.

And, over and above things in general, it has got luminosity and compass and a lot of other incidentals which you realise as well as I.

But we'll meet anon and talk a bit. For sheer 'cheek' the Mermaid yarn is the best. I am not thinking for the minute of anything except the audacity of it.

Ninethly and lastly, it isn't a collection that one can put in a category. Selah!

Sincerely and gratefully,

RUDYARD KIPLING.

A visit by the Kiplings to Dunstall in 1929 had been can-celled when Dunsany got measles, and then became difficult as Caroline Kipling was often ill. However, the Dunsanys often went to Batemans and sometimes he would come to Kent for a day. Kipling's son had been killed in 1918 and he always took great interest in Randal's letters from India. When Dunsany was out of the room, he said to Beatrice: 'It must be nice to have a son; I thought I should miss mine less as the years went by, but I don't; I keep thinking of how old he would be now.'

'You had the best of him,' was all that she could think to say.

'You mean his boyhood years,' he said, 'He'd have been over thirty now and might have been a great man.'

Kipling wrote several short but amusing letters, often thanking for snipe or arranging a meeting. One had a postscript: 'Sorry to see you've no nightingales in Kent. Here in our Yew Hedges they bay the moon like bloodhounds.' He also presented Dunsany with the ideas for two stories. In the first a stretch of country on the edge of a hunt has been built over. To an old and wearied member of the hunt –

'in some guise that you can arrange – (I suggest among the laurels) comes of his own good will, and for old sake's sake, a Fox – a fox of the old lot and from time to time showed himself quite openly. *Query*. Was he a real Fox or a dream Fox. (That's your job to indicate and imply etc.) Anyhow, it cheered the man's latter days and certainly, according to the little Peke who belonged to the man there was "A foxy smell in the laurels".'

Kipling's second suggestion was for three or four Irishmen who wish to dispose of a body and are followed by an 'odd-looking person in some sort of clerical garb'. He makes compelling signs and leads them to the edge of a bog where he delivers a sermon on the dead, on them and on Ireland at large.

'It is rather a notable sermon – as you will find when you try to write it; he being, or rather, having once been Dean of St Patrick's, in whose crypt his body, he tells them, lies. Cut it off at that point, or if you like add frills and grace-notes at discretion – such as one of the lads telling his priest the tale at Confession, or something of that kind.'

'You are the only man who could do it with comprehension and reason; so I put it up to you.'

Kipling approved the result (called The Mad Ghost). 'You've made the thing much more horrible with your implications.'

When Kipling died in 1936 Dunsany wrote two poems to his memory and was thanked by the widow, who said in her reply:

'Rud was not a man of many friendships, but he was very fond of you.'

That Kipling had had few close friends surprised and touched Dunsany though the same cause, the war, had had the same effect on his own life. His life throughout the 'thirties, as for most people, was a shadowed version of the previous years. Only his old pursuits seemed to go well. In 1931 he killed a snipe on the wing with a .250 rifle, a remarkable feat, and in 1932, 'over 100 golden plover, a few hundred snipe and a good many woodcock and other things, and did some hunting'. 'Ten birds with eleven cartridges, mostly right and lefts' in Yorkshire in 1934 only rates, 'I was shooting straight', as comment. His chess, which he played for Kent, the Carlton and the Athenaeum, and was asked to play for Ireland, won him a magnetised chessboard, when he won a lightning tournament. He also triumphed at Roehampton, playing with schoolgirls as pieces, by bringing up a small pawn where she could lurk unseen behind a larger piece; and he continued to beat the blacksmith at Dunstall. He enjoyed his painting and though lessons were not a success, taught himself and accepted advice. Though his hands were large, his fingers were neat and he discovered a facility for making from clay grotesque little figures. Under each was written a title: 'Even at fifty he could throw a knife that seldom missed the heart'; 'He had certainly digested the chop. The only question was about the oysters'; or 'Had he only had ears there are no heights to which he would not have risen.' He learnt glazing, as he learnt everything, by trial and error; the cook, who was not pleased by this new use for her oven, once had the pleasure of announcing 'His Lordship's God has been blow into 1,000 pieces'. He showed them at the first exhibition at Colnaghis and Queen Mary is said to have chuckled. Others proved similar appreciation by paying as much as £5 each. In 1934 he and a friend, Ted March, simultaneously painted one another but when he was sculpted by the Austrian, Strobl, he did not make a clay figure in return.

Other aspects of his life were not so happy. If his finances had started to go downhill in the early 'twenties the slump did not improve the situation and economies were desirable. In 1932 Uncle Horace, who had for many years meant more to him than any relation, died. The trend was still away from all that he admired. His plays were occasionally performed in the provinces. He refers in a letter in 1936 to 'that old illusion – a man who will help me to get a play put on' and three years later, 'It would be wonderful if in spite of it being a good book it were to go.' He began to feel, as so many frustrated writers do, that there was a conspiracy to keep his work from the public who would enjoy it if only they were given the chance. With all his work and hobbies he had never had enough to occupy his energy and enthusiasm. He began also to pick on little points, over which he was generally in the right, and then bring them up endlessly. The decay of language, one of his themes, and its fellows, shoddy punctuation, mis-prints and metaphors which have died but not faded away, are all reasonable topics for a writer though of limited interest to others. The Domination of Man by Machine is an important subject for our age, though not one on which it is easy to find new comments. It is perhaps more sad than funny that artificial wooden pips are placed in raspberry jam. Sour milk on trains passing through fields full of cows understandably upset him.

Two topics recurred more mercilessly than any – salt and dogs' tails. Long before, in 1914, he had decided that the salt normally bought in shops was injurious to health and that pure rock salt was not. He therefore carried his own and often demonstrated with two glasses of water that the former remained cloudy whereas the latter was soluble. He would do this with strangers and in strange houses. 'It was rather embarrassing on French trains,' Beatrice admitted. With dogs' tails it was once more nature he was defending. They should not be cut off. Most people would now agree, partly because of his tireless advocacy in print, on the wireless and in person, over the next twenty-five years; but it was wearing for those who heard these views on many occasions. Another worry was that water to make the tea could not be boiling still when it reached the dining-room. 'Now Eddie,' Lady Mexborough said on one of his annual visits to her, 'if you don't mention Cerebos salt *or* the Catholic Church during the whole of your visit, you shall be allowed to make the tea on your last day.' But when he had achieved a properly hot cup of tea he feared he would scald his throat and sometimes drank from the saucer; anyone who doubted the danger might have their finger thrust into a cup to show how great the temperature was. The Mexboroughs were Catholics and gibes at Catholicism came more from the fact that an Aunt Sally was so conveniently at hand than from any real objection. Though he did not let it prevent him reverting to these subjects he did not like people to ask him about his salt or think him pernickety. In a book[1] published in 1939 there is the exchange: 'Then you'll be a faddist,' he said.

'Not because I take wholesome mustard,' said Mona.

'Everybody will think you one,' he replied; 'You remember my words.' He was right, everybody did think him one.

In 1932 Yeats founded his Irish Academy of Letters, mainly to unite literary forces in a struggle against censorship. Dunsany was scarcely on any terms at all with Yeats. He was told

1. The Story of Mona Sheehy.

his name was in a list in *The Times* and wrote to point out that he had received no invitation. He also began a letter from Scotland to Beatrice, 'What a cad Yeats is! Today it rained all day. I started out to stalk at ten.' Then he was asked to be an associate member only. Two of the new members, who had managed to remain friends with everyone, behaved characteristically. A.E. wrote a long, kind letter explaining that associate membership was no slight and had been accepted by, among others, T. E. Lawrence and, the translator of Plotinus, Stephen McKenna, whom Yeats particularly admired. Full membership was for those whose subject matter was Ireland and the Irish. This made some sense but so did Gogarty's jokes on the subject, his boldest being at the dinner some years later which welcomed Dunsany as a full member when, with Yeats present, he said: 'Since this Academy was founded to keep Dunsany out we ought to dissolve it, now that he's admitted.' Hurt and angry at the time Dunsany never became friendly with Yeats again. Complaining about Yeats had always been a widespread Irish habit. Beatrice remembers a man in a green coat jumping off his bicycle in Kildare Street saying, 'You are Dunsany. I am Monk Gibbon', and agreeing animatedly on some of the great man's defects by the end of the street. Gogarty could still write to Shane Leslie in 1939, some months after Yeats' death:

'Have you read *Letters on poetry from W. B. Yeats to Dorothy Wellesley*? It is full of interest and shows how dearly Yeats could love a lady even if he disliked a Lord in the person of Dunsany.'

Dunsany himself writing over ten years later says only that he retaliated in private with a society to honour writers of the 14th century in Italy. 'Who, I asked, would they suggest? Dante of course was suggested; but I was shocked. "Most certainly not," I said, stroking my hair as Yeats used to stroke his. "Dante did not write about Italy, but of a very different place. Most unsuitable."' He went, however, to Yeats' memorial service to show no animosity remained.

This depressing incident may have prodded him in a satisfactory direction. Charles Masterman, who was in the Liberal Cabinet in 1914, had long before told him to write a tale about Ireland. Uncle Horace, never backward with advice, had said the same. In any case he now wrote a series of books, including Jorkens' stories on subjects he knew and about which he felt, in particular Ireland and the Irish. He still saw this as inferior to work drawn from thin air. 'I felt somewhat like a sculptor,' he wrote later, 'accustomed to work only in rare marbles, turning to work with chance handfuls of the soil that lay around him, yet somewhat enchanted soil so that it might do as well.'

His technique had steadily improved, and he was now much easier to read, his prose eloquent but under control. In June 1933 Beatrice could record: 'E. wrote his Irish novel in $3\frac{1}{2}$ breathless months; bits of it have been in his mind for years and I never let it be forgotten for too long and then it came suddenly.' The book, *The Curse of the Wise Woman*, was immediately successful, and is now the best-known and loved of all his work. The reviews were excellent but Dunsany was labelled and many of the opinions seem to have been trundled out rather than felt. This was particularly unfair for there is more direct feeling than he had ever conveyed before; if *The Blessing of Pan* had sung his love for Kent, then *The Wise Woman* did the same for Meath, adding his feelings about his lonely childhood. The story – of a boy spending his holidays from Eton in Ireland shooting snipe and geese on the bogs with the keeper, his mother dead, his father soon to disappear, is the most autobiographical of his books. The narrator is an old man (seventy whereas Dunsany was fifty-five at the time of writing it) looking sadly back from exile and occasionally the description of shooting and scenery slow the plot to a standstill; this concerns the Troubles, shifted to about 1890, and the Wise Woman who is successfully cursing the English who are going to drain the bog and 'compress the turf by machinery and sell it as coal.' So a boy's adventure story blends with magic and a feeling for the country and country people to make a book which appeals particularly to unbookish people, perhaps because few who appreciate shooting and weather so simply can write evocatively about them. It appealed sufficiently to bookish people as well to receive £100 and the Harmsworth Award as 'the best work of imaginative prose by an Irish author', selected from three books sent by the dreaded Irish Academy to John Masefield. So it was a score off them as well as a gratifying success all round.

The light it throws on Dunsany's feelings shows him in benign mood. Uncle Horace appears but is scarcely criticised, de Valera is rather a romantic figure dressed always in black and the Anglo-Irish hero, far from condemning Irish murderers, almost becomes one of them in face of the coal-threat: 'It was then that my Irish heart sorrowfully regretted what my English education had taught me, to interfere with my friend who would have killed these men.' Similarly the keeper who tells him not to fire at some snipe because, 'There is no man living could hit them walking up wind,' is not called a liar; on the contrary 'It was his old way of worshipping the golden idol of Tact before the Goddess of Truth if they got in each other's way.' But under the excitement and affection there is a pervasive sadness, more appropriate to the nostalgia of an old man, than to one in his mid-fifties.

Beatrice had continued her diary after noting that 'the Irish novel' was finished: 'It was rather sad leaving Dunsany this April as we had to cut down so much. The people are patient and fatalistic of course, but I doubt if they believe we can't help it. It is odd to have lived to see the British Empire at its apex and past it – and now to see democracy, which we may not have admired but expected to last our time, crumbling faster still – and these odd unexpected dictators popping up.' With this hint of war and a note on who came to tennis and dinner one day, Beatrice ceased writing her diary for seven years.

Articles, plays, poems and stories were pouring from Dunsany. Opinions and descriptions came easily on many topics, particularly nature, himself, other writers or misuse of language. In a tribute to Maeterlinck, whose works he saw 'shining through time like lighthouses at night over stormy seas', he insists that a true poet 'will never turn away from creation to dwell among intricacies and artificialities' – a charge brought against his own work. Dogs and adjectives were defended. *Decline and Fall* and *Vile Bodies* he admired for, among other qualities, their plausibility – a surprising virtue but one of his own problems. He still placed Coleridge among the greatest poets and preferred the age of Keats and Shelley to that of Pope and Dr Johnson, who were too intellectual. Many literary opinions are made clear in a story published in 1934 when the hero, Jorkens, stumbles on a club of poets from all ages. The secretary takes him round

'There you see Swinburne,' he said, 'talking to Herrick' . . . I should not have been surprised to see Homer himself. And sure enough there he stood, stroking his beard, eyes full of thought, giving me somehow the impression of a most tremendous Tory.

'And there's Stephen Phillips,' he said, 'talking to Dante.' And I recognised the two men and seemed to see through the rather dim glass of the door, a certain resemblance of feature.

'A bit lucky, wasn't he, getting elected?' I said pointing to Stephen Phillips.[1]

'Well, yes,' said the secretary, 'but you have luck in all clubs, there's always somebody who may be just not quite.'

And then Tennyson went by on the other side of the shimmering glass. I recognised him immediately.

'He's having a bit of a slump over there,' I said, pointing over the lawns to the way by which I had come.

'Oh, he's all right here,' said the secretary.

'And the waiters?' I said for they were passing to and fro.

'All writers too,' he said. 'All wrote good stuff. But not immortal. He's the best we have on our staff,' he said pointing to the hall-porter. 'That's Pope.'

The secretary himself rates above Pope but is only an honorary member, on the strength of one line. He is Dean Burdon who wrote 'A rose-red city half as old as time'.

Dunsany later wrote another story in which Jorkens returns to find the Dean loitering in the road, expelled from his club for theft. It had been discovered (by Dunsany as well as by the poets) that there was a line 'By many a temple half as old as time', published by Samuel Rogers in 1819 when the Dean was only six.

However Dunsany rated his own chances of becoming a junior member, he was confident of not being branded with intellectuality and wrote an article explaining emphatically that he was not a highbrow. Jorkens says:

'. . . No, I have my faults. Waiter, another whiskey. I have my faults, but nobody's called me a highbrow.'

'No, no,' I said, 'Jorkens, and nobody ever will.'

He gripped my hand and thanked me.

1. Stephen Phillips, it will be remembered, had taught him at his crammers, which may account for his luck.

This is not simple Philistinism but part of Dunsany's view of aesthetics.

While at Arden in 1933 to shoot grouse he wrote a poem called 'A Dictator's Fall' which must have been among the first prophecies of Hitler's fall, as he had only just risen far enough to catch the general attention. During the war he wrote of Mussolini:

> 'To whom,' he asked them, 'do the seas belong?'
> And, like a wave uprising, huge and long,
> The great crowd answered. And it answered wrong.

Dunsany had no liking for the little dictators, but in December Methuen asked him to be one of six authors of a series called *If I were Dictator*. He gave it the sub-title, *The Pronouncements of the Grand Macaroni*, and listed his main quarrels with the twentieth century. It is a good-tempered, short book which manages to include his disapproval of misprints, advertisements (at length), white flour, which destroys the teeth, tinned food, wooden pips in raspberry jams, ginger beer, weedkiller (only salt was allowed at Dunsany), skinning seals, cutting dogs' tails (surprisingly brief), lampshades that fail to shield the glare of the naked bulb and many, many more. Apart from his views that the League of Nations and disarmament are good in themselves but will not prevent men fighting and a few jokes against Indian independence, he is unconcerned with politics. His only serious positive plea is for a national theatre. It must have been about what Methuen expected and he enjoyed the four weeks he spent on it.

He was asked for a modern fairy-story and produced *Little Snow-White* in which the step-mother asks:

> O gramo, gramo, gramophone,
> Which of us is the fairest one?

and gets the unwelcome reply:

> 'Thou wert the fairest, Lady Clink,
> But Blanche is fairer now I think.'

Another request was even more promptly fulfilled. Lance Sieveking,[1] both a friend and a power at the BBC, came to

1. Novelist, playwright, composer, actor and producer of – among many – the first television play *The World*.

Ireland and regretted that there were two suitable plays dealing with Fame but they were not long enough to make a programme in themselves. Dunsany signalled to Beatrice to take him away and when they returned from tea with neighbours, he had completed a new play called *Fame Comes Late*. The three were duly broadcast. In spite of all this activity Dunsany was still little known in England and his reaction is perhaps in the play where a poet who has dreamed of Fame as a Greek Goddess with a golden trumpet is eventually visited by just such a one – but old and tired and a little pathetic. He takes it quite gently and says to a friend, 'All things age. And Fame cannot be now what she was when we were both young.' He was still eager for praise, but had become more resigned to the lack of it.

The tone of these years is compressed into a sentence in his autobiography: 'When shooting ended I was at a loose end and I only waited a week before settling down to the grim work of writing a novel, which occupied me nearly every day from March 8 to April 18th, actually forty working days, the shortest time in which I had ever written a novel.' Shooting came first, writing was largely 'grim work' to fill time but he was working faster and better than ever before.

The novel was *Up in the Hills*, a good-natured satire on the Troubles, one of his most Irish books in that the jolly light-hearted adventure of boys forming pointless gangs in the hills does not hesitate to take in the capture and execution of a sympathetic character. Death must not stop the fun. It also has an ingenious plot and some enjoyable Irish obstruction.

'Where is he?' the officer asked.

'Sure he's only after running out of that house,' he [old Mickey] said pointing. 'It's his mother's house and he's only after leaving it. And it's plaguing us all he is. And it's times I wish the English were back. I do surely.'

'Which way did he go?' asked the officer.

'That way,' shouted old Mickey, standing up and pointing with both arms, 'That way.'

'You've got your two arms pointing different ways,' said the officer.

'And why not?' shouted Old Mickey.

'You should point them both the same way,' argued the officer.

'The same way is it?' shouted old Mickey. 'What for did God give us two arms? If there were only one way to point sure he'd have given us only one arm.'

'Which way did he go?' insisted the officer.

'Bedad He would,' said Old Mickey, sticking to his point.

'Go on,' said the officer to the driver.

'Find him! Find him! Find him!' shouted old Mickey. 'Sure Mickey Conner gives us no peace.' . . . 'You got rid of them fine,' said Young Mickey stepping out of the cupboard.

The reviewers were as enthusiastic in Ireland as in England, his best yet. Apparently this view of a country playing violent fun-and-games which paused to let the hunt through was a joke all could enjoy.

The mid-'thirties were also his Great Canine Period. Dunsany had always liked dogs, had mentioned them in his work before and he was to revert to the topic again, but never in such detail. He had himself an Alsatian and an indestructible mongrel-terrier called Tyke who was bitten by an adder and once spent ten days down a rabbit-hole with his collar caught by a root but lived to be fifteen. After the war there was a profusion of spaniels, partly because puppies could only be given to those with enlightened views as to the proper length for their tails. In 1935 he published *Mr Faithful*, a full-length play, admittedly written earlier, in which the hero takes a job as a dog, and in 1936 two novels, *My Talks with Dean Spanley*, which he had started two years before in which the Dean has been a dog in a previous incarnation, and *Rory and Bran* in which it gradually emerges that Bran actually is a dog.

My Talks with Dean Spanley has only two jokes, that the Dean can half-remember his former incarnation as a dog and that it is necessary to get him rather drunk before he can, or will, do so; but they are well-sustained. Being a Dean by Dunsany he is a nice old boy, but greedy for some particularly rare wine the narrator has acquired from a Maharajah. It is generous of a near-teetotaller like Dunsany to make a fondness for drink almost always a sympathetic characteristic, and in this book a stranger wins the confidence of the narrator by opening their conversation with 'Never trust a teetotaller or a man who wears elastic-sided boots.' Dogs, or at least spaniels, for, with his name and a few hints, it is practically certain that that is what the Dean was, turn out to be the sycophants among animals, fawning on man, who is otherwise feared and disliked. The Dean says primly of rabbits, 'They lurk in the woods and plot, and give man no proper allegiance. They should be hunted whenever met.' Dunsany knew dogs and the opinions of the Dean ring true: 'There is no such thing as bad water. There is water with different flavours and giving off different smells. There is interesting water and uninteresting water . . . If the impurities are so thick that it is solid, then it ceases to be water, but while it is water it is always good.' There is a moment when hideous embarrassment threatens; the narrator thinks of throwing a tennis-ball to see if his dignified guest will retrieve it; but better judgment intervenes.

Rory and Bran is about Ireland as well as dogs. Rory, a simple-minded boy has to drive some cows to market. Bran is described as his companion and Dunsany has written, 'I did not state what Bran was, because I considered it unnecessary,' but this is disingenuous. The book is a tease as to Bran's identity. He drinks from puddles, but then so does Rory. He refuses mustard, which is reasonable enough in anyone, and likes a nice run. He likes rabbit, once wears 'a grim look', and is referred to as a 'lad'. The nearest to a cheat is: ' "Oh-ho" said Bran. The syllables were long-drawn and said wearily; but no printing of mere syllables can suggest the weariness with which they were uttered.'

It is possible to read the whole book without realising that Bran is a dog, for one reviewer complained that he was '*rather* silent for an Irishman.' The rest of the complicated plot involves thieves and tinkers and a thrilling point-to-point, which is a surprise as Dunsany was bored by racing. As in other of Dunsany's novels the hero has to quit his wandering ways to settle down to marriage, and this is a melancholy moment, as if noble opportunities were floating away for ever; which is rather an unfair attitude as Dunsany travelled considerably more after he was married than before without complaint or restraint from Beatrice. He asked a farmer if he had got his facts right and was told that the parents would have given £2 not £4 to Rory, but otherwise it was all correct.

Then he wrote a successful little story which he read on the BBC called *The Cut* in which a dog becomes more and more like a human, wearing clothes and doing the shopping. One day he meets a man, with whom he is on excellent terms, but as he is wearing no collar, the dog cuts him dead in the High Street. This is the highest moment for a dog, when he actually aspires to be a man and a better man than some, but such conflict is unusual. At the end the dog is to be shut up and a child wrote to the BBC asking if he could please be let out, which pleased Dunsany. In a play *The Use of Man* the hero dreams he is placed on trial for his life by animals and can only be saved if two will speak for him. The dog speaks for him immediately, 'He is man; that is enough.' However the hero has to try many before he can find other support and then it comes from the mosquito who regards him merely as food. Jorkens, to whom unicorns and Gods are commonplace, rarely meets dogs, and is then shown to be only a fairly lovable old rogue, for they do not much like him. He was attacked by an Alsatian in a London drawing-room but realised in the nick of time that the threatening fangs were too white to be real and slipped them out. Another Alsatian was the instrument of a murderer who changes his master's scent, thus inciting the dog to attack. No blame attaches to the Alsatian but they are not the same best friend to Jorkens that they are to other men. *Rory and Bran* and *Dean Spanley* were both well reviewed except by those who admitted that they had no interest in either Ireland or dogs. The shortest and a not unrepresentative appraisal ran: '*Dean Spanley* in which a dog turns into a clergyman, by Lord Dunsany. Good Lord.'

In the spring of 1936 Beatrice and Dunsany were in Ireland but were poised to come over for the coronation. They were having tea in the Kildare Street Club when he felt ill and went to lie down. Beatrice rang Gogarty who arranged everything while she got the servants off the boat again. Dunsany had a prostate operation, was in serious danger for a bit and then recuperated for three months in a Dublin nursing home. He was not an easy patient, complaining frequently of noise. The nurse thought him delirious but he scored in the end for she came to the quiet of Dunsany and exclaimed, 'Now I understand.' He grew a beard as he had before in the wilds but this time he retained it, small, pointed and distinguished. He said that his motive was 'to leave less room for the mosquitoes'.

The Dunsanys had long thought war was coming and they had every reason to be despondent. Beatrice had often been ill and now had trouble with her heart again; he was still convalescing. Book after book had failed to achieve any startling success. He marked his sorrow at the death of friends such as Kipling and A.E. with a series of melancholy poems. The tennis court at Dunstall had become a chicken run. He felt tired and old and that the world was against him and she had to sustain him.

Suddenly things improved. His literary agent, Spencer Curtis Brown, had asked him to do a book called *My Ireland* and without too much effort he did so. Now it was published and became the greatest success he had had in England. 'I do not say that some people had not read my story *Curse of the Wise Woman*,' he commented later, 'but they said very little about it until *My Ireland* came out.' It got enthusiastic reviews, went through several editions, and is pleasant enough, communicating his affection for the country, the people and their talk but no better than he had done before and with a distinct feeling near the end that he is writing whatever came into his head that morning whether it is interesting or not. Later that year he published a collection of ten plays under the title *Plays for Earth and Air*, as more were performed on the wireless than the stage. A mixed bag of fantasy, comedy and thrills, they were received with mild approval. A letter written to Beatrice, who was in France with Georgie Buller, seems busy and content:

Dunstall Priory
Oct. 8

My Darling Mink,
I'm glad Chartres looked so lovely. I got a cheering letter from Georgie as well as yours. I did 1,786 words yesterday and 660 this morning. Salmon has arranged 10 to 10.20 p.m. on November 13 for *The Cut* and I've answered. And I'm going to the annual meeting of the Sevenoaks Chess Club at 8.30 on Oct. 15th.

Salmon says 'Everybody will listen'. I *must* be solemn this time. I am playing a good deal of golf with Tyke.

4 p.m.

I went up against the partridges of Forty Acres and got 3 of them. The book is now 46,450 words.

. . . news of the new species (of beaver) has been let out by the *Ev: Standard*, and now sportsmen are out after it. One has just telephoned and I said he could look at my beard for an hour and a quarter from 1.45 p.m. tomorrow. The man to whom I have let the sporting rights in my beard appears to be called Guthrie . . .'

The Cut was often on the wireless and when the record was destroyed in the war, he made another. The book in progress was an autobiography, suggested by his agent, and though considering himself on an ever downward slope from the realms of imagination to the squalor of fact and continually apologising for this, he found it came easily to him. The title of the first volume, *Patches of Sunlight*, heralds his intention to leave out anything boring or unpleasant. This includes most of his youth and many people, but he is eloquent about Kent and the desert. In 1938 a new play *The Strange Lover*, about a mysterious millionaire in Yorkshire who, like Baron Frankenstein, creates a man, was given with great success by the Players of Dublin who were managed by his nephew, Lord Longford. In March he reviewed *War and Peace* on the Irish wireless. It had been his favourite novel since he read it in 1908 and he enjoyed the chance of praising it. His other Pakenham nephew, Frank, remembers bringing the brilliant young Oxford don, Maurice Bowra, to see him. Dunsany was looking to his conversational laurels, and proclaimed that he had always held that *Peace and War* was the greatest book of all. They talked for a time of rivals to Tolstoy's masterpiece and then Bowra referred to 'That one you mentioned just now,' (pause), 'you know,' (and then with slight desperation but the deference due from youth to age) '*Peace and War*.' Dunsany could hardly contain his derision, '*Peace and War*, what an extraordinary thing to call it! Have you never heard of the book? It's called *War and Peace*,' and so on.

In July he enjoyed being a member of a Brains Trust on television, and he foresaw a great future for this exciting machine, though regarding it as a death blow for the theatre. On his way out he peeped into the waiting room to discover what else the public wished to see and found two chimpanzees, a wallaby and a wombat. '*They* were held,' he said, 'but I was allowed to do my piece entirely alone.' In August his play *Alexander* was acted with success at the Malvern Festival with Sir Donald Wolfit as the eponymous hero, and he spent a few days there to enjoy the acclaim. In Dublin he was one of several chess players to struggle with the world champion Alekhine who, after a long game, defeated him. He wrote a series of pieces about country life for the *Daily Mail* and when he planned to describe the ways of nightingales but could not find any, wrote with true journalistic skill about the elusive qualities of the bird. A Jorkens story (about Pan) was translated into French which gave him great pleasure.

On August 1938 Randal married Mrs Vera Bryce[1] a lovely and attractive Brazilian. Dunsany recognised her charm and enjoyed her company, and though he and Beatrice thought it unlikely that she would settle down either as an army wife in India or as a châtelaine in County Meath, they accepted the inevitable and with perfect manners made her welcome. A collection of verse called *Mirage Water*, which came out at the end of the year is dedicated to her.

Dunsany accepted Munich at face value, though thinking in general that wars would recur and returned to and finished in the early months of 1939 a novel, *The Story of Mona Sheehy*, which concerns a girl who is thought to be the daughter of the fairies. It contains a portrait of Lady Fingal, a wicked but glamorous figure who causes all the trouble because, dancing at dawn in her tiara, she is taken, even by a stray lover, to be the Fairy Queen. Later she behaves better when, driving furiously about Ireland, she chooses her own death rather than that of a child in the road. Graham Greene in the *Spectator* found it 'a delightful book belonging to the disputable territory between fancy and imagination full of *underground malice* [my italics] and quite free from whimsy – a difficult achievement.' The change from shadow to sunlight in his life was not sudden or complete – but his friends remarked to each other how much mellower and happier he seemed to have become. His future again seemed set fair, when the war again made nonsense of prediction.

1. She was the daughter of Dr Genesio de Sa Sottomajor of San Paulo.

PART FIVE

War 1939 – 1945

IRISHMAN: I want a return ticket.

OFFICIAL: Where to?

IRISHMAN: Back here, of course.

In the summer of 1939 Randal and Vera came home on leave from India, and the whole family were at Dunsany Castle on September 3rd when war was declared. On September 10th Vera gave birth in Dublin, but Randal had already been recalled and so returned to India without seeing his son. The baby was christened Edward John Carlos and called Eddie like his grandfather.

In the autumn Vera and Eddie set out for India via America but they got no farther than Brazil, where the baby was cared for by Vera's parents until the end of the war.

After a slow start Dunsany had a good, even a splendid war. Left in Ireland, he was so confident of victory that he merely wrote a little heartening verse and waited for it. There seemed to be no call for the services of a poet of sixty-one, even one burning with patriotism. Meanwhile he was delighted to be made an honorary Doctor of Letters by Dublin University, the first recognition in Ireland of thirty-five years' work.

Then in 1940 an appeal went out for recruits for the Home Guard. His local doctor and his surgeon both said he should not go, but as they gave different reasons, eager now to have a role to play, he felt free to ignore them.

In neutral Ireland private arms were confiscated while Westminster appealed for more. So as the boat zigzagged across the Irish Sea in August, a figure 'with a stiff leg but a supple ankle and a furtive look in his eye' could be seen uncertainly pacing the deck. It was Dunsany with a Winchester repeater up his trouser leg; the stock sawn off as it was easy to replace and difficult to conceal. He declared it triumphantly at the Customs, but a flurry of forms were signed, permits required, and it finally arrived in Kent a month too late to be of any use to him.

Their first night at Dunstall was quiet and comfortable. The kitchen maids had refused to leave Ireland at the last moment but the housemaid, chauffeur and cook had come. The second night the sirens wailed and they found they had arrived just in time for the Battle of Britain. Two planes were shot down that night, one German, one English and they assumed that this happened everywhere every night. For a time to them it did; for Dunstall, just south of London, was directly on the German route to the capital and for over a month there was more than one meeting in their valley every twenty-four hours. Sometimes all the doors in the house slammed. Dunsany sat on the verandah with a rifle for a day or two and then he suddenly felt rather foolish and stopped. At night he watched and later wrote:

'Searchlights beyond the two sides of our valley went roaming about the sky, and sometimes one of them would flash its beam from left to right, from horizon to horizon, and then remain pointing at something it had found. Others would come up then, peering through the dark, and join it, forming a great silver pyramid.' After a bomb fell uncomfortably close, they took to sleeping in the cellar, 'and the gardener's family found room to sleep there too, and a toad that had been there for years continued his residence.' It was quieter and did not shake about.

The cook said that if she wasn't deaf she didn't think she could stand it. Dunsany, while not precisely enjoying it, would not have missed it for the world. He felt at the centre of things, no longer excluded. The *Daily Sketch* printed several of his poems among them:

> *Fauna of Kent*
> One thing I know which Milton never knew:
> When Satan fell, hurled headlong to the shade
> Of Hell eternal out of Heaven's blue,
> I know the screaming wail his pinions made.

This was written after he had joined the Local Defence Volunteers, into which he channelled his enthusiasm. At first he expected invasion and hoped it would come before the leaves were off the trees so that he could harass the German march on London with unseen rifle fire. Then his function changed to spotting and reporting falling aircraft. For this he would go to the top of the hill behind the house, because, he argued sensibly, he could hurry downhill but not up. On the other hand he could not spend all day up there so he would choose a battle, 'usually one between breakfast and lunch', to watch. One day he was rewarded by seeing the forced landing of a bomber, but his platoon commander had been out digging a trench and saw it too. He was not only at the centre of the stage but an actor in events, though in the opposite mood he recorded wryly: 'I said that all men in my platoon, that is to say Sir Herbert Cohen's, might shoot rabbits in my wood for as long as the war lasted: that was my contribution to the strategy of this war.'

Dunsany wrote to Sir Kenneth Clark to try and secure some sort of pension for Sime. He learned in reply that Sime, whom he had last seen two years before in a chaos of papers and drawings in his own house, was dying 'rather more quickly than the rest of us'; but there was nothing to compare with the slaughter of friends in the First War.

In September 1940 the British Council amazingly asked him to take the Byron Chair of English Literature in Athens, Greece not yet being at war. He accepted a new adventure with speed and his old enthusiasm. He had written in '39 of men who 'began to notice that they walked with some slight difficulty almost as though they were old', but if that was an observation of himself it was now forgotten. Beatrice started a diary again but proclaimed: 'This is going to be only a cold record', its purpose being to note the names of people they met. Her comment was: 'This job is they say more useful [than the Home Guard] at his age. I don't like being away at such a time, but D. says a change of danger may be pleasant.' So she became his secretary, but wrote to her niece, Mary Clive: 'You'll be surprised to hear that in our old age we are jaunting off to the Balkans (I am sixty tomorrow and feel all that) . . . I must say I still can't believe it is much use, or indeed any, as we can't speak Greek; but the idea is for him to give a weekly lecture and just show that we have as much culture as the Germans . . . I am not one of the world's adventurers and it is 30 years too late, but there! one never knows one's luck.'

When he got to Athens, Dunsany was to lecture on English Literature. The immediate problem was to get there. The planned route was by way of Lisbon and Lake Chad, but it was abandoned. After a difficult drive to London, with a bomb missing them narrowly, and numerous diversions to avoid damaged roads, they were given tickets for Glasgow, which was the first time they had heard that they were going there. Euston was pitch dark and torrential rain was falling. They waited in the tube during a raid, among the tired Londoners who were going to sleep underground. Eventually they moved on to the platform from which they could see the red flash of British shells through the glass roof. The train was four hours late and like all trains on tiresome journeys, pulled out of the station and then stopped for an hour. Dunsany stretched his long legs on the floor, slept well and rather enjoyed roughing it. They had worried about missing their boat at Glasgow, but where the train was delayed hours, the ship waited days.

In wartime curious routes were obligatory. They did not know where they were going, nor for how long, though they hoped to be back in February. Dunsany wrote to Lady Jersey: 'Instead of betting on the ship's run, which is absurd as we can't be told it, we should bet on where we are going; bets to be paid on a certificate being given by our officer of the port that it really is that port.' It looked as if the Captain wanted to go to New York, preferred Brazil, and, again changing his mind, fetched up in Sierra Leone. Beatrice began recording who they met – 'a lot of Free French on board, to be put off *en route* to join Gen de Gaulle, a good many sailors and air force, and some twenty wives, most with babies . . . and there are about sixty women ambulance drivers under the command of a beautiful Mrs Newall – such nice girls probably going to Kenya.' They slept off the exhaustion of the Battle of Britain and then had a pleasant rather gay trip. Dunsany found some opponents to beat at chess. As they sailed down the West African coast, Dunsany saw some packages from Glasgow addressed to St Helena and began to wonder just who did know the secret of their destination.

At Cape Town they went ashore and ate oranges. The wind was so strong that it was hard to walk. After a glance at Port Elizabeth which Dunsany found pleasantly wild, they missed a flying boat at Durban and waited three days for the next one. Beatrice wrote to her mother: 'I liked my three days in Durban: we walked about after dinner admiring the blazing lights and windows and were amused to read in the paper next day that Durban had been having its first sample black-out!' Dunsany had never flown before and in the next flying boat was amazed by the cloudscapes and the glimpses of forest beneath. Beatrice was less enthusiastic. 'The drawbacks to the flying-boat are that it starts at 4.30 a.m. so that one is sleepy all day and it is noisy . . . it is quite cool flying at 8,000 feet, so that descending suddenly into blazing heat on the ground is trying each time it happens.' A night in Mozambique, a fourpenny pineapple in Dar-es-Salaam and they reached a place Dunsany had been to before – Mombassa in East Africa. The next night was spent at Kisumu on Lake Victoria, where Dunsany experimented with his stock of Swahili. They swooped down to see the Murchison Falls in Uganda but 'swerved so much that I [Dunsany] did not at first see which way they were falling up or down'. However they glimpsed 'elephants buffaloes antelopes and waterbuck, and the river full of hippos playing and splashing.' A few minutes in Khartoum, a hotel in Wadi Halfa from which 'we saw the Nilotic sunset we had known of old glowing orange as ever over the sandy hills', a dart down to glimpse Abu Simbel and Dunsany was able to look at the Great Pyramid outside Cairo on the fifth afternoon from Durban and attend a party in the evening. Beatrice was tired but dutifully went. Though Greece had been neutral when they set out, she was now at war with Italy, but there were no counter-instructions so they assumed they were meant to continue their circuitous advance on Athens.

They had begun in Cairo as they were to continue, the whirl of new places giving way to a whirl of new people. They both carried on in the same vein, Dunsany revelling in the excitement, Beatrice coping with it all as cheerfully as she could, a pair not unlike Don Quixote and Sancho Panza. In three weeks her record of names becomes formidable. People from the Embassy, Hassinan Pasha, Lord Wavell, Sir Henry Maitland Wilson, Prince Mohammed Ali, people from the university. . . . Dunsany lunched with some and lectured to others. He particularly liked tea flavoured with mint; she noted that no taxi-drivers knew the city and so it was necessary to get a guide as well. The minister of finance was 'easy to recognise because he had a thin face with a grey moustache

instead of being round and cleanshaven like the rest.' They
admired the Rufai Mosque and a state farm with pure Arab
stallions; Dunsany spent a day in Alexandria, and pursued
ducks with the king, young Farouk, who had to be allowed the
first shot. Beatrice was in a taxi that swerved to avoid an
accident so that she was thrown on to the floor. Before their
hectic stay was over she could write: 'I know a bey from a
pasha and both from an effendi.'

Their journey continued to wind. On December 8 they
left Cairo in the evening, rowed across the Suez Canal under
the stars, and got into 'the eternal *wagon-lits*' for Haifa. Beatrice
wrote: 'I don't wonder the Israelites were pleased to see this
green fertile country after Egypt. I must say it is quite amusing
seeing all these unexpected countries.' Next day they filled a
car with oranges and motored to Tripoli, lunching in Beirut.
An Englishman there was travelling an even more curious
route for Budapest. Beatrice liked Syria with its 'houses of
solid yellowish limestone with red roofs (like Yorkshire)' but
they did not falter, changed trains at Aleppo and so on to the
Ankara Palace Hotel. They arrived at noon, four hours late,
washed and had lunch at the Embassy. Dunsany went to a
party that night given by Lady Mary Walker but this time
Beatrice was too tired. Next day at 11 a.m. he lectured on
British poetry with a translator interrupting every ten minutes
with a summary, which apparently worked very well. Beatrice
found it 'an amusing town built on the grand scale with boulevards and every kind of large cultural building, one restaurant
and no business background at all.' The one restaurant seems
to have been literally true for 'Dined at Karpish' is a daily
entry. Turkey was neutral and full of Germans, who also dined
there, not to mention a brilliant Japanese juggler. They saw
the sights and Dunsany shot a ruddy sheldrake.

On December 16th they left for Istanbul where their
experiences were much the same. From the Pera Palace Hotel
they lunched at the Embassy. Michael Grant from the British
Council had looked after them in Ankara and looked after
them here. Dunsany lectured. They saw rather older, superior
sights. Dunsany enjoyed a concert of Turkish music, but
Beatrice had left too many of her thick clothes in the hot

countries behind them and now caught cold. When he went to stay with Abbas Bey, a new friend, she stayed behind. Her Christmas was not gay.

Wed. Dec. 25: More or less in bed.
Thurs. Dec. 26: Rather less in bed.
Friday Dec. 27:   ,,   ,,   ,,   ,,
Saturday Dec. 28: Still ,,   ,,   ,,
Sunday Dec. 29: Still wet and sleety.
Monday Dec. 30: Sunny. Went out. M. Grant returned. D. is more or less marooned by floods at Karacabey.
Wednesday Jan. 1. 1941: The manager sent me a large cake for breakfast as a New Year present.

The floods abated, and Dunsany returned. He had been a little better at chess and a little worse at shooting than his host, and equal in his appreciation of poetry. Abbas Bey translated Turkish poems and he turned them into English ones. They had stayed in a farmhouse to shoot and the owner always wore a bowler-hat because it would be disrespectful to his guests to appear bare-headed. He wrote to Beatrice: 'A wolf came into our street last night. I divide all towns and villages into two classes, those into which a wolf comes now and then, and those into which a wolf comes never. It made me very happy to hear it. We are completely surrounded by floods. The wind would nearly pull the hair off a wolf's back ... the town is running out of provisions and here we no longer have milk. They say that "several people were drowned".' Cold, he was given a sheepskin waistcoat 'the finest waistcoat I ever had, though the British Ambassador in Athens looked a little askance at it once.' He was delighted about the wolf and wrote several times, 'There was a wolf at my door last night and he was not a metaphor.'

They reached the Greek frontier by train on January 4th and were met by a Mr Vedova from the British Council. At Alexandroupolis they feasted with policemen on spaghetti captured from the Italians and then drove past military posts for Salonika but floods had destroyed the bridges and they had to stay at a 'doubtless well-meaning inn.' Another day's drive to a train, 'no sleepers and it took twenty hours but we were lucky and got an apartment to ourselves' and on January

7th, eighty-three days after they left Dunstall, the Dunsanys arrived in Athens.

For a month they were the guests of the British Ambassador, Sir Michael Palairet, and his wife, whom Beatrice had known as a child. The University was shut and so many of Dunsany's potential audience were away, but other halls were found and he lectured two or three times a week to about a hundred students. They were fanatically pro-British and eager to enjoy the dignity of Milton or the felicities of Tennyson. For Byron there was standing room only. Afterwards a friend said: 'We decided we knew exactly what he would say and what quotations he would use. We were quite wrong.' Dunsany had been reading *Earth and Heaven* and other less well-known poems and dwelt on them; this was how he worked, ranging about English literature and reporting on new reactions as well as old, naturally giving time and emphasis to those he liked, with half a sheet of notes before him in case he needed prompting. On one day he lectured on Ruskin, Clough, Watson, Flecker, A.E. and Kipling. On another the list ran Kipling, Hardy, F. Thompson, Bridges, Houseman. He was a great success, he was of use, the Greek Army was active in the north. A pleasant stay and victory seemed certain.

Beatrice's list, rather thin as she was whisked from capital to capital, grew to unmanageable proportions with notes for herself: 'small, dark', 'nice smile' and an exhortation, '*must* remember faces.' Few entries are longer than: 'Tea: the King, pleasant and evidently glad to be informal. Genl. Heywood, Mr Channon (climber) Sir Thomas Bloomfield (R.N.V.R.), Air Commodore George. We sit in Mary's (Palairet) nice warm little sitting-room with a fireplace.' On another occasion Dunsany was in the library of the legation and, seeing some volumes of Herodotus, amused the King by quoting him on Hercules: 'It is incorrect to say that Hercules was a god. The priests of Egypt have a careful record, which they showed me, of all that has happened for four thousand years, and in all that time no god has walked on the earth. In all that time the sun rose only once in the west, setting on that occasion in the east.' At the legation they also met Harold Macmillan fleetingly, Sir Harold and Lady Caccia, whom Dunsany knew, and quantities of generals.

By February 9th Beatrice could write to Arthur of . . . 'The Acropolis, which is closed to the public, I can't think why, British soldiers and officials are allowed on it, but poor Greek soldiers, some of whom have never seen Athens before, have to stay outside. Greeks are not allowed to dance in war time though they may sit in cabarets and drink if they want to – it seems a pity for one sees them sitting about on the edge of the pavements with nowhere to go.

'We are in a little flat we have taken for two months with a Greek cook who refers to Eddie as the "lord-boss", and one maid who speaks French . . . So far it has been cold, and frost-bite is the commonest injury at the front. General Wavell was here three weeks ago – we were all too discreet to mention it . . .' The flat, number four Plutarch Street, was modern, with an air-raid shelter and a fireplace for which they were grateful. A swallow nested in the eaves above the balcony and 'from some of the windows we looked down on the gardens of other houses in which almond and peach were flowering in the sunlight of the Greek spring. From the roof we could see the Acropolis and the whole range of Hymettus, and I [Dunsany] never let a day go by without going up to the flat roof to gaze awhile at the Parthenon.' Also on the roof was the wash-ing, laid out to dry. They were very snug there, though food was scarce. Beatrice too could enjoy this part of their adven-ture.

Dunsany had asked Sir Michael Palairet to place the passage in which Aeneas in Hades is guided through the door of dreams, and been impressed when Wavell said promptly and accurately that it came near the end of the sixth book of the Aeneid. They went to the site of the battle of Marathon and Sir Michael Palairet stood on a mound and read the account from Herodotus. A less happy visit in retrospect was one paid by Dunsany to the *Coventry*, which was later sunk. Typically he borrowed a rifle to have a crack at any Italian planes that came over. None did. They enjoyed Laurence Olivier as Heathcliff in the film of *Wuthering Heights* '. . . . and all the while the spring filled the country with more and more anemones and beautified the gardens of Athens . . . and humming-bird hawkmoths hovering before the flowers, and swallows soaring in sunlight, and the calm hills of Egina changing their colours above the sea in the twilight, all seemed to pretend that Greece had nothing to do but to wait for the summer and the ripening of olives.'[1]

They had expected, hoped, to be home in May but now Dunsany was offered the Chair of English at the University of Istanbul. It was flattering that his lectures had made a good impression and he felt that this was the way in which he could most help the war effort, and it probably would not be too bad anyway, so he accepted.

On March 25th, Greek Independence Day, Yugoslavia signed the German demands, which naturally depressed the Greeks. Dunsany was lecturing on the 26th and, regretting that Byron was not there to write of events, he said that as occupant of the chair that bore his name, he would read a poem of his own on the subject. He did so and scored a sensational success. Later it was read on the wireless. The next day it turned out that Yugoslavia had broken with Germany and on the 28th Dunsany delivered a new poem, welcoming them back to the cause of freedom and this one went just as well. That too was read on the wireless to keep the record straight.

The war seemed to be going well in the north, summer arrived with the end of March, Dunsany was happy lecturing and wondering about the fate of some war poems he had left with an agent in England. Then on April 6th Germany declared war on Yugoslavia and Greece. That afternoon there were German planes over Athens and they came a second time in the night. Dunsany 'went again to the roof of our flat to watch, and a lovely sight it was. Slow coloured lights went climbing up the sky from our guns and suddenly I saw go up from amongst them the most gorgeous display of fireworks that I have ever seen. It rose up pure golden and curved out to left and right and fell like the fountains of Versailles . . . it must have been a munition ship.' Another was hit later and all Athens quivered. 'Our maid and the doorkeeper of the flats, who were awakened with the rest of Athens, discussed whether one of them should go upstairs and knock at our door and tell us there had been an explosion. In the end for some reason they had decided not to.'

In spite of such a dramatic first night, Beatrice wrote calmly to her mother on April 9: 'I don't know if the war having spread

1. *The Sirens Wake*: Dunsany Autobiography Vol III.

will stop our job (in Istanbul) ... It is a great thing to have all the Germans shut up here at last; they were everywhere getting information but the day Germany declared war big omnibuses went round and collected them all. How is everybody?' and to her niece Mary Clive on April 10th a long letter in which she said it was nice to be offered the Chair in Istanbul, but she rather doubted their ever arriving.

Refugees with carts piled with chairs and little bundles appeared. Beatrice found, 'The Greeks are not organisers, but their courage atones.' There were raids each night. Dunsany gave, to more women than men, a lecture on the English Authorised Version of the Bible as it was Greek Holy Week. The sirens sounded but no one left their place. Rumours of disaster abounded.

On April 16th Mr Burn of the British Council told Dunsany that he had now completed his job and perhaps he should make plans to go. Neither mentioned any other factor that might speed his decision. That night Beatrice had just gone to bed when an hysterical Greek woman rang up in a panic with news that the line had broken. What were the English going to do? Beatrice was greatly irritated, said she knew nothing and doubtless they would be told what to do in time.

Dunsany went to inquire about evacuation in the morning. He saw an officer riding on the pavement and found in that a sign that the sanctity of the city was over. At the office the applicants were many and ships were few. He was offered a place on a Polish cargo-boat – leaving for Haifa at six that afternoon, no food, sleep in the hold – and advised not to take it. An immediate decision was necessary and he said yes. Getting visas he was struck by the sight of a perfectly ordered house, 'beautifully furnished, tidy and full of charm, but utterly doomed. If there is any trace of ruin, any singe of flame, the mind is easily prepared for disaster; but when there is not the slightest sign of trouble, when the table-linen is clean, the carpets swept ... the imagination is called on almost with violence to picture what is coming and the vision of disaster shocks it.'

A few brief farewells, 'a suitcase, a linen bag, a small holdall attaché case, bundle of rugs and basket of food' packed and they were in a taxi for the Piraeus and their boat the *Warzaura.*

Beatrice left a row of dresses behind, Dunsany wore two hats, and regretted two more. So began the most appreciated journey of Dunsany's life. He had been interested to be bombed in Kent, and pleased by the rigours and difficulties of their roundabout approach to Athens. As a refugee he was euphoric. Beatrice kept her diary and wrote a continuing letter to her niece, Mary Clive, while Dunsany wrote to another Pakenham niece, Pansy Lamb. The events naturally overlap, each using adventures, Beatrice the least. She did not mention that she was not well but in her diary admitted: 'The ship is filthy – I suppose we have the crews' cabins, three girls and I share one with dirty straw mattresses, and the sanitary arrangements are dirty and meagre in the extreme. But we are all relieved to get away and there are many worse things. No news is the worst.' Dunsany wrote on April 18th, their first day on board:

'I feel one has not travelled, who has only travelled first class or steerage, the extravagant luxury of these two being practically indistinguishable; but travelling refugee is a new experience. The chances of your ever receiving this letter are not at the moment too promising, but I dare say you'll get it. I'm glad I did not stay in Ireland while such an interesting world was in such a crisis, but it is a pity Beatrice is here. [She doesn't think so, B.D. – added in her handwriting.] April 19. The lives of refugees are full of interest. One learns what a lot of places there are to sit down, and how to be comfortable, with the help of one's life-belt. And one learns what good food bread is; water is grand stuff too when you can get it. Everyone in the ship has lived a life in the last few days which would make at least one good book each. The Germans come over two or three times a day. Oh, how I criticized the food of the ——; and rightly too. I wouldn't exchange it for the fare of a refugee, and a refugee's table-manners, which I just heard summed up thus, *à la guerre, comme à la guerre*; and to this is added tolerance and help. I expect most of us in this ship have a price on our heads.'

The *Warzaura* sailed on the first night by the light of an uncomfortably bright moon, and, pacing the deck, Dunsany met a contented Australian who remarked: 'I always wanted to do a Mediterranean cruise.' But in the morning they were back surrounded by the low Greek hills and the shattered wrecks of the Piraeus; their convoy had not yet materialised. At 5 p.m. with great relief they left again. There was nothing to do but

talk and they counted eighteen nationalities on board, largely
Poles, Greeks, Czechs and British. There was also a great
number of dogs brought, Beatrice was told, because the Germans
would eat them if they were left. They behaved very well,
neither fighting nor barking, but the white ones turned to
grey and the black became yet darker, for there was limited
water. Some Czechs used to sing sad songs in the evening and
all around children played soldiers and when later events sent
them real if empty cartridges, they happily seized on them. A
wireless picked up Italian news, all bad, and four translators
passed it on each to his own group so that you could see the
reaction spreading. Beatrice does not mention the Germans on
the 19th, but 'is depressed by the news' and 'Met Mr Sedgewick, correspondent of *N.Y. Times* (cousin of our friends in
U.S.A.) and his Greek wife, who nobly gave me a towel, a
precious gift on this ship. But the ship treats us well and it is
not intended for 300 or 400 passengers.' Mr Sedgewick said
they were beginning to look like refugees, 'our clothes are
rumpled, our shoulders droop and we are very dirty.' Nor was
their destination certain – 'probably Crete or Egypt'. They
were not allowed to throw even orange-peel overboard as it
might give away their position. Dunsany continued on the
20th April (their third day on board) ... 'they spoil me here;
I was sleeping quite comfortably on the deck yesterday when a
lady insisted on giving me a mattress. And last night they let
me sleep on the officers' deck also on a mattress, under lovely
stars.' Beatrice just noted: 'Sun. Apr. 20. Greek Easter and it
was most touching to see them all gather for a meal in the
saloon and sing Greek hymns and songs – two old women with
tears running down – I wouldn't have missed being a refugee.

'We go very slowly so as not to pass Crete by daylight. Some
alarms but our convoy of twenty-four is guarded by a cruiser
(the *Carlisle*) two destroyers and two Greek submarines – and
some seaplanes at intervals.' They were joined the next day by
a Free French cruiser and a Greek warship. Theirs was the
only passenger ship, but they had two machine-guns and six
gunners. It was as well, for Dunsany wrote:

'And then on Monday morning we were found out, under a blue
sky with one cloud in it and in that cloud was a Stuke.

L.D.   R

'No sirens at sea and our only intimation was a roar from our machine-gunner, and the bomber swerved on to the next ship. I suppose I may give you information that has already been given to the world by the Italian wireless, which is that they sank the ship, but it is a lie. We didn't feel too pleased to have been found out. Then they came again and it looked like a fleet action, but they didn't actually attack our ship this time.'

Beatrice continues:

'Our 2 escapes gave a sort of zest to the evening and spontaneously people brought out their own food and many of us had a picnic supper on deck (that is at 6 on board); Capt. Paltov, a Russian painter who likes to talk metaphysics and religion, shared his chicken with me and Mr Lyell[1] – I only produced raisins – and a Canadian girl and party from Belgrade gave us stewed pears. The suitcases are piled on deck under awnings and we sat on top of that (there are of course, no seats), and then a sing-song began and after sunset when it was going well there was a shout of "Alert" and again we dashed for shelter; the planes swooped low and there was much firing; our soldiers believe they got one, it was losing height but darkness hid it before it touched the sea and I didn't see it at all. What a life!'

Dunsany commented:

'. . . Nobody is calmer than Beatrice on these occasions, though all are calm enough . . . Had he dropped some bombs he could scarcely have missed us, or he could have swept our decks with his machine-guns; but he fired a torpedo instead, and missed. No one quite knows why he did not fire with his machine-guns. One theory is that he died just at the wrong moment. That is what our machine-gunners believed. I never saw calmer weather or a bluer sea. Men were not for the life-boats; there would not have been room. But there were plenty of ships near us, and I recollected all the time that it was the height of the Mediterranean bathing-season, a very different matter from the Atlantic. In spite of which one or two men stupidly argued that they ought to have a seat in a life-boat, because it said so in a notice on the wall of their cabin!'

Mr Sedgewick had been opening a can of sardines when the attack came and was troubled that such a paltry act should be his last, though he comforted himself that the last recorded

1. Archie Lyall turned out to have been at Oxford with Edward Longford and been on a British mission in Yugoslavia.

act of Matthew Arnold was to catch a bus and that of Gladstone was getting through a wire fence.

Next day they were in safer water but still apprehensive. Dunsany

'came up to have a look round after a perfect night's rest. A lovely dawn. Saw a lady "made up" a bit; she evidently thinks she is going to live. After our bit of bother last night we heated up our engines and are all racing for land at about the pace of a tricycle, about five knots in fact. Don't let this information out as the Germans can, and would, find out from encyclopaedias exactly what the pace of a tricycle was. This morning a sailor (Sailor R.N.) in reach-me-downs, gave me two lemons, suggesting lemonade for Beatrice. I said I had a bag of sugar and went to get it. I had just got it when they said, "Bombers coming". When I looked at the blue Mediterranean and thought of the sugar in my pocket, I felt like a treasure ship. However nothing came near our ship and the sugar is still dry except what went into the lemonade, which was very good. Yesterday while playing chess I saw a shoehorn in my box of chessmen and thought how useful it would be if I were ever to take off my shoes. I put them on in Greece about a week ago.'

The rest was anticlimax, though far from pleasant as the squalor increased, with the garbage that could not be thrown away lying in heaps. On the next day they were 'so safe that you see people forgetting their life-belts' and on 24th they reached Port Said. 'A sad moment ... I feel this has been about the best week of my life and that I was educated at Eton and on the s.s. ———.' They were driven to Cairo and had a row about the fare. Everything was back to normal. Another trip to the familiar Mena Hotel and they could relax. Beatrice felt ashamed that she had lost nothing but some clothes and books, and that 'a bath and a day in bed can put me right, and I can do nothing for the rest.' Meanwhile Dunsany wrote to Lady Jersey:

'Beatrice, who has been sleeping in the same pair of boots for a week, is now resting without them, in a comfortable bed. She is beginning to adopt the view of Anatole France's dog "wherever I am, I am in the middle of it all". Because the day we arrived in Kent, Kent became one of the world's hottest spots, and when we were off the West Coast of Ireland was the worst week of the war at sea (198,000 tons) and when, after a rest, we went to Greece, things warmed up there, and when we left it, the sea was distinctly hot.'

and later he wrote to Mary Clive,

'You will have heard that we are alive; this is to let you know that we are well ... I keep seeing very smart people in hotels and realizing, always with surprise, that they are from the ragged groups reclining on heaps of refuse, that I got to know so well. A fellow refugee who came to tea with us yesterday told me that the Captain told him the number of inches by which the torpedo missed our ship ... today we were astonished to hear that a job I was offered in Turkey is not yet off. More likely "refugee" will become our permanent occupation. It is not very cool ...'

When they recovered, to Beatrice's surprise and pleasure, Dunsany sought out the Cathedral to give thanks for their deliverance. His relationship with the Protestant Church was always friendly and never precise, but it certainly grew stronger. He enjoyed reading the lesson at Dunsany when he got home. They sought out their six gunners and took them swimming, at which they excelled. There was constant news of who had and who had not escaped from Greece, of which ships got through and which were sunk. The rest of their luggage was reported sunk. The hot wind blowing from the desert sent the temperature up around 106° and neither of them was well – Dunsany had a bad cold, Beatrice asthma – which marred an otherwise peaceful period of recuperation for though there were sirens in Cairo, there were no near bombs and though there were soldiers, there was no fighting close at hand. Just heat, and lemonade, occasional shopping or mosque-seeing expeditions and meals with friends. Dunsany wrote a poem a day and his *Songs of an L.D.V.* were published, in his opinion very badly.

After two months, with several more before Dunsany was due in Turkey, Beatrice suggested and organised winter in South Africa. This journey by boat they did not enjoy. Dunsany recalled later:

'There were two kinds of beetle in our beds and my wife at first seemed to take some sort of dislike to them, but I asked her what harm the beetles did, whereas the Chinese stewards ... ! ... The immediate effect of drinking a cup of tea as far as one's shirt was concerned was as if one had poured it externally over one's shirt. Anybody contemplating a holiday of a fortnight in the Red Sea at midsummer should have at least a hundred shirts . . . roast beef and sausages made me wonder if the Company had been allowed to know that their ship had slipped away from cold Northern waters. . . . I remember once in the Sahara coming to an old camping-ground, for the Arabs never camp on fresh ground, and seeing the ticks run out to meet the camels: somewhat in that spirit are travellers met by taxi-drivers and others in Aden.'

Beatrice's exhausted notes, written at the time are almost as eloquent:

Sunday June 22nd 1941: There are some 1,200 Italian prisoners on board who come on deck a good deal and one evening sang well. One result is that water is not sufficient in this weather and there is no washing of clothes though we need it as never before. Also no deck-chairs, decks crowded with extra boats.
Monday June 23 1941: What looked like steam rising from the sea, we are dripping and some men walk about with towels round their necks.
Tuesday June 24 1941: Aden, hot but less steamy.
Wednesday June 25 1941: Aden, coaling, Very hot night.
Thursday June 26 1941: Aden, sailed 2 p.m.
Friday June 27 1941: Gulf of Aden, hot.
Saturday June 28 1941: Met monsoon in Indian Ocean.

Everyone was tired; many, including Dunsany, had developed boils and he went straight to hospital in Durban. There he made a rapid recovery, while Beatrice plunged into a social round though she knew no one. A stranger, Mrs Van Amstell, heard her telephoning unsuccessfully for a hotel room and asked her to stay for a fortnight. Soon she was writing: 'The usual form of entertaining is tea-parties in the morning' and of the evening 'the custom is to get there at 6.30, sherry, dinner at 7.30.' The list of names lengthens once more, among them Marda Vanne who had played in *If* in 1921 and Gwen Ffrangcon Davies. Dunsany began giving talks to the Rotary Club and Literary Societies as soon as he was up and made a record of some of his poems. Soon he found some guinea fowl to shoot, but there was no chess player to beat. Robin Mount who had married Julia Pakenham, another niece, and had been in hospital, turned up to accompany them to the Karkhof Falls, which Dunsany painted. Beatrice picked flowers and five Zulu boys performed for them – 'I think it was a warriors' dance as they advanced in a row stamping and waving and the little leader making wild faces. One tiny one didn't know the dance and watched the feet of the others, coming in late with a rather timid little stamp.' – Other jaunts were to the spot where Churchill was captured in the Boer War; the battlefield where Dunsany had fought, other falls, and the Big Hole, 'the largest man-made crater, an abandoned diamond mine.' On August 7th Beatrice wrote to her mother that their visit to Turkey was finally cancelled so they might soon be home and that nothing was rationed 'except I believe silk stockings.' Though they did not admit it even to each other, they were relieved to be going home. Before starting back there was a month in the country which gave Beatrice asthma so they moved to the spectacular Valley of a Thousand Hills for further convalescence. Dunsany realised that the year's events had given him the material for an epic poem and he began to write 'The Journey' before he had in fact completed it. He thought the metre of 'Childe Harold' suitable for a poem describing a long pilgrimage written by a sometime Byron-Chair-holder.

After a further delay, alleviated by sunshine, books, butterflies and peaches at 1d each, the SS *Umtali* sailed on January 24th. Dunsany, showing more anxiety for his work than for himself, left copies of all he had written with a friend on dry land and posted carbon copies of any new work whenever he had an opportunity on the way home. There were few passengers but among them some that played chess. He read as much as he had written of 'The Journey' and was corrected on two scientific points by Brigadier Sir Christopher Lewis. The rainbow at Howick Falls, it transpired, could not have moved lower down the water after midday as he described. Dunsany had left before twelve and found it lower on his return, but did not realise that though it had sunk while he was away, it was now climbing. Also he said that the sun changed its direction when he passed under it where it was then vertical, whereas this happens at the equator. The second error remained as 'the rhymes seemed somehow to have frozen round my mistake.'

Beatrice noted in Freetown: 'If dust can be damp then that is what this is. The sunset like a frosty crimson ball.' Dunsany bought the biggest bunch of bananas he could carry. From there on they had a convoy, and no difficulties. Beatrice's entries are once more brief:

27th Feb. Two days east wind; and now mist which is calmer and safer.

28th Feb. Told to be ready for possible air attack today.

March 1. Our own climate again, north east breeze, gentle sun, crisp and clear.

March 2. A very stormy night, everything flung about.

March 4. Anchored outside Oban. Very cold.

March 5. Landed!

PART SIX

Last Days

DUNSANY went straight to Ireland and hardly left it for six years. Beatrice had not seen her mother for almost eighteen months and paid her a visit before joining him. Though she was now ninety-two the force of Lady Jersey's character had not diminished. She had refused to leave London, until it was put to her that she would be a nuisance and a danger to those who had to rescue her if her house was bombed. She then consented to be evacuated to a cottage attached to the new house which Lutyens had built at Middleton on the site of the old Georgian mansion. Beatrice was woken one night by a maid who told her that her mother had had a slight heart attack. 'Send for the doctor at once,' cried Beatrice, preparing to take control of the situation. 'Oh I wouldn't dare to do that without asking,' said the maid, and as Beatrice opened her mouth to remonstrate, she realised that no more would she.

Dunsany was quiet and they were tired. Though Ireland was neutral, many young men had gone. Petrol was not rationed but simply non-existent. If there was someone you wanted to see, you went by dog-cart. On occasional visits to Dublin, Beatrice was greeted with, 'But I hardly knew you, you're so thin.' Shortages had been foreseen by the Irish, but the Dunsanys refused hoarded tea offered by friends and instead drank cowslip or lime blossom brews. There was no electricity at Dunsany until 1946 and the paraffin ration had to be turned over to the kitchen, but the cook managed to make some candles out of mutton fat. They each had battery lamps in the drawing-room which made a pool of light for reading but could not dispel the gloom entirely; also a battery wireless. They listened eagerly to news of the war and Churchill's speeches found no more appreciative audience.

A good piece of news from the Mexboroughs was censored but Dunsany unerringly divined what it must be:

Dunsany Castle

My Dear Marjorie,
I've been guessing what your news was, and Sarah's. This is my guess – that the HQ of the most adulterated salt in England has been hit. If it has then Hitler will have one afternoon off in every year to sit on the ice with Judas.

Yours ever
D.

The great salt factory had indeed been struck.

This muted version of normal life at Dunsany was suitable while they gradually recovered from their exertions and not unpleasant afterwards. If there were fewer servants than before, there remained at least a local footman, a scullery maid and housemaids to support the cook, and a butler, when one was found. General Hammond had died while they were away, and the estate was now run by a steward and a solicitor in Dublin, whose black city clothes looked out of place when he came to look at the acres in his care. Though a permit was necessary for Beatrice's visits to England, it was not hard to obtain. Perhaps Dunsany missed snipe a little more frequently, and, though he was publishing as fast as ever, his fatigue often showed. *Wandering Songs* (1943) included his translations from the Turkish and, as the title implies, the poems he wrote on his travels, describing spring in Athens, the soup on the refugee boat or the Sphinx.

In the same year he delivered the Donnellan Lectures at Trinity College, Dublin, dealing in turn with Prose, Poetry and Drama. They are moderate and sensible. Saying that it is difficult to draw a line between prose and poetry he remarks: 'If a man who is writing prose strays into poetry it is rather as if at that moment he had become a little drunk; while if he is writing poetry and drops into prose it is as if a heavy meal of meat suddenly overtook him and he became dull and sleepy, without dreams.' Both are apt descriptions of weak passages in his own work. In his third lecture he maintains, 'that the material of the dramatist is events and that poetry can greatly ornament a play, but it cannot construct one' – which he would not have said thirty years before, but is a change of emphasis rather than belief. He is still upholding the same standards, praising Milton and Shakespeare, Coleridge and Shelley. He did not believe in seeking beauty and truth in unlikely places; several of the poems from his most recent collection were about the Parthenon, and this was characteristic; when he saw the Taj Mahal he had written about that. His displeasure is scarcely called forth, a slap for those who say Bacon wrote Shakespeare, a few words on the use of nouns where adjectives are demanded and a quotation from 'Maud': 'And chalk and alum and plaster are sold to the poor for bread', to show that Tennyson was ahead of his time and on the right side about the white loaf. The lectures were a success and published two years later.

Dunsany was never interested in cutting the work he wrote so fast and his long poems suffer from this. 'The Journey' (1944) and 'The Year' (1946), a diary of twelve uneventful country months in verse are repetitive and therefore best to dip into rather than plough through. Compton Mackenzie found the former a 'curiously felicitous record', though 'some of the verses may seem jog-trot, some of it pedestrian'.[1] 'Another Year' was typed but not published. The second and third volumes of his autobiography[2] are much less good than the first. He had two books to jog his memory, his game book and a great list of where and when he had written every story, poem, article or play he had ever penned. These sources are all too apparent. He never asked to see his wife's diary, but this is consistent with his stated view that all that could be interesting about his life is the demonstration of how the mind of a poet had worked. He therefore goes to some trouble to recollect what inspired various works but nevertheless dismissed the two volumes (in the second one) as 'garrulity rather than art.'

In worldly terms the most successful book of these years was *Guerilla*. Written in thirty-eight working days it was designed for that purpose, though Dunsany was rather ashamed of so low a motive. Heinemanns offered £1,000 for a thriller so Dunsany wrote one about the resistance in Greece. Though he transferred the Troubles and gave the story a strange quality – with references only to 'The Land' never to Greece and 'The Mountain', which almost speaks – it is essentially his only realistic novel, and achieved its aim. It won the prize and sold out a first edition of 10,000 copies. Paper was short and so no

1. *Evening News* October 13th 1944.
2. *The Sirens Sleep* and *The Sirens Wake*.

second edition appeared, which was disappointing, but in America a pocket edition 2 × 3 × 4 inches was issued to the army, so many thousands more saw it. John Betjeman writing in the *Daily Herald*[1] found 'the freshness proper to an adventure book' and it was widely liked. In 1943 the horse that was taking Beatrice to Church (no petrol) tripped and she was flung over its head. She broke an arm, the horse broke a leg, and she listened to a conference between the vet (she'd better have a tetanus injection) and the doctor (nothing is worse for her asthma, I think we'll risk it without). So she was unable to take Dunsany's dictation of the rest of *Guerilla*, and Dunsany returned to writing with his own hand leaning back in his chair and using coloured chalks.

He translated the 'Odes of Horace', using a French crib when in difficulties, and a few years later the Horatian Society asked him to speak, which he duly did, writing them an ode for the occasion. Beatrice accompanied him to the dinner and sat next to C. B. Fry whom she had not seen for almost fifty years when, an enthusiastic girl of eighteen, she had presented him with a cup as the Captain of a victorious football team. Two collections of stories, *The Man who Ate the Phoenix* and *The Fourth Book of Jorkens*, contain excellent tales but they are collected from the previous fifteen years and the best usually turn out to have been written before the war.

A Glimpse from a Watch-Tower, a collection of essays published in 1945, shows what he was thinking as 'The Year', if not a major work, shows what he was doing. Dunsany shared with others an unreasoning unshakable faith that Britain would win the war, and in the month after Dunkirk, a feeling that we had now rid ourselves of unreliable allies and could get on with it. Nevertheless the news was often depressing. He felt, as he was, isolated from events, hence the title of his essays, on the first page of which he wrote, 'I look at the world from a great distance for I am in Southern Ireland.' In 'The Year' he refers to 'this lifeless gloom we call neutrality.' Great massacres in India will come simply because there has not been one for some time and nature demands blood periodically. On a more specific political note, he commented: 'There have been three

1. Feb. 17th, 1944.

great scourges of India, Genghis Khan, Tamberlane and Pethwick Lawrence.'[1]

Old Lady Jersey died on May 22nd 1945 at the age of ninety-five. As a small child she had shaken hands with the Duke of Wellington and knitted a pair of red muffetees for the soldiers at the Crimean War and she managed to outlive Hitler by a few weeks.

The end of the war, though naturally a relief, hardly affected Dunsany in his state of near-retirement. New threats came to replace old anxieties.

Chapter VII from his *A Glimpse from a Watch-Tower* begins: 'Strange news came to us today. We have just heard of the atomic bomb. . . . I think that a new era started yesterday . . . henceforth we are all people with a mission, a strange mission, not to destroy the world. . . .' Dunsany's belief that machines have got beyond the control of poor-spirited man coupled with his belief that it is in the nature of man to fight from time to time lead to the conclusion that unless 'some overwhelming spiritual revival should sweep the world, turning man from cheating man in the old familiar ways . . . all the history of Man may culminate in a radiance of energy suddenly flashed from our planet, which may scorch our wandering neighbours, Venus and Mars, as they pass.' A solemn and sincere conclusion, but it seems to be stated with more rhetoric than regret.

He still had bursts of energy, not always universally welcomed. His long-standing dislike of furniture polish meant that it had to be applied furtively in his absence. Returning home early on a winter afternoon he detected the smell, commanded that the whole stock of the offending substance be brought to him on a tray and threw it tin by tin from the window on to a bank of snow beneath, where it remained, gradually sinking with the thaw. 'I'm not advertising,' he declared on another occasion and had a firm's name removed from a manhole.

Randal had had an active war in the East and Vera, his wife, had been – and still was – in Brazil. To arrange their future, whether together or apart, Randal sailed to South America in 1946 and returned on the *Queen Mary* in the spring

1. A Labour MP who favoured independence and was made Secretary of State for India and Burma that year.

with Vera and his six-year-old son, Eddie, whom he had never seen. However the reconciliation did not last. Vera returned to Brazil and Randal, who was due to rejoin his regiment in India, took 'little Eddie' over to Ireland.

Dunsany and Beatrice were aged sixty-eight and sixty-six when they found themselves suddenly confronted with the task of bringing up their small Brazilian grandson but they met the challenge gallantly. Both had always been fond of children, 'little Eddie' was sensitive and affectionate, and soon they were devoted to him and he to them, and what had begun as a duty became the greatest pleasure and interest of their lives.

When he first arrived Eddie could only speak a few words of English and communication was difficult. He had nightmares, and when Beatrice asked what was frightening him he said only that he could not say. She coaxed him to tell her, if not in English, in Portuguese, and when he did, all she could catch was the word '*Diablo*'. However, he was soon chattering fluently and endured the rigours of a boarding school, so the Dunsanys were once more arranging their lives to fit in with days out, half terms and school holidays.

In 1947 Randal returned from India. Beatrice decided, and set to work to persuade Dunsany to agree, that they should make over the Castle and property in Ireland to Randal and live permanently at Dunstall. She had noticed that tea with the vicar was an event to which he looked forward, and thought this no life for a writer. Once he had felt for Kipling, who complained that his wife seemed to think he could spin stories out of himself like a spider and would not let him go out. Now he was in the same position but clinging to it. When Randal married Sheila de Rutzen[1] in 1947, he gave in and very reluctantly left. The actual move was made in the middle of the night. To avoid being taxed twice, they discovered that it was essential not to be in residence in England or Ireland on April 5, so they took a boat at 11.45 p.m. and spent the night at sea.

It was immediately clear what a good decision had been

1. She was born Sheila Philipps, daughter of Captain Sir Henry Philipps, and had a daughter, Victoria, by her first husband, Baron de Rutzen, who had been killed in Italy in 1944.

made. In Ireland Dunsany had been growing old. Now energy returned, his spirit revived. He went up to London almost once a week to visit his club. He was a fellow of the Royal Literary Society and of the Royal Geographical Society and President of the Authors' Society and enjoyed the dinners, speeches and duties that these entailed. He lectured at schools. His stories in the evening papers brought him a further degree of renown and when Beatrice broke her knee at Victoria Station in 1950 she was gratified that a nurse in the ambulance asked Eddie if he was the grandson of the writer. Instead of the snipe of the bogs, Dunsany pursued partridges and occasionally neighbouring pheasants. Nor had it been a question of leaving the home of his youth for he had always loved the woods and hills of Dunstall best of all.

Dunsany was still interested to meet new people and he would write to strangers whom he admired and invite them to Dunstall for the day. However they did have an introduction to Odette Churchill, the heroine of the French resistance who had been tortured by the Gestapo. She came down and they were impressed that she of all people should feel she owed the world something, 'because I came through where so many of my friends did not.' She also had a sympathetic preference for gardening over politics, 'You put in a carrot and a carrot comes up. You vote for a cause and nothing happens.'

There were also frequent visits from old friends and their children and from relations. Beatrice had kept in close touch with her fourteen nephews and nieces and now there were many great nephews and nieces who came to Dunstall and rolled down the banks as their parents had done before them.

Dunsany enjoyed helping inexperienced writers. Anne Crone, whose novel had been refused by twelve publishers, was losing heart and sent it to him. He read it straight through in one day, thought it was good and arranged its publication. In 1949 he wrote an article praising her, and Mary Lavin, another he had helped to get started, in an American magazine called *Tomorrow*. Both were planning to become teachers and not the least of his help was to persuade their families not to oppose a more precarious career. Anne Crone went back to teaching, Mary Lavin continued, and continues, to write with great success. On another occasion he found a privately printed copy of sonnets by Lady Wentworth[1] in a country drawing-room. They were handsomely bound and clearly unread. He liked them, wrote letters recommending them and they duly appeared in public.

In the spring of 1950 there was a correspondence in the *Spectator* as to whether Hewlett Johnson, the 'Red Dean' of Canterbury, should be removed on political grounds, and Dunsany sent a long letter pointing out with his old relish that there was only one formula for such a deed, and that had been laid down by a 'clear and binding' precedent.

'The Crown has to utter eight words before any action can be taken, and the rest of the business is entrusted to four knights. The eight words are "Who will rid me of this turbulent priest?" As soon as these words have been formally uttered the four knights proceed to Canterbury. Originally they were self-appointed, but this is scarcely in accordance with modern usage. Any four knights would scarcely do for a royal mission to Canterbury. Sir Stafford Cripps might as a Senior Member of the Government, appear as an obvious choice. But a Field-Marshal should surely be one of them and, if a Field-Marshal, then an Admiral of the Fleet and a Marshal of the Royal Air Force. But more than all these choices I would recommend Sir Don Bradman for it would be an active mission . . .'

A fortnight in Paris in the spring of one year and in Holland the next was successful. He had never seen Holland before and, though he thought the bulbs might as well have been cabbages, they were so commercially grown, he loved the pictures, the huge sky, the neatness and in all found it a beautiful little country. Nor were these the limits of his journeying.

Ever since he had discovered it, Dunsany had been susceptible to the mixture of admiration and energy, which he found across the Atlantic. One day in August 1952 an American admirer, Hazel Littlefield Smith, was brought to lunch at Dunstall by Patrick Mahony, a mutual friend. Dunsany rose to the occasion, and she noted each syllable: ' "Bah," he said, "technique cannot make a work of art . . ." Suddenly with a startling "Hah!" Dunsany came back to drama, "Hah," he exclaimed, "I know where Synge got one of his most dramatic ideas . . . Ah yes," he said, "we had plenty of excitement here

1. Daughter of Wilfrid Blunt and great grand-daughter of Byron.

in the days when Goering was raging overhead: plenty of inspiration for writing poems. I had only to reach up into the air and pull it down . . ." Somewhat dazed by the impact of his dynamic personality I had listened all this time in silence.'[1] He copied out a poem and she sent a thank you letter in verse, as well as a few pounds of sugar. A friendship was formed and prospered. They posted their own verses and praise of one another's back and forth. She asked them both to stay in California next March with some vague lectures to help pay for the journey. Beatrice had hurt her leg the year before and thought she might find it exhausting but urged him to go and, after many letters and plans, he went.

Patrick Mahony, who had introduced them, met him off the *Queen Mary*. He remembers that, faced with the vast number of volumes that accompanied Dunsany, he asked if he was going to make a gift to some library. 'No,' said Dunsany, 'I always travel with a complete set of my own books.' The Irish-American customs man was listening. 'Is this,' he asked, 'the Lord Dunsany who wrote *The Book of Wonder*?' A nod. 'Anyone who could write *The Book of Wonder* wouldn't be apt to make a false declaration,' he mumbled and in a trice they were on their way to the airport.

Landing in California,

'he came with the long forward stride of the hunter, swinging a walking-stick. From his shoulders floated a green woollen scarf. His face, lifted to the light glowed with eager expectation: a prophet on holiday . . . On his first morning in our house we heard the wild tinkling of his bell, then thumping, and a shout . . . From Dunsany's bathroom came a voice in tones of fury and desperation, "My razor! Where is my razor? My *razor*?"

Kwi (the maid) had unpacked it and put it in the cabinet over the lavatory. She explained this through the closed door.

"There is no cabinet," he shouted.

"Behind the mirror," I directed.

The rumblings continued like the mutterings of a volcano and he could not hear my instructions to put a finger under the lower edge of the mirror and pull forward so that the cabinet would be revealed. I pleaded with him to listen.

1. From *Lord Dunsany: King of Dreams* by Hazel Littlefield Smith; an enthusiastic and detailed account of her friendship with him in his last years. This account of Dunsany in America is based on it.

There was a silence then a triumphant "Ha!" and with sheer delight, "Ha, a secret cupboard; a family secret unmasked". '

Dunsany was not an easy guest, particularly without Beatrice to hover tactfully between him and the world. Mrs Smith had to 'spend a good piece of each morning bringing order to his room where boots, books, dinner-jackets and damp towels were left in a heap' and twenty-five pounds was the smallest amount of the essential rock salt that she could find for sale. She searched for the desired shades of pale blue writing-paper and purple ink, she tried to quiet his complaints in a hotel, 'but he would not be quieted.'

Outings brought out the best and worst in him. In the car he would mutter his incantations against the advertisements that flanked the road or sit silently for an hour before raging against the speed and discomfort of cars. Then his fancy would be caught and he would insist for example on swimming in the Salton Sink which was 250 feet below sea level. At Glacier Point there is a spectacle which might have been arranged to catch his imagination. Over a ledge above a drop of five thousand feet a heap of burning logs are rolled so that, as they strike the rocks that jut out below they break into showers of sparks and fire. However the electric-lights on the terrace from which he was watching were not turned off and he spent the fifteen minutes railing against the management of the hotel. His hostess's patience was tried if not exhausted and 'the vigor with which I closed the car door must have warned him of my feelings'. However when he was caught in a dust storm sixty miles from home, and a man of seventy-five might be permitted a few complaints, he saw the whole thing as an adventure, enjoyed every moment and wrote a story about it; and he was truly penitent after he had been difficult.

So the visit was a success on both sides. On uneventful days he would lie on a swing-sofa in the garden, sometimes thinking about a poem or story, sometimes just watching the humming-birds in the sun. A friendly amateur agent named Willow Wray arranged lectures to clubs and literary societies for him, and these were invariably successful. Interviewers and photographers arrived and were welcome, for though he would not pose formally, he did not otherwise mind even 'explosive photography' (flash lights) and he had always liked questions about his work and views. Better still were admirers.

'Invited and uninvited they came to morning coffee and afternoon tea. They adored him. His impeccable dignity and natural charm were all that they could have desired . . . the conversation at tea more often became a brilliant monologue . . .'

New York was as happy. A letter to Beatrice after a dinner in his honour at the Yale Club is bubbling with the high spirits engendered by success.

'Tho I had no idea I should have to talk, I got up at once and my speech, which was rather long, went right down. The success was astonishing and as they were all stars or astronomers, it cannot quite quickly die out . . . Gloria Swanson came to stare at me very nicely . . . I am told that two Dunsany experts are coming to dinner. This has simply been a triumphal tour all the way.'

He went to America again in each of the two following years and his letters if less euphoric are contented, after a slightly nervous start.

The Boat-Train.
Feb. 18 1954.

'The only thing I know I have forgotten so far is my silver. You can spend it. The gloom of the station is lit by the occasional flash of camera-men. They got me out of the train to make a pressman's holiday. I find that unusual on this side of the Atlantic. I have verified that my vaccination certificate is in my passport without which I should be left ringing a leper's bell on Ellis Island.'

Queen Mary. Feb. 18.

'. . . Among others that this ship carries as part of its staff is one you would not guess in ten, a gardener.

'Will you tell Smith to tell the bootmaker to cut a piece out of those shoes of his to make them fit. I know it will spoil them and so does he. But hoping for a year that they will be all right does no good and spoiled shoes are better than spoiled feet . . .'

When he landed he started to calculate his costs and earnings and reckoned he would show a £200 profit on the journey. All is well. 'But I say definitely – use up as much of Barclays red ink as you want and we shall be able to buy him plenty more. . . . I've met a new tactic of the *chasseur d'autograph*. He encloses a dollar bill for me to sign. This beats a postage stamp for reply . . .' He found that the library of the University Club had seventeen of his books and happily signed them 'two of them in prose, fourteen in verse, and I have yet to inscribe *Lord Adrian.*'

Without Beatrice, he worries constantly that something may go wrong.

> March 9 1964, Santa Fe.
>
> (on the train) 7.10. I look a little ill-equipped without reindeer, because I have not been able to get rid of my fur coat. I hope Willow will meet me. Only you and she know my plans . . . March 10. The desert soon turned from what would feed a goat to what would feed a gazelle and then what would feed a lizard . . . I thought of a very good idea for a play, something the Queen of Greece once said to me . . .

The play, which was to be called *Power*, was never completed. It concerned a king who saw the way things were going and managed to lead a double life, becoming also the leader of the successful revolution that removed him, not quite accurate, but not bad as unintended prophecies go. There was to be a scornful aunt who doubts her nephew's abilities and 'is contemptuous even of his appearance.' Willow said it was tremendous.

He stayed with Willow in California but, though she was always full of plans and energy, she could not get him as many lucrative lectures as they had hoped. 'It has got out that I lectured for $50 and there are plenty of offers for that. But I have refused them and Willow agrees.' Instead he read poems and plays aloud at her house and hoped publishers might hear of them. He reports also that T. S. Eliot's plays are '*frightful* nonsense' and that he has 'brought poetry to the very lowest ebb that it has ever known. I don't mean that he writes it, but that he has overthrown it.' Eliot had become one of his main topics, scarcely a letter was without its reference to his lack of talent. He owned copies of his work, studied them and covered them with acid comments. Dunsany assailed Eliot as a symbol of all that was worst in those who tried to create poetry by treating trivia with solemn obscurity. A writer is seldom at his most dignified or attractive when attacking another more admired than himself, and the fact that Eliot was enjoying great success with plays in verse lays Dunsany open to the charge of jealousy as well as failure of appreciation. But, given that he had continued to admire Elizabethan and 19th rather than 20th century literature and that he still enjoyed grand themes, strange fancies, the flash of jewels or the fall of kings, it was hardly likely that he would find fear in a handful of dust; nor, having failed to do so, is it surprising that when this 'frightful nonsense' was acclaimed on all sides, he felt the wish to protest; and it was never his way to protest only once.

Work and the sun took up his time.

'The play lumbered forward rather heavily, the Willows say it is wonderful. . . . There's a big cloud overhead, which is a collector's piece in California. I knocked off a light poem today called *Thanks*:

> 'I often thought of Fame,
> Coming with her late wreath,
> Where a slab told my name
> And that I lay beneath.
> But all my thanks to you
> Fair California State
> Who something you thought due
> Has given, not too late.

'I was looking at a photograph of T. S. Eliot. The mouth looks as though he were really trying to tell someone something but all the upper part of the face looks puzzled and perplexed by his "raid on the inarticulate with shabby equipment always deteriorating in the general mess of imprecision of feeling"; in fact his ignorance of plain English and his inability to write clearly.'

On March 20th he moved to stay with Mrs Smith in 'the same pleasant rooms' as the year before. There had just been an earthquake which cracked the ceilings 'but not nearly as much as the surviving Dunstall ones'. He read 'Under Milk Wood' and found that Dylan Thomas 'has a Rabelaisian imagination, but a touch of insanity prevents him from using English properly and of course like all that school he is obscure.' There was also an altercation with a barber who 'was a complete savage and started shaving my head quite bald on one side with clippers. He was barbarously rude too.' And he asked

Beatrice, 'Do you remember the leopards' and wild cats' eyes
that shone by the roads in India? Here it is small empty beer
cans'; he enjoyed giving a talk on television, driving to San
Francisco and seeing the film *Roman Holiday*. Above all it was
restful, as New York was not, and he was allowed to go to bed
early if he wanted to.

His 1955 American trip was similarly successful and he
planned a third which never materialised.

From California he had written, 'Yes we must get the
Betjemen[1] again. She is no longer cow-conscious, he tells me
it's chickens now,' and still enjoyed having people to Dunstall.
Again the French showed interest in his plays which he thought
was '*Diablement chic.*'

He published at least one book every year from 1943 to
'54, except for 1953, when he had produced two the year
before. After 1947 these consisted of two collections of Jorkens
stories which find that traveller in less than his peak form and
with the wrong views on the cutting of dogs' tails but still
excellent company; *The Strange Journeys of Colonel Polders*, a
cross between Jorkens and Dean Spanley in that an Indian at
the Colonel's club sends his mind into a series of animals and
we are told his adventures; *To Awaken Pegasus*, a book of longer
poems including 'Ulysses Bound to the Mast' which Dunsany
thought his best; and two collections of stories and two novels –
one science fiction, the other sending its hero on a doomed search
for tolerance. Though he was ever more versatile his best work
had been done before the war.

When he started to write he had one subject, his gods, and
one tone, and relied on his originality and the power of his
language to make up for lack of plot, character or facility. The
language of his last years is almost flat, but easily read, the
imagination replaced by invention. Far more accessible than
his earliest writing, it was naturally more widely read, and,
equally naturally, rated much lower by Dunsany himself.
He liked his plays best, then the novels and put the stories last.
The most read today (1971) are the works of the 'thirties
which have all his virtues and vices in some degree – two dimen-
sional characters meandering through plots that threaten to

1. John Betjeman, the poet and his wife Penelope, whom he had met in
India.

lose themselves or cross irrevocably into whimsy, the modern world appearing only in complaints, yet doing so against such fondly evoked countryside, sometimes with humour and high-spirits, sometimes with a melancholy charm, always with a pleasing contempt for the drab, that it is easy to succumb to them. Almost all his prose achieved some success, none achieved enough to satisfy him.

Eddie Plunkett was now at Eton and they kept up a correspondence. He showed marked talent for painting and has since become an abstract artist, but at that time he was still painting in a traditional manner.

Dunstall Priory
Feb. 8 1956.

'. . . Beware of the false originality of the people who paint the sun square and green. It has never been done before, or not until recently; but that is because the sun is not square or that colour. Others assist them by writing in words long enough to be puzzling. . . . Similarly the deathshead moth makes a humming noise when he enters a bee-hive, which lulls the bees while he raids the honey. I had an uncle who was skilled at that. I am glad you agree about Toomey. I should like to have a portrait of him, and I think you would do a very good one of him. You would never be dull while you painted him. Turpentine for you and whiskey for him, if you can get it, would be good aids that would give fluency to the portrait.

If ever you know a boy or a swan who have a swan's feather to spare I should be glad of one or two . . .'

The portrait of Toomey was a great success and hangs at Dunsany.

Life was quiet but pleasant. Once he and Beatrice picked hops for half an hour for the Church. They were not skilled or quick, but the sweet smell was pleasant. As he had grown older, he had simply slowed down and now though he could see and hear perfectly well, he took little exercise and was unwilling to walk far. When, in the autumn of 1957 he went to Dunsany to shoot, he did little more than potter about with Toomey and failed to hit much. On Saturday October 22nd he missed some golden plover in the rain and on Sunday he drove over to Killeen to lunch with the Fingalls. A pain in his side that night he attributed to having twisted something when he got out of the car. The next day it was worse and Beatrice, to her surprise, found it quite easy to persuade him to go into a Dublin nursing home, without realising how serious the situation was. The pain came from his appendix and they operated that night. He never recovered consciousness and the next day, Tuesday October 25th, he died, aged seventy-nine years and three months. Though no more aware of the danger than Beatrice, before his operation he had called for paper and had written:

'I want to be buried in Kent in the Churchyard of Shoreham so as to share with every one of my neighbours whatever may be coming, when dead, as I shared it through the summer of 1940, when alive.'

Accordingly his funeral took place at Shoreham and ten days later, a memorial service was held at Kilmessan at which, as he wished, *Crossing the Bar* was read.

As the family returned to Dunsany, four wild swans rose from the water in the park and flew in formation over the Castle.

The Works of Lord Dunsany

Date	Title	Publisher
1905	THE GODS OF PEGANA – Tales	Elkin Mathews
1906	TIME AND THE GODS – Tales	Heinemann
1908	THE SWORD OF WELLERAN – Tales	George Allen
1910	A DREAMER'S TALES – Tales	George Allen
1914	FIVE PLAYS – Plays	Grant Richards
1915	51 TALES – Tales	Elkin Mathews
1912	THE BOOK OF WONDER – Tales	Heinemann
1917	PLAYS OF GODS AND MEN – Plays	Talbot Press (Dublin)
1922	PLAYS OF NEAR AND FAR – Plays	Putnam
1918	TALES OF WAR – Tales	Putnam
1919	UNHAPPY FAR-OFF THINGS – Tales	Elkin Mathews
1916	TALES OF WONDER – Tales	Elkin Mathews
1919	TALES OF THREE HEMISPHERES – Tales	Luce (Boston, USA)
1922	THE CHRONICLES OF RODRIGUES – Novel	Putnam
1921	IF (reprinted with PLAYS OF NEAR AND FAR)	Putnam
1924	THE KING OF ELFLAND'S DAUGHTER – Novel	Putnam
1928	SEVEN MODERN COMEDIES – Plays	Putnam
1926	THE CHARWOMAN'S SHADOW – Novel	Putnam
Date	Title	Publisher
1936	MY TALKS WITH DEAN SPANLEY – Novel	Heinemann
1929	50 POEMS	Putnam
1934	IF I WERE DICTATOR (The Pronouncement of the fraud Macaroni)	Methuen
1927	THE BLESSING OF PAN – Novel	Putnam
1930	THE OLD FOLK OF THE CENTURIES – A Play	Elkin Mathews
1933	LORD ADRIAN – A Play	Golden Cockerel Press

Date	Title	Publisher
1931	THE TRAVEL TALES OF MR JOSEPH JORKENS – Tales	Putnam
1934	JORKENS REMEMBERS AFRICA – Tales	Heinemann
1925	ALEXANDER – Three small plays	Putnam
1935	MR FAITHFUL – Play	Samuel Franck
1935	THE CURSE OF THE WISE WOMAN – Novel	Heinemann
1937	PLAYS FOR EARTH AND AIR – Plays	Heinemann
1935	UP IN THE HILLS – Novel	Heinemann
1938	MIRAGE WATER – Poems	Putnam
1936	RORY AND BRAN – Novel	Heinemann
1939	THE STORY OF MONA SHEEHY – Novel	Heinemann
1938	PATCHES OF SUNLIGHT – Autobiography	Heinemann
1937	MY IRELAND	Jarrolds
1940	JORKENS HAS A LARGE WHISKEY – Tales	Putnam
1940	WAR POEMS (a muddle, printed while we were abroad)	Hutchinson
1943	WANDERING SONGS – Poems	Hutchinson
1944	THE JOURNEY – Poem	Macdonald
1944	WHILE THE SIRENS SLEPT – Autobiography	Hutchinson
Date	Title	Publisher
1944	GUERILLA – Novel	Heinemann
1945	THE SIRENS WAKE – Autobiography	Jarrolds
1945	THE DONELLAN LECTURES 1943	Heinemann
1947	THE ODES OF HORACE, translated into English Verse	Heinemann
1946	THE YEAR – Poem	Jarrolds
1946	A GLIMPSE FROM A WATCH-TOWER – Pamphlet	Jarrolds
1948	THE FOURTH BOOK OF JORKENS – Tales	Jarrolds
1947	THE MAN WHO ATE THE PHOENIX – Tales	Jarrolds
1950	THE STRANGE JOURNEYS OF COLONEL POLDERS – Novel	Jarrolds
1951	THE LAST REVOLUTION – Novel	Jarrolds

INDEX